Outside Moscow

OUTSIDE MOSCOW

*Power, Politics, and Budgetary Policy
in the Soviet Republics*

DONNA BAHRY

New York   COLUMBIA UNIVERSITY PRESS   *1987*

Library of Congress Cataloging-in-Publication Data

Bahry, Donna.
  Outside Moscow.

  Bibliography: p.
  Includes index.
  1. Budget—Soviet Union—Republics.
  2. Intergovernmental fiscal relations—Soviet Union.
  I. Title.
  HJ2130.B35 1987   336.47   87-8020
  ISBN 0-231-06290-7

Columbia University Press
New York   Guildford, Surrey

Copyright © 1987 Columbia University Press
All rights reserved

Printed in the United States of America

For Jay

Contents

Preface

Part of the enjoyment in completing this book is the ability to acknowledge a good many professional debts. The first is to James Millar, whose professional support has helped in innumerable ways, and whose commitment to rigorous scholarship is, I hope, reflected in the pages that follow. Without the benefit of his advice in tracing out the intricacies of the Soviet financial system, and his insights on the economic side of regional politics, this would be much less of a book.

Thanks are due also to Carol Nechemias and to Henry Morton for braving early drafts of chapters 1–3. Their detailed comments added clarity to my sometimes opaque arguments. I had the advantage, too, of relying on Ellen Jones' detailed knowledge of the Soviet federal system and budget, and her generosity in providing some of the most recent data on republic investment. Frank Holzman's advice on budgetary matters and data on local finances were most welcome; and I am grateful to Samuel Beer, whose writings and whose advice on Western materials assisted me in piecing together the arguments in chapter 1. Nasrin Abdolali provided her usual careful assistance in preparing the tables and figures.

The National Academy of Sciences, the Soviet Academy of Sciences' Institute of Economics, and the Faculty of Arts and Sciences and Department of Politics at New York University all provided welcome research support for travel to Moscow.

My debts to Jay Bartlett are much greater. Without his substantive and editorial comments, affection, and patience even in the face of multiple drafts, there would be no book. I dedicate it to him, but keep for myself all responsibility for the errors of fact and interpretation that remain.

Outside Moscow

THE LOCAL REVOLUTION IN SOVIET POLITICS

O NE OF THE QUIET REVOLUTIONS in the USSR since Stalin has been the rediscovery of regional and local politics. Stalin's successors upgraded consumer welfare, spun off central government programs to republic and local management, and thus put more responsibilities and funds into the hands of governments outside Moscow. The change has been striking: in 1950, for example, republic and local agencies accounted for only 23 percent of Soviet budget expenditures; by 1984 they claimed 48 percent—nearly half the Soviet budget (*Narkhoz* 1984:575). Their share climbed even higher during Khrushchev's Sovnarkhoz reform; yet in spite of the dismantling of the Sovnarkhozy after Khruschev, politicians at subnational levels still manage more of the business of government than they did at any time under Stalin.

While this "local revolution" enhanced the role of regional and local officials in the Soviet system, it also presents them with a dilemma: they have more programs to administer and more complex problems to face, all of which require added funding. But with Moscow controlling revenue and appropriation decisions, funds below the national level are severely constrained. Leaders in the periphery are caught between pressures from above to assure regional economic growth and political stability, and pressures from below to improve public benefits and services, all with limited local resources. They thus have an increased need to coax more funds out of higher agencies.

Given their greater role, and the freer political atmosphere since Stalin, they have become more open in defense of local interests. Their appeals for more funds, more supplies, and more help from the central government pour out at every CPSU congress and Supreme Soviet budget convocation.

Some even protest if their republic's level of economic development or its appropriations from Moscow fall below the USSR average (see, e.g., Khaburzaniia 1978:131–34; Iskanderov 1969:171–74; N. S. Ermakov, *Pravda*, March 5, 1986, p. 3). Instead of waiting for policy to "trickle down" from on high, leaders in the periphery look for ways to influence national policies. Their role is far more complex than one of obedient lieutenants carrying out directives from Moscow: confronted with demands from above and from below, they are activists out to protect local interests in the face of a limited budget.

Thus, as Bialer (1980) and Hough (1971) both note, much of Soviet politics below the national level concentrates on gathering more resources from above. Regional and local authorities are constantly engaged in the business of lobbying for more funds. Judging from the attention that budget matters receive, they constitute some of the most important issues that come between Moscow and Baku, Tashkent, and other regional capitals. Billions of rubles in investment and in social welfare funds are at stake each year—and politicians outside Moscow work diligently at securing their area's fair share.

Yet in spite of the now abundant evidence on grassroots lobbying, little has been written that would tell us who wins. Do appeals by subnational politicians really matter? How does Moscow respond to such input?

To answer these questions this book focuses on the republics' role in economic decision-making—in the "budgetary process." Since regional lobbying concentrates so heavily on funding, the budgetary process offers a unique opportunity to explore the appeals that regional leaders put forward, their political maneuvering in the budgetary arena, and the impact of their lobbying. By examining budget debates and decisions, I hope to show:

— what issues regional leaders emphasize in their lobbying efforts, and how their agendas have varied both across regions and under the different regimes from Khrushchev to Gorbachev;
— how Moscow responds to regional requests;
— which regions benefit most from budgetary decisions, and what explains their success;
— how the economic relationship between Moscow and the republics has changed over time; and
— how Soviet center-regional dilemmas compare with those in other industrial countries.

This approach should offer new evidence on the political economy of Soviet domestic policy-making. Budgets provide a valuable "window on the policy process"—one that encompasses nearly all major activities of government (Heclo and Wildavsky 1974). Almost every public decision, be it to build a new town or to expand Russian-language education among minorities, carries a price tag, and the budgetary process reveals how such decisions emerge; who is involved in them; and what government priorities really are. It also serves as a useful barometer of changes in decision-making and in public priorities. In a system where public policy-making is so secretive, the government's budget allocation speaks volumes about reigning political values.

Equally important, the Soviet budget offers a rare opportunity to assess change in the Soviet federal hierarchy. Given the strict rules of fiscal federalism in the USSR, the allocation of budget funds is one key indicator of shifts in the operational authority of regional and local governments as against Moscow. Since each level of government is assigned expenditure and revenue sources to match its programmatic responsibilities, the size of republic and local budgets reveals how much government activity is in regional and local hands. Changes in these budgets yield valuable clues to the shifts that have taken place in the federal system over the years.

Budgetary policies also provide insights into the strategies Moscow uses to cope with regional and ethnic conflict. Since each republic is so closely identified with an eponymous ethnic group, regional economic choices are also choices about the future of Soviet minorities. Soviet leaders have made the connection quite explicitly: promises to close the "ethnic gap" have focused on reducing inequality among republics and regions. Nikita Khruschev (*XXI S"ezd*, 1959: 1:44) tied ethnic progress directly to re-public socioeconomic development; so too did Leonid Brezhnev (1972:72–75), who called for interregional equalization as a means of promoting equality among nationalities. Consequently, ethnic overtones are never far below the surface in the regional competition for economic benefits (Hough and Fainsod 1979). And given the growing territorial imbalances in the supply of labor and the availability of natural resources, regional conflict over economic choices may be intensifying. Budgetary allocations reveal how Soviet leaders respond to these regional tradeoffs—and reveal which regions gain or lose in the process.

Questions of center-periphery relations and budgetary politics are also important issues cross-nationally. In the face of regional and ethnic conflicts everywhere from Quebec to the Caucasus, the territorial distribution of money and power has become an increasingly sensitive political problem. The USSR, with its regional cleavages and its 100-plus nationalities, offers a unique case for comparative analysis. The evidence presented in this book suggests that the Soviet "local revolution" may parallel some of the major trends in other industrial countries since World War II, and it creates conflicts and dilemmas for Moscow that are similar to those facing Paris, Washington, and other national governments. I outline some of the similarities—and the differences—in order to ground the study of the USSR in a comparative framework.

Any such analysis naturally raises difficult questions about the comparability of Soviet and Western experience. Moscow's pervasive controls over the economy and over the careers of regional and local officials make center-regional relations overwhelmingly one-sided. The center dispenses both resources and career advancement, and public officials outside Moscow must keep a careful eye on cues from above. The emphasis is on conformity and deference to higher authorities, and Moscow clearly has the wherewithal to enforce them (Breslauer 1984).

This Soviet penchant for extremely centralized political controls must be borne in mind in any attempt to compare across systems. But it says little about the conflicts and tensions that arise *within* the Soviet system. Even with the greater degree of centralization in the USSR, there are still inevitable divergences between regional and national interests, still dilemmas confronting both central and regional officialdom. And the dilemmas grow out of structural problems similar to those that confront other advanced industrial societies. Officials in the periphery of both capitalist and communist nations have become the primary executors of the welfare state, the target of increased popular demands for government benefits, but must depend on national authorities to underwrite local programs. And the expansion of the welfare state in both the East and the West has intensified debates over the distribution of government benefits and the commitment to social equality. In addition, one can find similarities in experiences with reorganization and reform and similar complaints about the resistance to change that seems to characterize center-periphery relations.

These issues—center-periphery dilemmas, obstacles to reform, debates over social equality—are familiar ones for students of Soviet politics. Yet we sometimes overlook the parallel themes that dominate the discussion of center-periphery relations in capitalist countries. The intensity of the problems varies, of course, between federal and unitary systems and from country to country. Nonetheless, even in nations where the economic and budgetary discretion of local officials has traditionally been extremely limited, where the central government has played by far the dominant role (as in France, for example), center and periphery are still at odds over the issues of central versus local power, over territorial appropriations, and over reorganization. While each system copes with them in substantially different ways, one of the objects in this book is to explore the problems that cut across political boundaries.

Research on the USSR and Territorial Politics

Much has been written about Soviet center-regional relations and regional policy, and I draw heavily on this rich literature in the analysis that follows. Indeed, research on the topic has become a growth industry in the Soviet field, ever since critics first began to challenge the totalitarian model. In the totalitarian schema, with its nearly exclusive focus on high politics, governments below the national level were all but ignored. Since decision-making was by definition extremely centralized, regional and local agencies were treated as basically only administrative arms of the center.

This image has been revised dramatically since the 1960s. Researchers now emphasize the sheer impossibility of total central control over fifteen union republics, a hundred-plus oblasti and regions, and more than forty thousand local governments. Nove (1981:4) points out, for example, that

> the nominally total power of the central organs is not as absolute as it might seem. It is physically impossible to control and supervise everything. Local organs and local management do in fact have some room for maneuver, a range of decisions to take within necessarily rather broad (and sometimes contradictory) guidelines from Moscow.

The totalitarian model's emphasis on strict local conformity to all central dictates has also been called into question: Western scholars have repeatedly demonstrated that tensions between center and periphery are frequent and widespread, especially over budgetary matters (Taubman 1973; Rakowska-Harmstone 1979). As Hough (1969) suggests, the conflicts are so common that national leaders may see their subordinates in the periphery less as tribunes of central power than as incorrigible representatives of localism. And recent research by Breslauer (1984) indicates that local "demandingness" may be on the rise, as the old generation of regional leaders is replaced by younger and more activist cohorts.

The literature thus implies that politics outside Moscow might really be "political." However, research up to this point has yet to answer a fundamental question: does activism below the national level *matter*? If regional and local politics is about coaxing more out of higher-ups, how does it affect the appropriations process? Put simply, we have no clear picture of the impact of regional and local activism. Studies of politics below the national level are rich with data on elites, political conflicts, and local lobbying efforts; but they stop short of explaining how these political variables influence Soviet policy choices.[1]

Similarly, studies that concentrate on policy choices provide valuable detail on territorial differences in public expenditures, social welfare, and economic develement;[2] but few explore the political factors that give rise to regional policy differences. Many analysts do emphasize the highly politicized nature of industrial location, budgetary, and regional development decisions, but "politics" in this sense is typically treated as a residual. If standard economic explanations fall short, then the assumption is that political factors must somehow intervene. What these factors are, and how they work, is far from clear.

The literature, then, remains highly compartmentalized. Studies concentrate either on politics or on policy—but seldom on the connection between the two. It is almost as if they were entirely separate topics.

This book seeks to reconcile them by integrating policy with politics. If we can link regional activism with budgetary choices, we can then begin to assess the impact and importance of politics below the national level; and we can explore the political influences that dictate how money will be spent and which regions will benefit.

Research Design and Data

Questions about local influence in national politics are difficult to answer in any political system. Data on political relations between center and periphery are often scarce, the lines of authority and influence are hazy, and regional and local officials seem to find it more expedient to play up their lack of power vis-à-vis the central government than to acknowledge the influence they wield.

These problems are compounded in the Soviet case by the shortage of reliable data, the secrecy surrounding the policy-making process, and the tendency in Soviet discussions to confuse the "is" with the "ought." The real involvement of all-union, republic, and local officials in Soviet policy-making is difficult to untangle. Formal descriptions of their various powers tend to be very general and sometimes contradictory, giving bits and pieces of information that offer only a partial fix on the role of governments below the national level. To use Grodzins' (1972) metaphor, studying regional influence in the Soviet system is a little like analyzing a marble cake with most of the pieces missing.

Yet a careful examination of the literature published in the Soviet republics offers revealing details on center-regional relations. In the post-Stalin period, Soviet regional officials have been surprisingly candid about the tensions and problems that come between Moscow and the periphery. The Soviet literature on regional development also includes a long list of requests and complaints from below, providing an inventory of the concerns that populate regional agendas. In addition, publications on regional problems, national planning, and budgeting offer rich and previously unexplored detail on how Moscow handles regional appeals. These different sources, plus published Soviet budget and investment data, yield new evidence on the fiscal relationship between Moscow and its constituent republics.

Making the most of so large a body of data demands a combination of qualitative and quantitative analysis. I employ a qualitative approach to explore the workings of the budgetary proccess and the nature of regional demands and complaints. Stenographic reports of CPSU party congresses and of Supreme Soviet budget sessions and the specialized Soviet literature on regional economics are reviewed to identify regional agendas and to examine patterns of elite communication between center and periphery.

Such materials must be interpreted carefully. The "ritual of communications" (Swearer 1964) has produced statements and documents cloaked in the bland rhetoric of total unity and unceasing progress. Getting beyond the surface demands a knowledge of the context in which materials appear, the audience for which they are intended, and the degree to which they fit with our accumulated knowledge of Soviet politics. Given the traditional concern with the appearance of unity, the analyst must be sensitive to any deviations from the official line. In Swearer's (1964:24) words, "even minor changes in the ritual may have considerable importance, since this is one way of getting a message across unobtrusively."

The best research strategy in these circumstances is one of cumulation—analyzing a wide array of different sources, written by people at different levels in the Soviet economic hierarchy, in Moscow and in different republics. If these diverse sources all point to the same tensions, we can be reasonably confident that we have identified truly system-wide problems. If different spokesmen *disagree* publicly on causes and especially on cures, we can be sure that we are tapping real conflicts.

In addition to analyzing policy statements and discussions, I employ quantitative analysis to track the outcomes of budgetary decision-making and to explain Soviet policy choices. Budget and investment data are examined to determine which regions have fared best in the appropriations process and why. The analysis identifies the areas that have experienced the most rapid budgetary growth, and it weighs the impact of different political and economic variables on their success.

The quantitative data are also employed as a check on Soviet policy commitments, since the priorities that Soviet leaders endorse in public and the ones that actually get funded are sometimes very different. Statements by political leaders and even plan directives reveal what the leadership might like to do, but they may or may not be put into practice. Discovering who really gets what in the federal system thus means exploring the actual distribution of public funds.

As with qualitative sources, the quantitative data too require very careful analysis. Statistics on budgets and on investment are not always what they seem, as the abundant Western literature on Soviet defense spending attests (Holzman 1975). And the problems are not limited to defense expenditures: statistics on the same phenomena but from different sources do not always agree; data are not always clear or well-defined; and what is collected and published does not always measure what we would like (Bahry 1980; Bahry and Nechemias 1981). Using these Soviet statistics raises questions of both reliability and validity, and I cope with them here by cross-checking all the data against other sources, against what we know of Soviet politics and economics, and against both theory and logic. (A discussion of specific problems and data sources is provided in appendix A.)

The results are encouraging in spite of the gaps and inconsistencies in the data. The findings match the major political and administrative trends from NEP onward, and they conform to empirical theory on public finance. Thus, for example, chapter 2 shows that when Stalin imposed extreme centralization, the central share of the budget rose dramatically; and when the war prompted even greater centralization, budget data reflected the change. The same close correspondence also shows up in the post-Stalin era: Khrushchev's campaign to upgrade regional and local administration stands out as a dramatic increase in the subnational share of the state budget, and the subsequent disillusionment with territorial reform and the return to a more centralized system show clearly in the rise of the center's share after 1965. Trends in Soviet budget revenues also fit with what we would predict from empirical studies of taxation and economic development (Millar and Bahry 1979); and the allocation of taxes between central and subnational governments, with the center retaining the most lucrative sources, is one common in the West as well as the East.

Moreover, many of the discrepancies in budgetary data can be traced to the predictable problems that characterize any large-scale social and economic accounting effort. The importance attached to different kinds of data evolves as the political and economic climate changes, so that the inclusiveness of statistics varies from year to year. For example, when the annual editions of *Narodnoe Khoziaistvo SSSR (Narkhoz)* first appeared in the latter half of the 1950s, they did not always count investment by collective farms under "total" investment,[3] since the farms were not technically "state enterprises or institutions." But kolkhoz investment did come to be included later, as the publication of statistics expanded and as agricultural investment grew.

Definitions change too, since theories underlying the economy and the collection of statistics are also evolving. And organizational needs for information vary, as in the case of central ministries with different territorial-administrative structures geared to the geography of their particular products. To complicate matters even further, territorial boundaries also change, expecially below the republic level, making it difficult to determine "who gets what" because the units are frequently redrawn.

This is not to say that all the gaps and inconsistencies are simply products of changing definitions or growing economic complexity; the ambiguities of defense spending, and the decline and recent increase in the quantity of data published over the last few years, can hardly be accidental. Nor can we conclude that, because the data as a whole are reliable, any given statistic can be taken at face value. This becomes especially clear in attempting to determine what the Soviet budget actually represents, how much the government spends, and how expenditures are allocated across regions.

In using the terms "budget" and "budgetary process," I have been referring to the public expenditures made by Soviet authorities. But it is important to note that in Soviet usage, these terms refer only to a limited portion of the resources allocated by the state (Bahry 1980). Thus a study based on budget data alone would seriously underestimate how much the Soviet government spends. More important for our purposes, budget data alone give a distorted picture of Moscow's economic appropriations among the different republics, because official statistics do not reveal how much the central government itself spends in each region. Over 50 percent of the budget is spent directly by all-union agencies, but with no published breakdown to indicate which regions receive central funds. The total amount of allocations to a region therefore includes the republic budget—which is published in Soviet budgetary statistics—plus an undisclosed amount from the central government.

This would present only a minor problem if the undisclosed amount were proportional to what is disclosed, but the two figures are not necessarily related. The amount that Moscow spends varies from one republic to another, depending on which sectors dominate each region's economy: some sectors are more centralized than others (see chapter 3) and thus receive more funds from central rather than republic sources. Resources spent on union-subordinate industries, from aviation to medical equipment, machine-building, and instrument-making, do not show up at all in republic budgets, while funds for less centralized industries such as food-processing or construction materials do show up among republic allocations. As a result, Soviet budget figures exaggerate the real degree of inequality across regions (Bahry 1980; Bahry and Nechemias 1981). (For a quantitative assessment of this problem, see appendix A.)

Put simply, accounting practices create artificial differences among republic budgets for economic programs.[4] Any study of Soviet regional appropriations must take this fact into account; otherwise it will yield an excessively negative picture of regional spending differences. In my analysis below (see chapters 4 and 5), I therefore examine total investments in each region, including both budgetary and extrabudgetary funding.

Three related points should also be mentioned here. First, as noted earlier, Soviet planning often leads to situations where resources are allocated on paper but not in practice, and this can create some confusion about the true picture of Moscow's expenditures. All the data in the book, unless otherwise noted, represent actual expenditures. I refer to these on occasion as "appropriations,"using the term interchangeabley with "expenditures," but both refer to resources expended.

Second, I refer to the central government as "Moscow" for terminological convenience, but this is not to imply a single monolithic center. Indeed, as the rest of the book demonstrates, part of the problem for authorities outside Moscow is the proliferation of decision-making arenas at the central level and the pervasive departmentalism that characterizes their work.

Third, extending the analysis to include quantitative data on Western systems (chapter 1) poses almost as many problems as Soviet data do. Definitions and reporting procedures for state, provincial, and local finances vary substantially, and are subject to frequent revisions. In many cases, governments provide figures on different levels of government separately, without net data on each level's share of total spending. Some provide them in the categories used in public budgetary accounting; others provide data in the categories of national income accounts. Given the problem of finding comparable data, I rely here on studies by Pommerehne (1977) and by the European Communities (Commission 1977), which provide consistent and comparable figures for the United States, Canada, Australia, and Western Europe.

The Level of Analysis

The book takes a somewhat unusual approach by focusing on politics and budgetary policies at two levels of government—union republic and local (in Soviet budgetary practice, all governments below the union republic level are termed "local"). For the most part, these two levels are treated separately in Western research; often the assumption seems to be that the policy process operates differently, or that leaders at one level or the other have more clout in Moscow. The only way to identify the differences, however, is to compare the two levels, and that is one of the aims of this book.

The primary emphasis is on the republics, because they have been the

chief beneficiaries of the local revolution since Stalin. Under Khrushchev
and Brezhnev, republic leaders acquired more responsibility for managing
both republic and local affairs and more seats in the Politburo; and issues
of republic development received more national attention. Local gains
have been less dramatic, as chapter 5 demonstrates. Certainly some oblasti
and cities (such as Moscow and Leningrad) have been singled out for
greater attention, and may be more important economically than some of
the smaller union republics. Yet on the whole, the "local revolution" has
meant more dramatic *change* at the republic than at the local level. The
differences offer all the more reason for a comparative analysis, to discover
whether republic and local politics do indeed deserve to be studied
separately.

The Structure of the Book

To provide a comparative framework, chapter 1 explores the literature
on the political economy of center-periphery relations in Western countries
and in the USSR. Chapter 2 then turns attention to the evolution of
center-regional relations in the USSR: it offers an overview of the republics' role in the budgetary process since the early years of Soviet rule; and
it examines the development of Soviet "fiscal federalism." Chapter 3 takes
up the republics' role in the contemporary budgetary and planning process,
exploring regional agendas and the impact of republic lobbying efforts on
Moscow's appropriations decisions. In chapter 4, the analysis turns to the
issue of how different regions fare in the budgetary process, and to the
factors that explain budgetary choices. Chapter 5 focuses on politics and
policy at the local level. And chapter 6 outlines the broader implications
of center-regional relations for the study of policy-making and of political
centralization in the USSR.

CHAPTER ONE

CENTER, PERIPHERY, AND POWER
IN THE MODERN STATE

O NE OF THE PARADOXES of the modern state is that political centralization and local power are both growing. In federal and unitary
systems alike, money and power have become increasingly concentrated
in the hands of national governments. Yet the role of governments in the
periphery has grown too: regional and local officials control more domestic
programs and more funds than ever before. In both cases the reasons are
to be found in the expansion of the public sector. At the national level,
the rise of the welfare state created and expanded government programs
ranging from health, education, and welfare to environmental protection,
economic infrastructure, and urban development. Increased demands on
the public sector and changing attitudes about the role of the state fattened
the role of central governments (Ashford 1981; Lewis-Beck and Rice
1985).

However, much of this expansion has been achieved by relying on
regional and local officials to implement national policies. Central government programs in the domestic sphere are typically carried out by
authorities in the periphery with central direction and financing. The
growth of the welfare state created a dynamic in which more programs
are mandated and funded by national governments but carried out by
regional and local ones.

The pattern has been strikingly similar across industrialized Western
countries: governments below the national level accounted for an increasing share of domestic spending from 1950 through the mid-1970s, with
some leveling off as the economic stringency of the 1970s and 1980s
limited further welfare state expansion. As figure 1.1 shows, state/local
authorities acquired a bigger role in the allocation of public funds in both

FIGURE 1.1
State and Local Share of the Budget, Selected Years

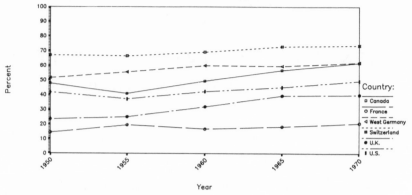

Data points are for 1950, 1955, 1960, 1965, and 1970 only. Transfers from the national government are counted as expenditures at the state and local level. Data represent the state and local share of all government expenditures.
SOURCE: Pommerehne (1977:307).

federal and unitary systems, from the U.S. and Canada to Great Britain, France, Switzerland, and West Germany in the postwar years. Other Western nations have followed suit (Kee 1977). State and local leaders came to command more public programs and funds, primarily through implementation of national policies.

The extent of shared programs varies, however, both by country and, within each country, by type of program. In France the national government has traditionally dominated in almost every type of program, from transport and communications to health, education, and welfare (see figure 1.2). But elsewhere the pattern is much more variegated, with responsibilities for natural resources and primary industries predominantly in central hands, but with other concerns—health and welfare, housing, education, transport, and communications—divided among different levels of government.

Expansion of these joint responsibilities has created dilemmas for officials at each level (Ashford 1981). Regional and local chief executives are faced with increased demands for public goods and services, but their revenues seldom grow as quickly. Central governments find themselves more dependent on subnational implementation, but with correspondingly less ability to coordinate or control all the many national programs now in regional and local hands.

FIGURE 1.2
State and Local Share of the Budget by Type of Expenditure

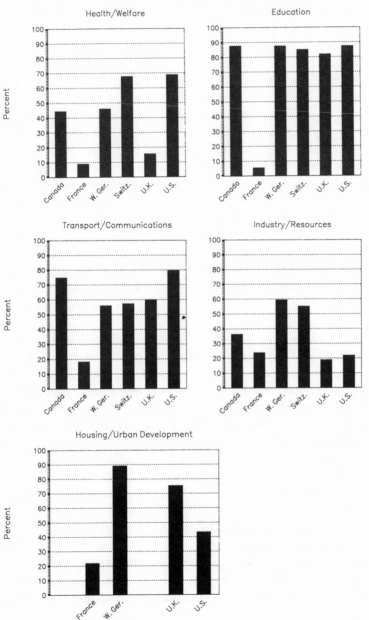

Data are for 1971. The data in these figures are defined differently from those in figure 1.1. Here, only unconditional national transfers are counted as state/local expenditures, while conditional transfers are counted as national expenditures. Thus where the balance between these two categories changes, as in the U.S., the data automatically increase the national government's share of the budget.

SOURCE: Pommerehne (1977:316–21).

For subnational officials, there are more programs to run, but funding is problematic. Most communities have limited revenue bases that rarely keep pace with the demand for government benefits and services. And they have few options for finding extra revenues. Raising local taxes creates high political costs—often too high for local officials. In addition, local governments typically operate under legal constraints that restrict both the taxes they may impose and the funds they may borrow (ACIR 1981; Sharpe 1981; Prud'homme 1974b). Nevertheless, many carry sizable debt burdens, which further inhibit their ability to respond to new demands.

State and provincial governments, with their larger tax bases, tend to have more fiscal options and thus somewhat more flexibility; yet even at this level, demands can outstrip revenue possibilities, and many state/ provincial leaders too face a fiscal squeeze. The squeeze is not always apparent from the aggregate data that are typically published: resources below the national level would appear to balance out or even be in surplus, but the aggregate data obscure the continual and difficult scramble by individual governments in the periphery to find the funds to meet local needs (Meltsner 1971; Bahl 1984). Thus both local and state/provincial governments experience fiscal dilemmas in the face of their expanded responsibilities, and for our purposes their fiscal problems may be described in similar terms.

Recent attempts to curb welfare state growth have cut some of the spending obligations imposed by the center, but they have also put more pressure on the governments below. In the U.S., while federal cuts have decreased the funds flowing from Washington for some state and local functions, federal efforts to return programs to the grassroots have met with only limited success. State and local officials find it difficult to replace federal initiatives because of the externalities involved, fearing that redistributive programs such as income maintenance or welfare create disaffection among taxpayers and attract more potential beneficiaries into the community. Moreover, for state and local governments to fill the gap left by federal budget-cutting would be to admit that governments below the national level can do without federal funds—something that many leaders outside Washington are reluctant to concede (Nathan et al. 1983). Their objections have been at least partially successful: despite the rhetoric of budget-cutting at the federal level since 1980, aid to state and local governments dropped in only one year (1982) and then grew by 3 percent (in constant dollars) during the rest of the first Reagan term (Hall 1985:10–11; Nathan and Doolittle 1984:100).

Thus politicians at the grassroots have continued to look to the center for relief, and for good reason. The national level typically has superior revenue powers and a preponderance of the most income-elastic taxes.[1] Given the many obstacles to raising extra local revenue, regional and local leaders turn to the national government "as the constituency from which they hope to win the most at the least cost" (Haider 1974:77). Yet national aid invariably comes with strings, with prescriptions on how it should or should not be spent. Officials in the periphery must promote local development, secure national assistance, and at the same time prevent national assistance from eroding their autonomy.

For national governments, the dilemma is one of reliance on subnational agencies to carry out national policies. The more programs and funds in regional and local hands, the harder it is to ensure that national goals are met. The proliferation of government programs and the sheer number of regions and localities frustrate attempts to control policy at the grassroots. The success or failure of national policy depends on local implementation, over which central agencies exercise only limited control (Ashford 1981; Prud'homme 1977). Overlapping jurisdictions and political fragmentation at the national level often lead to similar programs being managed by different national agencies; and the wording of national legislation can be so general that monitoring agencies have difficulty in deciding whether policies are in fact being implemented "correctly" (Hale and Palley 1979).

The task of implementation thus gives leaders in the periphery a key vantage point for resisting or reshaping central policies. National initiatives that seem unreasonable or unworkable have a way of being undermined or evaded. Oversight is limited, and funds can be subtly reprogrammed to meet state or local rather than strictly national goals (Hale and Palley 1979). Governments in the periphery can obstruct, impede, and otherwise bend national policy to local ends—a kind of "interest articulation" in the process of carrying out central decisions. Kesselman (1974:369) emphasizes this point by citing the lament of a French cabinet minister: "everything is possible with the cooperation of local officeholders; nothing is possible without it." Even where subnational officials are hemmed in by elaborate central controls, implementation provides a key means of influencing policy outcomes.

National governments do, of course, have the formal power to deny funding to agencies that undermine or evade national policy directives. But they stand to lose as much or more than they gain: penalties are counterproductive and are rarely invoked. Sanctions interfere with the provision of public goods and services that national programs are supposed to deliver. Since the national government has a vested interest in seeing that its policies are implemented, disputes are more likely to end in compromise, rather than disrupt central policy goals (Pressman and Wildavsky 1973; Ingram 1977; Hale and Palley 1979; Hanf and Scharpf 1978).

From the central government's standpoint, it pays far more to sound out leaders in the periphery earlier in the process—to use regional and local perceptions and needs in shaping the agenda and allocating resources. Collecting local input in these earlier phases provides feedback on how national policy is working in the periphery, on the problems it may create, and on the possible ways in which it might need to be modified. Subnational leaders serve as a critical source of information for the national government (Haider 1974).

National governments also reap other advantages by courting input from below. The inclusion of regional/local complaints on the national agenda can pay off by coopting grassroots support for central decisions. To the extent that officials in the periphery offer input on national agendas and policy choices, they may come to identify with central decisions, as part of a political coalition with a stake in seeing that national policies are made to work.

Thus the rise of the welfare state has meant a growing web of mutual dependence between center and periphery (Schain 1979; Derthick 1974). National governments control a larger share of funding, while regional/local leaders are in a position to determine whether—and how—national policy is actually carried out. Clearly, images of local powerlessness in the face of the welfare state's Leviathan underestimate the real degree of influence that leaders in the periphery wield. As Beer (1976) observes, the very fact of increased national financing makes the national government more dependent on local implementation and thus heightens local political leverage. The relationship between center and periphery has therefore become far more than a zero-sum game: expansion at the national level means expansion of power in the periphery as well (Ashford 1979; Prud'homme 1977; Samuels 1983).

Yet despite the mutual interest in cooperation, the relationship is more likely to be conflict-ridden. The ongoing fiscal squeeze below the national level challenges state and local officials to gain more national support with fewer strings attached. In the process, they face increasing competition with other areas for the same national benefits. Since the welfare state has multiplied the number of national programs, the arenas for competition and conflict have increased as well.

The national government's involvement in more policy domains also multiplies opportunities for redistributing resources to distant and disadvantaged segments of the population; hence equality in national government programs has come to be an important but much disputed issue. And conflicts arise over organization as well as over policy. The new demands on government and the rise of problems that cut across old local boundaries render old territorial subunits outmoded. However, reorganization is a troublesome issue, and it too leads to constant tensions between center and periphery.

Given the gap between demands placed on subnational governments and the availability of local funding, political leaders in the periphery have an increased stake in finding ways to influence national policy-making. What national leaders do, or can be made to do, has become a major preoccupation (Haider 1974; Break 1980). Regional and local officials are under greater pressure to find adaptive strategies to win support from higher-ups (Tarrow 1977).

One result is the growth of liaison offices and lobbying staffs sent to the national capital to defend local interests.[2] Even where representation in national legislatures is apportioned to state or local governments, leaders in the periphery seek to establish other ongoing links with national agencies—a channel to transmit local demands and to keep abreast of policies and problems at the national level. Lobbying plays a valuable role in the policy process by funneling information between center and periphery.

Often regional and local officials form coalitions with other communities to put their case to the central government. But for the most part, they are competitors, and the expansion of national government gives rise to interlocal and interregional conflict. Every area seeks to gain its fair share of national benefits.

Central governments, in turn, find themselves confronted with increased controversy over how to distribute national funds among territorial subunits. The "right" allocation formula is always elusive: should underdeveloped or lagging regions get a larger share of national funding? Or should the central government concentrate its efforts on more economically viable or growing areas?

How should the twin issues of equity and efficiency be handled? Since some areas will benefit more from one or the other of these two alternatives, equity and efficiency become a growing source of conflict as national government programs expand. And even if a consensus can be reached on the need to adopt one criterion or the other, disagreements still arise over what "equity" and "efficiency" mean in practice. There often seem to be as many definitions as there are governmental units.

Another source of conflict lies in the fact that old territorial subunits are less and less fitted to cope with the growth of programs and demands at the regional/local level. The expansion of policy domains means new problems that cut across regional and local jurisdictions. Some national pro grams even create new jurisdictions or territorial subunits. The result: balkanization that fragments power and frustrates attempts at policy coordination (Ashford 1977; Break 1980). These problems have prompted frequent proposals to reorganize and redefine center-periphery relations, often by creating yet another level of government that at least in theory can overcome fragmentation (Samuels 1983; Tarrow 1974). However, reorganization seldom proceeds smoothly. Politically, it threatens the interests of established communities, and authorities in the periphery tend to delay and impede reforms that might challenge their prerogatives. As Kesselman (1974:367–68) observed in the French case, the power of the localities has been all too clear: one need only consider how many times national authorities have "failed to achieve the changes [they] sought." The history of center-periphery relations is full of examples of failed or partial reforms (Brand 1976; Samuels 1983).[3]

In some cases, the externalities at the local level and the need to coordinate policies over a wider geographical area simply push programs and funds upward to intermediate-level government. For West Germany, this has meant an expansion of the role of Lander at the expense of the localities, and for the U.S., a parallel rise in the role of state governments (Hall 1985; Johnson 1983; Stephens 1985).

Center-Periphery Conflict and the Distribution of National Funds

Thus while the growth of the state has increased the mutual dependency between center and periphery, it has also multiplied the opportunities for conflict over the territorial distribution of national economic benefits. Western research offers two different perspectives on the outcome. One holds that areas with better polictical resources, namely access to key national leaders and agencies, also do better in collecting additional benefits from the national government. Yet with the interdependence of center and periphery, the central government needs a coalition of supporters to get its programs adopted, and cooperation from authorities below the national level to get them implemented. It needs policies that will enlist broad local support, and this implies a more diffuse allocation of national benefits.

According to the first hypothesis, the growth of government makes it all the more important for regional and local leaders to reach central decision-makers. It would be difficult to get a hearing, much less a favorable response, without influence at the national level. Direct access constitutes a key political resource that ought to lead to a greater success rate in winning central funds.

The literature on center-periphery relations is filled with examples. In France, research suggests that local officials with ties to Paris have a demonstrable advantage when it comes to gaining support from the central government (Becquart-LeClercq 1977). As Frears (1983:57) contends, a local leader "with political weight and good contacts in the ministries can obtain more for his town in the way of subsidies or new developments." And in the U.S., the notion of pork-barrel politics, with power in key congressional committees assuring federal benefits to members' home districts, is firmly entrenched among scholars and politicians alike. The distribution of public works and military projects are legendary examples (Goss 1973; Ray 1981).

Yet pork-barrel politics rests squarely on norms of reciprocity and universalism. The system works by spreading the wealth to guarantee political support. Public works bills in Congress tend to include a little something for everyone in order to get passed. Similarly, districts that do not get military contracts do get agricultural subsidies, urban aid, or any number of other federal benefits. And research on congressional decision-making reveals that the tradeoffs have intensified because of changes in the Congress itself. The traditional power structure dominated by a relatively stable leadership has given way to temporary majorities "assembled on particular issues and successful only to the extent that diffuse benefits are in prospect"[4] (Owens and Wade 1984:418–19). The net effect of the pork-barrel, then, is to even out national expenditures across different constituencies, and thus across regions.

Diffuse benefits also emerge even in the face of unequal party and political connections among officials in the periphery seeking central funds. These are certainly valuable assets, but they hardly exhaust the political resources that local leaders bring to bear. Leaders below the national level succeed in gaining national benefits without partisan connections or close personal ties in national government. For example, Tarrow (1977) shows that communist-led communities in Italy have received some of the highest levels of state aid, despite Christian-Democratic dominance; and Schain (1985) notes that local communists in France have won benefits from Paris even under opposition rule, and with only limited and conditional access to central administrators.[5] They succeed not so much through personal contacts as through skill in bureaucratic bargaining, "by exploiting the same interdependence between administration and local elected officials exploited by other mayors, but perhaps with more determination and for different policy objectives" (Schain 1985:93–95).

They have yet another asset too: central ministries have incentives to work closely with local officials from a broad array of regions, to create constituencies that will lend political support to continuing and perhaps expanding their mandate. These conditions provide an array of local political advantages that go beyond personal patronage or partisan alignments, and since each local leader may rely on a diferent subset, such "cross-cutting" advantages tend to cancel each other out.

The dispersion of national funding is reinforced by other factors as well. One is the sheer diversity of national programs in advanced industrial societies, from urban development, mass transit, housing, agriculture, and environmental protection to education, medical care, and welfare—each directed to different segments of the population and each likely to benefit different regions or localities. A second is the need to maximize cooperation from below. Where the success of national policies depends on regional or local implementation, central governments need to distribute funds in a way that will enlist local support. The result is a diffusion of benefits to strengthen political loyalites and ensure grassroots adherence to national goals. Central government funds are thus likely to be spread among diffrent territorial subunits, so that most or all regions/localities get some payoff—a kind of "functional logrolling" to coopt leaders in the periphery into supporting national policies (Haider 1974; Bennett 1980).

National programs to foster regional development or renewal are good cases in point. In France, the center's efforts to construct territorial development plans have produced recommendations to disperse benefits throughout the country. Prud'homme (1974b: 40) noted that the National Commission of Territorial Planning (CNAT), with its representatives from all over France, "merely underlines the necessity to do everything everywhere." In the FRG, federal policies initially designed in 1969 to strengthen joint finanical planning and coordination with the Lander ultimately had somewhat different results: "Federal funding, rather than reflecting differential goals and practices, usually took the form of equal treatment of all the states, and additional funding over the years tended to preserve the shares of the various states" (Diamant 1981:118–19). And in the U.S., major federal initiatives toward regional or local redevelopment since the 1950s have been broadened to cover a wide geographic net. The idea of General Revenue Sharing in 1970, for example, began with a focus on a small number of localities; but "political salability required a much larger group of beneficiaries," and ultimately it was applied to all general-purpose local governments (Break 1980:147). Political pressures also affected the formula used in dispersing revenue sharing funds: equal per capita grants were the easiest to defend politically to different congressmen (Beer 1976). When the House and Senate arrived at different formulas for allocating revenues, the conference committee compromised by adopting both versions and allowing each state to choose the formula that gave it more funds (Nathan et al. 1975). Similarly, a public works program initially designed to counter unemployment in depressed areas during the 1970s ended up dispersing benefits among a far wider array of states and localities (Sundquist and Mields 1980). Hale and Palley (1981) suggest that the proliferation of intergovernmental programs has led to an era of politics by printout, with congressmen often reluctant to cast a vote until they have seen district-by-district calculations showing the effects of alternative distribution formulas. Consequently, federal programs that start with the object of favoring selected states or localities quickly lose their selective focus; in order to get adopted, they are often rewritten to distribute benefits more equitably among a larger number of constituent governments (Arnold 1979).

FIGURE 1.3
Inequality in Regional Expenditures, Western Countries

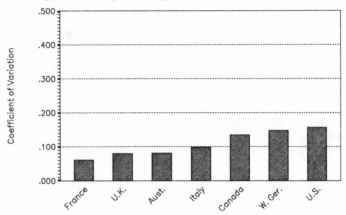

Coefficients of variation are unweighted. For comparable units of measurement, U.S. data are based on 9 regions; Italy, 20 regions; France, 21; and the U.K., 10. The year covered is 1975 for the U.S.; 1973 for Canada and Italy; 1973–74 for Australia; 1970 for France; 1964 for the U.K.; and 1970 for Germany. Data represent total direct central government expenditures in each region.
SOURCE: Commission of the European Communities (1977: 1:241–46).

Given the premium on compromise, policies with an explicit regional focus come to reflect multiple goals, and these too can lead to a diffusion of funds. Thus regional development aid in Britain was conceived in the 1970s as a means of reviving depressed areas; but it was also viewed as a means of replacing old industries with more modern ones (e.g., microprocessors)—and the two goals did not necessarily concide. Lagging regions did not necessarily have the requisite skilled labor force for high-tech plants, so other regions gained benefits as well (Grant 1982). Territorial planning may therefore be at odds with sectoral economic interests, and in this situation, territorial policy frequently takes a back seat.

The combination of bureaucracy and bargaining in national politics therefore serves to damp down inequalites in central appropriations across different regions. The effect is evident in expenditure data compiled by the European Community: as figure 1.3 shows, total direct central government expenditures provide "roughly equal per capita benefits" by regions in both federal and unitary systems (Commission 1977:127–35). The coefficients of variation presented in the table reveal extremely modest interregional differences in national spending—with coefficients in many cases at or even below .100. Naturally, the pattern is much more varied if we focus on individual programs rather than on total expenditures: social security programs benefit areas with a higher proportion of dependent children and retirees: industrial renovation policies are likely to benefit regions with a preexisting industrial base and a skilled labor force. And many specific types of appropriations seem to follow political criteria (Owens and Wade 1984; Arnold 1979).

Yet taking each type of expenditure in isolation misses an important aspect of the allocation process: decisions on different expenditure programs are interdependent. The fact that some regions get public works or agricultural aid may hinge on the condition that other areas qualify for other kinds of benefits. The allocation process should be viewed as a sum of interdependent parts, and its aggregate impact is to level the central government's outlays in different regions.

The evenness of central expenditures, in turn, provides a mild form of redistribution from richer to poorer ares. Poorer regions receive more than they would on the basis of their level of economic development or tax capacity alone. In this sense, as the Commission of the European Communities (1977:134) concluded, national policies combine to yield a mild form of interregional redistribution, "automatically and invisibly." [6]

This brief overview has only touched on a few of the conflicts inherent in center-local relations, and on only a few of the features that distinguish various industrial nations. To stress common problems and policy choices is not to deny the many fundamental differences between federal and unitary systems or among individual nations. But despite the enormous variations in state structures and in national-local relations, many of the same tensions come between center and periphery, fed by the growth of the welfare state.

Center, Periphey, and Power in the USSR

Soviet leaders find themselves with similar tensions and dilemmas. Like the rise of the welfare state in capitalist countries, the Soviet commitment to social welfare after Stalin expanded programs at both the central and the regional/local level in the USSR. The consumer orientation of the Khrushchev and Brezhnev regimes spurred new initiatives at the national level in agriculture, health, education, and welfare, putting more funds into the hands of regional and local leaders—who are primarily responsible for implementing Soviet welfare state policies. Increases in funding for farms, hospitals, schools, pensions, consumer goods, and other economic and social benefits upgraded the role of governments below the national level.

In the Soviet case, however, the rise of regional and local politics went beyond the expansion generated by welfare state programs. Khrushchev, Malenkov, Bulganin, and Kaganovich all shared a consensus on the need to streamline Stalin's top-heavy bureaucratic machine, though they fought over how far such reforms should proceed (Fainsod 1963; Brzezinski and Huntington 1965; Breslauer 1982). Within months after Stalin's death, the number of all-union ministries dropped from 30 to 15 and more responsibilities were handed over to the republics (Fainsod 1963). By 1956, then-Premier Bulganin (1956:48) reported to the Twentieth Party Congress that coal, timber, oil, iron, steel, food, textiles, construction, and transport, among other sectors, had been transferred from central to union-republic or republic subordination. All told, over 11,000 industrial enterprises had been shifted to republic administration just since 1953.

The move seemed in part to be a response to the lagging performance of Stalin's rigidly centralized economic system. During the years just after World War II, the central bureaucracy had proliferated into a number of increasingly specialized ministries,[7] while the rapid economic growth of earlier years gave way to more erratic progress. The growth rate actually declined during 1951 and 1952, as did farm output and meat production (USSR: Measures 1982). At the same time, the economic crisis and political rebellion in East Germany, Czechoslovakia, Hungary, Poland, and Rumania soon after Stalin's death raised the prospect of a virus that could potentially spread to the USSR.

The cumulative problems strengthened the hand of those who, like Khrushchev, were ready to spin off some responsibilities to officials outside Moscow in the name of greater efficiency. Devolution also offered distinct political advantages: upgrading the role of regional governments was a valuable means of building support in the periphery given the new atmosphere of collective leadership. Any such proposal could not help but appeal to regional and local elites—who made up 54 percent of the CPSU Central Committee selected at the Nineteenth Party Congress. They could be key allies for a new leader trying to consolidate his power, as Khrush-chev's confrontation with the "antiparty group" demonstrated.[8] When his rivals opposed further devolution and pushed through a resolution early in 1957 to increase the powers of the central planning apparatus, he countered by mobilizing the Central Committee to reinforce support for regionalization (Fainsod 1963).

Khrushchev, in his memoirs, suggested another reason for his concern with hypercentralization: he had spent a significant share of his career in regional and local posts, subject to the heavy hand of ministerial tutelage. As premier and party boss in the Ukraine and boss of the Moscow party, he had learned firsthand the frustrations of trying to persuade higher-ups to respond to local problems. In agriculture, for example, "we were forever receiving from the ministry memos and directives that almost invariably ran counter to our understanding of what should be done" (Khrushchev 1976:127–28).

His attack on centralism began with agriculture and peaked with the adoption of the Sovnarkhoz experiment in 1957, in the process nearly tripling the republic and local share of the state budget. And the impact proved to be more lasting than the Sovnarkhoz reform itself. When the experiment faltered, and economic administration returned to a centralized ministerial system, governments below the national level still played a larger role than they ever had in Stalin's time. Their share of budgetary expenditures in 1980, for example, was twice as large as it had been in 1950, and roughly what it was during NEP.

The rise of the republics is also clearly reflected in high politics and in policy agendas under both Khrushchev and Brezhnev. Under their lead-ership, six republics gained representation in the Politburo (see table 1.1). First secretaries from Belorussia, Uzbekistan, Kazakhstan, Georgia, and Azerbaidzhan, and Latvia's president of the Supreme Soviet all acquired full or candidate membership.[9] This was a marked contrast with the Stalin era, when the only regional officials who were regularly included in the Politburo's ranks had been from Russia or the Ukraine. In addition, the new leadership gave republic premiers permanent seats and votes in the national Council of Ministers (Shafir 1968b; Nelidov 1962).[10] The prin-ciple of postpreds (*postoiannye predstavitel'stva*) was also reinvigorated,with republic governments assigning permanent representatives to union-re-public ministries in Moscow to help facilitate cooperation between center and periphery (Tsikulin 1966; Shafir 1968b).[11]

TABLE 1.1
Republic Representation in the Soviet Politburo, 1924–1980[a]

	1925	1930	1935	1940	1945	1950	1955	1960	1965	1970	1975	1980
RSFSR												
Premier	FFFCC						C	FCFFFFFFFFFFCCCCCCCCC				
Chair, Supreme Soviet		CCCCFFFFFFFF										
First deputy premier									CCCCC			
Ukraine												
First secretary	CCC	CCCCCFFFFFF	FFF					CCFFFCCFFFFFFFFFFFFFFFFFFFFF				
Premier	CCCCCCCCCCCC						F	CCC CCCCCFF				
Chair, Ukr. TsIK	CCCCCCCCCCC											
Belorussia												
First secretary								CCCCCCCCCCCCCCCCCCCCCC				
Uzbekistan												
First secretary								CC	CCCCCCCCCCCCCCCCCCC			
Kazakhstan												
First secretary							C	FFFF	CCCCCFFFFFFFFFF			
Georgia												
First secretary								CCCCCCCCCCCCCC				
Azerbaidzhan												
First secretary											CCC	
Latvia												
First secretary							C				CCCCC	
Chair, Supreme Soviet							CCC					
Lithuania												
Moldavia												
Kirgizia												
Tadzhikistan												
Armenia												
Turkmenia												
Estonia												
Karelia												
Chair, Supreme Soviet							FFFFFFFFFFF					

[a] Including all Politburo members who simultaneously held office in a republic. F = full member; C = candidate member. If a republic official was a full member for even part of the year, that year is coded with an "F."

SOURCES: For years after 1952, Kress (1980:226); for earlier years, *Ezhegodnik Bol'shoi Sovetskoi Entsiklopedii* (annual); Lewytzky (1968); Schapiro (1960); Schueller (1965); Lowenhardt (1982).

Given the new concern with regional issues, Khrushchev accorded special emphasis to republic socioeconomic development. He took a characteristically sweeping approach at the Twentieth Party Congress, declaring that Stalin had perpetuated inequalities among regions and advocating fairer policies—such as equal per capita budgetary expenditures for each republic. The platform also included a greater republic role in industrial management (*XX S"ezd* 1956: 1:88–90). And for those who questioned the center's territorial allocation of resources, he suggested that the Economic Commission of the Supreme Soviet be directed to investigate complaints.

The increased concern with regional issues also showed in five-year plan directives. Starting with the Sixth Plan (1956–60), published directives began to include a separate section devoted to republic and regional development. In earlier years such documents had concentrated instead on the development of different economic branches, with less emphasis on the regional dimension.[12] And as regional development received more emphasis, so too did the notion of a scientific approach to regional planning.

With Khrushchev on the offensive against the central bureaucracy, regional officials grew more voluble in bringing local problems to the attention of national leaders. The contrast between the Nineteenth Party Congress in 1952 and subsequent congresses bears witness to the new atmosphere: regional elites at the Nineteenth Congress offered criticisms of some national ministries and put in a few requests for more funds, but most of their speeches reflected the notion of "criticism from below," i.e., attacking the short comings of their own organizations and colleagues. The tone was best expressed by Z. I. Muratov, first secretary of the Tatar ASSR (*Current Soviet Policies* 1953:159–60): "The Great Stalin teaches us not to let successes go to our heads, to see the darker side of achievements, to bring to light and decisively to eliminate shortcomings." Georgia's party boss A. I. Mgeladze castigated the failures of past republic leadership; and L. G. Melnikov, the first secretary of the Ukrainian party, criticized his colleagues in the Ukraine for their defects and errors (ibid.: 141–42, 153–54).

Such self-criticism certainly continued under Khrushchev, but the bulk of the complaints shifted to the deficiencies of the central government and its regional policies. Regional leaders became far more open in criticizing the national government and its shortcomings, and in calling for more authority. At the Twentieth Congress, Russia's premier, M. Yasnov (*XX S"ezd* 1956: 2:67–74) declared that republic and local officials still did not have enough power over the local economy; central ministries, he said, seemed to be reluctant to give up control. Other delegates from the periphery were equally vocal: Belorussia's N. S. Patolichev (*XX S"ezd* 1956: 1:161–67) contended that Gosplan, the Central Statistical Administration, and the Ministry of Agriculture all needed to be restructured; and Lithuania's A. Iu. Snechkus (*XX S"ezd* 1956: 1:351–59) called for the consolidation of higher educational institutions under a single republic ministry.

The complaints continued after Khrushchev's ouster and the dismantling of the Sovnarkhozy, though the tone has varied over time.The most vehement and wide-ranging remarks, rivaling 1956, came at the Twenty-Seventh Congress. Gorbachev's emphasis on openness and on airing alternative reform schemes prompted a litany of many of the same complaints as at earlier congresses (see chapters 3 and 5), but with somewhat sharper criticisms and a broader variety of recommended cures. The new first secretary himself went on record for greater regional and local authority (*Izvestiia*, February 26, 1986, p.5), a theme echoed by several delegates from outside Moscow. And some republic and local leaders took the idea further, suggesting that economic administration could better be served by territorial organs rather than ministries and that republics and localities might perform more efficiently if put on khozraschet.[13]

Party leaders after Khrushchev also continued to support the idea of republic socioeconomic development, though here too the tone has varied with time and with different individuals. Thus Brezhnev (1972:78) announced in 1972 that the goal of regional equalization had largely been carried out, but in the same breath he offered reassurance to regional elites by emphasizing the need to protect "the interests of all the republics." In later years—at the Twenty-Sixth Party Congress in 1981, for example—he again stressed the need for more even development among different regions of the USSR and predicted their eventual "convergence" (*sblizhenie*) (*XXVI S"ezd* 1981: 1:72–75). The emphasis had changed since Khrushchev's day, for the energy crisis had brought the development of regional fuels and natural resources to center stage, and uneven economic conditions brought greater recognition of the need to tailor regional development strategies to local circumstances (e.g., labor-intensive industry in labor-surplus areas of the Caucasus and Central Asia). Yet in spite of the changes in emphasis, regional concerns continued to occupy an important position on the political agenda, well after Brezhnev declared the USSR a success in combating regional inequality.

The themes of adaptation to local conditions and of interdependence have received even more attention under Brezhnev's successors. Andropov (*Pravda*, December 22, 1982, pp. 1–2) advocated the "free development of each republic, of each nationality" and the liquidation of inequalities; but this was to be done by furthering the economic integration of republics and regions and by achieving a better fit between central planning and local resources. Chernenko (1984:565–67) claimed that the first problem was to develop the material and cultural potential of every republic, but in a way that maximized its contribution to the economy as a whole. Old policies favoring redistribution now had to be subordinated to the greater interests of the nation at large. Gorbachev and Ryzhkov have also adopted the theme of integrating republics and regions into a single economic complex—but with their own variations. Ryzhkov (*Pravda*, March 4, 1986, p. 4), for example, has stressed the need to develop "all the republics and major regions," while Gorbachev has downplayed the issue of equality—and cut the number of Republic leaders in the Politburo—but advocated greater power for republic and local agencies (*Izvestiia*, February 26, 1986, p. 5). Each regime has thus conveyed subtle differences in emphasis on the regional issue; but each also seems to have been careful to signal leaders in the periphery that their economic interests will be protected.[14]

The Dilemmas of Center-Regional Relations

The enhanced role of the republics creates dilemmas at both the central and the regional level. For republic officials, the increase in programs and funds is a mixed blessing. More of the business of Soviet government has come under their jurisdiction; and they are also the target of more demands both from the citizenry and from Moscow. Yet no major program can be mounted without approval and funding from Moscow. Thus while regional leaders have gained more responsibility, they also have a greater need to garner the attention and resources of the center. For Moscow, the drive to spin off central programs has been useful in coping with some of the rigidities of the Stalinist system. Yet it has also increased the national government's dependence on subordinate governments to implement national policies. Central controls are therefore more difficult to maintain: the more the programs and funds in regional and local hands, the harder it is to guarantee that each subnational government actually follows central directives.

More than ever before, the expanded role of the republics demands that Moscow temper centralized planning and financing with enough local flexibility to make policies work. Brezhnev (1976:60) admitted as much in 1976, noting that democratic centralism should be centralized enough to overcome narrow institutional or local biases but open enough to encourage local initiative and flexibility in decision-making. He was recognizing a simple political fact: excessive centralization is counterproductive. Central authorites can attempt to "command" subnational governments, but directives that regional officials perceive to be misguided may get stalled or subtly altered to conform to local needs (Hahn 1972). And given the greater role for the republics since Stalin, there are now more opportunities to question or evade unwelcome rules.

In any event, at least some of the objections by authorities outside Moscow are likely to be well founded, since they grow out of firsthand knowledge of local problems. Thus if national policy is to be effective, it must fit local needs; regional leaders must be able to adapt it to local circumstances. To borrow a phrase from Dan Nelson (1979:44), achieving the goals of the central government requires a degree of local autonomy.

Achieving national goals also requires feedback from the grassroots. Moscow must have input about regional needs in order to identify real and potential problem areas—and to check on the performance of its ministries in the field. A republic complaint about shortages of industrial capital or educational funding, for example, provides national leaders with critical information about how their policies are working in the periphery. Regional criticism of ministerial delays and mistakes helps to pinpoint trouble spots in the central bureaucracy.

Input from below therefore constitutes an essential part of the bureaucratic system. But information on local problems and needs is not likely to flow upward smoothly or even accurately unless it evokes a response from above. Regional officials have little incentive to speak out unless they have at least some chance of persuading higher-ups to investigate their appeals and complaints. For Moscow, then, the dilemma lies in maintaining central control while assuring at least some degree of responsiveness to local needs.

Certainly we should not underestimate the ability to remove any "malcontents" among regional elites, especially those who seem overly imbued with the taint of local nationalism. Khrushchev (1976:138), for example, replaced Kazakhstan's first secretary, R. O. Shaiakhmetov, in 1954 for trying to discourage the adoption of the Virgin Lands program (since it was perceived as bringing outsiders—mostly Russian—into the republic). And this was by no means an isolated case: charges of local nationalism have been frequent and widespread.

Yet removing all regional leaders who voice demands or complaints is hardly practical; it would deprive Moscow of critical data. Moscow's dependence on input from below therefore gives regional leaders a degree of latitude in appealing to central authorities. They have what Campbell (1978:31) terms the "coercive power of the weak"— the threat of failure in carrying out central policies.

Of course, the type of request matters: an astute regional politician will emphasize the congruence between regional and national interests. He can usually find some way to show that "what's good for his region is good for the USSR" (Sullivant 1962; Biddulph 1983). Thus every request for more funds comes with a preamble underlining the region's major contributions to the national wealth. Whatever the centerpiece of the regional economy, be it cotton or natural gas, machinery or tourism, republic leaders are certain to emphasize how much it benefits the other "fraternal republics." Cotton becomes white gold; forests, green gold; oil, black gold, and the list goes on. Regional appeals that by themselves might seem to reflect a narrow localism can be justified by linking them to broader national goals. And the more complex the economy has grown, the more diverse its goals have become, the easier it is to legitimize a request by tying it to one of many national priorities. As Tarschys (1979) demonstrates, the national political agenda has become broader over time, with more products, more industries, and more issues (e.g., environmental protection, the quality of life) than were evident at the end of the Stalin era. This modernization of the agenda offers a shrewd regional leader more opportunities to cast his appeal in terms of its importance to the nation as a whole.

The advent of the Gorbachev era offers some intriguing examples.

Tadzhikistan's S. A. Niiazov (*Pravda*, March 2, 1986, p. 5) invoked both the Food Program and defense needs in his appeal to the Twenty-Seventh Congress, arguing that the Food Program could not be realized without more investment in the Tadzhik water system and that a problem with food supplies could be risky in a vulnerable border region like Tadzhikistan. Other regional spokesmen adopted Gorbachev's insistence on "social justice" (*spravedlivost'*) and greater accountability among cadres to justify their requests. Thus Tataria's first secretary G. I. Usmanov (*Pravda*, March 3, 1986, pp. 2–3) contended at the Twenty-Seventh Congress that the new concern with accountability should prompt the USSR Minister of Energy to speed up construction of a Tatar atomic power station; and he argued that Tataria's oil industry needed new equipment—in the interest of social justice to the oil workers. Sverdlovsk's Iu. V. Petrov (*Pravda*, March 2, 1986, p. 6) claimed that social justice requires equality in different regions: lagging areas deserve special assistance. Politicians outside Moscow interpret new planks in the national platform in a way that will benefit regional and local interests.[15]

But this is only half of the process: regional problems—such as labor deficits or water shortages—turn into national priorities as their effects spread and governments outside Moscow begin to press for relief. Given the interdependence of Soviet regions, regional problems are exported every day to other parts of the USSR. Thus very few problems are ever truly "local," and to the extent that they affect other parts of the country, they give appeals from below added weight.

Regional politicians can, then, appear to promote both local development and national interests at the same time. And, far from being penalized, many who complain most vocally about the treatment of their regions receive promotions. K. T. Mazurov (*XX S"ezd* 1956: 2:74–82), as first secretary of Belorussia in 1956, demurred from Khrushchev's recommendation of doling out equal appropriations to different regions—because, he claimed, Belorussia needed more than other regions; he went on to become deputy prime minister of the USSR and a full member of the Politburo. Or, to take another example, D. A. Kunaev (*XX S"ezd* 1956: 2:173), then prime minister of Kazakhstan, criticized the central government in 1956 for inadequate investment in water supplies for his republic. When he later became first secretary of Kazakhstan and also a full member of the Politburo, he continued to lobby on the same theme, from the

Brezhnev era to that of Gorbachev. Other regional officials have been just as active in defending local interests and experienced as much or more success in their later careers, from Brezhnev (Kazakhstan), A. P. Kirilenko (Sverdlovsk), Frol Kozlov (Leningrad), I. V. Kapitonov (Moscow), and M. S. Solomentsev (Rostov, RSFSR), to Ia. P. Riabov (Sverdlovsk).

The defense of regional economic interests is clearly a legitimate role for republic party bosses. Indeed, national leaders have even institutionalized mechanisms for responding to such requests. National party congresses and the Supreme Soviet have commissions that amend both the plan and the budget in response to regional appeals for more funds; and the Council of Ministers arbitrates regional demands, serving as a court of appeals for disputes and questions that arise concerning the republics versus central ministries and planners (see chapter 3).

However, the fact that such procedures are necessary emphasizes the underlying economic tensions between center and periphery. The very structure of Soviet central planning works against regional interests. Given the continued reliance on the branch principle in economic administration, central ministries tend to downgrade regional concerns in drawing up plans and budgets. One highly detailed account of the planning process provides a vivid illustration: out of 203 steps in compiling a ministry's plan, the regional dimension is introduced only at step 179, after most of the key decisions have already been made (Kalinin 1973:64–138). Nor is the regional part of the plan binding on the ministry—it represents desirable but not obligatory targets for regional development (Emelianov 1976; D. L. Kartvelashvili, *Deviataia sessiia* 1983:107). Thus branch and territorial planning are still at loggerheads, leaving regional officials in the middle. Given the increased responsibilities, politicians outside Moscow are under more pressure to coordinate regional development targets with central ministries; yet coordination is inadequate, as Gorbachev readily admitted (*Izvestiia*, February 26, 1986, p. 5). In spite of almost constant emphasis on the need for integration (*sochetanie*) of branch and territorial concerns, branch planning still carries the day.

That leaves regional and local authorities to cope with the familiar disproportions that grow out of sectoral plans: ministries may build factories but skimp on the housing needed to find and keep an adequate labor force. When housing is built, it often lacks the roads, stores, and other services that would make new neighborhoods livable. Leaders in the periphery find themselves responsible for correcting the problems created by sectoral planning, but with limited authority and little funding available to mitigate all the imbalances.

The dominance of central ministries puts an even higher premium on the representation of regional interests in Moscow. Regional leaders rarely pass up an opportunity to focus central attention on problems at home. Occasionally they even present joint appeals, as in the case of lobbying by Central Asian party bosses for the diversion of Siberian rivers (*XXV S"ezd* 1976: 1:137–44, 176–81, 345–50). However, overt factionalism carries political risks, and regional leaders are more often competitors for a bigger share of finite central resources. And given the growing territorial imbalances in the labor supply, in natural resources, and in water supplies, the competition seems unlikely to diminish.

Regional competition adds fuel to the ongoing debate about the proper goals of regional policy. Soviet leaders have traditionally promised to promote both more efficiency and greater equality in allocating resources. But there is little consensus on how the two goals are to be combined. They are, of course, often viewed as antithetical; yet they can be complementary in the right circumstances. It can actually pay to redistribute resources from more to less developed regions, where the returns may well be higher (Buchanan 1950; Richardson 1973).

Equally important, leaving underdeveloped regions to lag behind can be costly, since, as was emphasized above, regions are increasingly interdependent. Brezhnev (1972:29) called attention to this point in his speech on the fiftieth anniversary of the USSR:

> The state of economic affairs in, say, Uzbekistan, depends not only on the cotton crop in the republic itself, but also on the work of the machine-builders of the Urals and Leningrad, the miners of the Kuznetsk basin, the grain-growing state farms of Kazakhstan and the makers of electronic computers in Belorussia.

The quantitative evidence bears out his argument. Some regions import as much as 90 percent of the materials they use in basic industries, and an equally high share of the fuels they consume (Gillula 1979:642–44). As a result, economic stagnation or decline in one area can spill over all too easily into other regions. To use Brezhnev's example, a labor shortage in the Urals or in Leningrad threatens the continued supply of machinery to Uzbekistan, just as a shortfall in the cotton crop may reduce the supply of cloth to textile industries in the European USSR. Given the high degree of interdependence, the effects of economic problems and inequalities "travel" all too quickly. Serious regional inequality can be inefficient.

For Soviet leaders, then, the key question is not whether to promote equality, but how (and how much) to pursue it. No single approach seems to be universally accepted. Some regional leaders advocate parallel industrial development in each republic; others call for equal development of each republic's "potential"; and still others—including Nikita Khrushchev—have defined equality in terms of equal per capita expenditures for each region (Zakumbaev 1975; Lychagin 1975). The choice of a definition is of course political: republic spokesmen seem to advocate the formula that will most benefit their own region.

Similarly, there has been little consensus on the ideal form of territorial organization for the Soviet economy (Holubnychy 1975; Medvedkova 1984). The existing system comes in for constant criticism: regional and local governments that were set up decades ago find it difficult to cope with the increasing number of problems that cut across their borders. As Soviet planners acknowledge, old administrative boundaries correspond neither to current settlement patterns nor to the areal distribution of economic activity, and the literature is filled with proposals for redrawing economic regions (Alampiev 1960; Kazanskii and Khorev 1976; Pavlenko 1983).[16]

Moscow's response has been to reorganize, and the frequency of reorganizations reveals the dilemmas in trying to establish an optimal mix of center-regional authority and optimal regional borders. Programs have been shifted from central to republic jurisdiction and back; new regionalization schemes have been introduced to create more "rational" planning units; and still more reforms have attempted to streamline territorial planning through production associations and "territorial-production complexes" (TPKs). At the same time, Soviet leaders have been extremely reluctant to cede any real decision-making powers to lower levels of government or to TPKs; reforms seem always to be designed to perfect vertical coordination without surrendering central control. The Sovnarkhoz is the most dramatic of these efforts to reorganize, but it is by no means the only example. Reorganization started well before 1957, and it has continued ever since.

Center-Regional Conflicts and the Allocation of Funding

Thus despite the advantages—indeed the necessity—of center-regional cooperation, tensions still arise between Moscow and republic capitals over economic policy-making. How do they influence the allocation of funds among Soviet regions? As in the literature on Western countries, studies of the USSR suggest two different answers. One emphasizes the hierarchical nature of the system, the importance of personal ties, and thus the value of direct access to top leaders. In this case, regional officials with better connections in Moscow are also assumed to be more successful in their lobbying for more support from the center. Political clout presumably pays off in bigger increments of funding. Having an "in" should enable regional leaders to find a more responsive audience in the capital. As Rakowska-Harmstone (1979:182–83) suggests, "the success of this or that republic in having its demands met frequently depends on the quality of its leadership's contacts at the top." And the best contacts are established through direct representation in high politics—in the Politburo. Regions with a spokesman in the Politburo—such as the Ukraine and Georgia— therefore ought to have a measurable advantage when it comes to competing for funds.

Other forms of political privilege are also viewed as possible explanations for differential regional success: some non-Russian regions seem to enjoy greater trust from Moscow, as evidenced by the degree to which native elites hold key party and government posts (Miller 1977). And such trust may well be reflected in budget allocations (Hough and Fainsod 1979). In addition, Western studies also point to the anointing of a new republic party boss as another source of at least a temporary increase in regional funds (Bunce 1979). New leaders presumably have more political capital and perhaps more energy at the start of their term in office and are therefore seen as more likely to try to change appropriations policies.

In contrast, interdependence among regions, the commitment to multiple goals such as efficiency and equality and the need to coopt local loyalties to the center would lead to a wider dispersion of funds among regions and localities. Most or all regions would get some response, because a diffusion of benefits would serve the economic and poitical interests of national leaders. The result should be compromise over regional allocations and regional development and a relatively equal distribution of funds among the republics. As Bialer (1980) predicts, the outcome of the competition should be a draw. And the example of Khrushchev would seem to bear him out: Khrushchev's advocacy of equal per capita allocations among the republics seems to have been a calculated political appeal in his bid for regional support.

From a comparative standpoint, then, both the Soviet local revolution and the conflicts over regional appropriations in the USSR run parallel to trends and conflicts in Western countries. However, the evolution of Soviet center-regional relations and "fiscal federalism" since the early days of Soviet power sets the USSR apart, and the history does much to explain both the current role of the republics and the issues that dominate regional agendas. Chapter 2 therefore turns to the development of Soviet fiscal federalism, to help explain the factors that have shaped center-regional economic ties.

CHAPTER TWO

THE EVOLUTION OF SOVIET FISCAL FEDERALISM

CENTER-LOCAL RELATIONS are rarely static in any modern state. The real distribution of money and programs among levels of government is constantly in flux as new problems arise and political conditions and leaders change. According to Soviet theorists, that is precisely the way it should be: in their view, there is no single right way to divide tasks and budgets among central, republic, and local government agencies. Instead, the Soviet system ought to be reorganized often as society develops and circumstances dictate (Piskotin 1981; Shirkevich 1972). Western scholars have taken a similar if less positive view of Soviet needs. Grossman (1963:107) has argued, for example, that determining the optimal degree of centralization is the "chief persistent systemic problem" in a Soviet-type or command system.

Soviet history certainly bears out the difficulty of finding a single long-term solution. Nearly every decade since 1917 has witnessed attempts to redivide programs and funds between center and periphery. Leaders from Stalin to Gorbachev all presided over reforms, though the magnitude of change and the room for maneuver both seem to have grown narrower over time.

This chapter examines the changes in the federal system and their impact on the economic role of republic governments. The changes are tracked by measuring the republics' share of budget funds (which, in Soviet practice, also includes local budgets) since 1924.[1] I will be looking at expenditures, revenues, and transfer payments from Moscow to assess the evolution of "fiscal federalism" and the rise of the republics in the Soviet system. The distribution of expenditures can reveal how much of the business of government has come under republic jurisdiction through the years, and can therefore offer insight into the changing degree of centralization in the Soviet system. The size and sources of republic budget revenue over time also say a good deal about the constraints under which republic officials operate and the revenue needs that bring them to Moscow seeking additional funding.

Budget data do, however, need to be interpreted with caution. (See the discussion in appendix A.) As noted in the introduction, the budget does not include all the funds that Soviet planners actually spend. And what is included is not always clear: defense expenditures are the most notable example, but there are also others, such as agricultural subsidies, that are hidden in budgetary residuals.

Budget figures prove to be much clearer on the vertical allocation of funds, by revealing how much of direct budget outlays are left in republic and local hands. The division of funds between central and lower governments should not, of course, be equated with the real division of power. The fact that republic governments account for nearly half of all budget expenditures hardly makes them coequal partners with Moscow. Central controls are greater than any simple tally of budget funds would indicate. Yet the data can tell us when and how the controls have changed—whether the responsibilities entrusted to regional politicians have expanded or contracted. Budget funds can be of substantial value in mapping the repeated attempts to alter center-regional economic relations.

Centralization in Soviet Budget Expenditures

The most striking feature of budget allocations between Moscow and the republics is the uneven pattern over time—the dramatic peaks and valleys in the republic share. Budget revenues have followed a similar path, with the same peaks and valleys in the degree of centralization. Reforms in the federal system have had a profound impact on the way funds are distributed between center and periphery.

As figure 2.1 illustrates, Soviet fiscal federalism has gone through several stages, with an emphasis on increased central control during the First Five-Year Plan (1928–32), the war, and during the last years of Stalin's rule. There have also been several eras when central controls became less restrictive. Moscow's share of the budget dropped during the Sovnarkhoz reform, of course, but also during the mid-1930s, when a brief campaign was mounted to counteract the hypercentraliztion that the First Plan had produced. In contrast to these rather dramatic changes, the period since the Sovnarkhoz reform has been one of relative stability.

The history of these various stages offers a revealing look into the transformations of center-regional relations since the NEP. During the 1920s, after the formal creation of the federal system, Moscow and the republics accounted for roughly equal shares of the state budget (figure 2.1). Moscow's share included exclusive jurisdiction over defense, foreign affairs, and foreign trade. Other functions, such as industry, agriculture, transport, communications, labor, finance, and Rabkrin (Workers' and Peasants' Inspection) were officially under joint central and republic ("union-republic") jurisdiction. Still others, such as public education, health care, social security, housing, and municipal services were left to republic and local administration (Okrostvardidze 1973; Kochumov 1982). However, what was clearly divided on paper was ambiguous in practice. The joint union-republic programs were a gray area with the rights and duties of each level never very clearly specified, and with leaders in the periphery complaining about frequent central encroachment on the functions formally assigned to lower levels (Bescherevnykh 1976). The confusion was aggravated by continual reorganizations. Individual enterprises and other institutions were shifted from one level of government's jurisdiction to the other, creating havoc in the still underdeveloped budgetary system (Davies 1958a).

The ratification of the First Five-Year Plan (FYP), with its headlong rush to industrialize and collectivize, quickly put an end to the ambiguities. Stalin's rapid development strategy led to a massive increase in the state budget, most of it concentrated at the national level (Tulebaev 1973). Total expenditures quadrupled just between 1928 and 1932 (from .878 to 3.800 billion rubles), while central government expenditures increased by almost six times (from .533 to 3.005 billion rubles). (For sources, see appendix A.) During the same period, republic expenditures barely doubled.

In the stampede toward industrialization, Moscow shifted major republic-level programs to direct central jurisdiction. The bulk of the republics' responsibilities in agriculture, light industry, transport, communications, and professional-technical education were taken over by the central government. Agriculture was transferred from republic to

FIGURE 2.1

Republic and Local Share of Soviet Budget Expenditures, 1925–1980

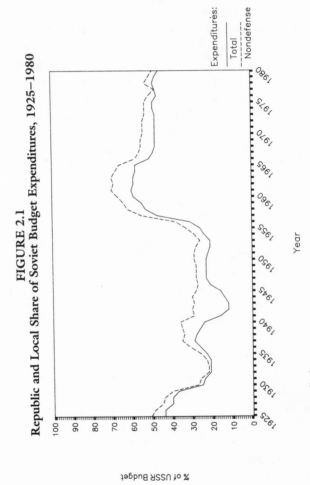

For sources, see appendix A.

union-republic control in 1929, and light industry and higher and technical education were reorganized along the same lines in 1931 (Aspaturian 1950; Sullivant 1962). And of course the bulk of industrial production came under national jurisdiction. Thus, for example, by 1932 over 90 percent of the government's expenditures on industry came from the all-union budget (D'iachenko 1978:296).

All told, the sweeping centralization cut the republic share of the budget from 44 to just 26 percent between 1926/27 and 1932 (D'iachenko 1957:577). The republic share of spending for industrial development dropped from 19.6 to 7.2 percent; in agriculture, republic expenditures declined from 64.6 to 29.1 percent of the total; and in transport and communications, the regional share went from 11.6 to 7.0 percent (D'iachenko 1957:577). At the end of the First FYP, republic and local governments retained a major role only in health care, primary and secondary education, welfare, housing and municipal services.

Thus the contours of the centralized administrative machine had already been established by 1932. Moscow was to absorb even more functions during the war: conversion to a wartime economy, temporary losses of territory, and the squeeze on civilian services all cut republic expenditures to less than 15 percent of the total in 1942. And when military expenditures declined and the system had reconverted to a civilian economy, Moscow's share of the budget remained higher than it had been before the war. It was even on the increase at the time of Stalin's death, while both the republics' share of the budget and the absolute level of republic expenditures dropped in 1951 and 1952.

Yet the Stalin era was not one of unremitting increases in centralization. The early 1930s did witness a brief retreat, when the Central Executive Committee (TsIK) moved to counteract excessive central controls by restricting further transfers of republic programs to the central government's jurisdiction and reassigning some health and education expenditures from central to republic and local administration (Davies 1958a). Together, these measures gave a modest boost to the republic share of the Soviet budget during the mid-1930s, but the effect was soon reversed with the onset of the war.

By the early 1950s, the war and postwar reconstruction had left the republics with only a fifth of the total budget. Republic leaders had major responsibility only for health, education, welfare, housing, and municipal services. Even in these areas, Moscow exercised stringent control over budget funds, down to the number of pupils enrolled in school and the amount to be spent on them (Davies 1958a).

As chapter 1 showed, the combined succession struggle and economic crisis in 1953 unleashed a number of proposals to reduce the administrative burdens on Moscow. The first of them to be implemented was a plan for consolidating the many overlapping ministries that had multiplied under Stalin: those responsible for domestic and for foreign trade were merged, as were ministries in machine-building, electrical equipment, and other fields of production. All told, over 50 ministries were amalgamated into 25 (Vvedensky 1958).

However, the consolidation failed to produce any measurable economic improvement, and as the initiative shifted to Khrushchev, the result was a more sweeping attempt to cut back the central bureaucracy and enhance the role of regional and local officialdom. The new tack was explained in an article in the December 1953 issue of *Kommunist* (Shitarev 1953): while stoutly defending the need for centralization the author emphasized that the center could only be as strong as the subnational officials who carried out party policy. Strengthening the role of leaders in the periphery would in theory enhance Moscow's power as well.

By 1954, the new line brought the transformation of all-union ministries into union-republic or republic ones, and the devolution of programs and funds in everything from ferrous metallurgy, coal, and oil to machine-building from central to republic administration (Sabirov 1966). Within two years, republic governments were responsible for enterprises producing 55 percent of Soviet industrial output (*Narkhoz* 1960:214).

The new leadership also reduced some of the stringent central controls over republic expenditures. As of May 1955, Moscow was to approve only the totals for major spending categories in republic budgets, leaving the republic governments themselves to decide how funds were to be distributed within categories and within the republics (Sabirov 1966; Khimicheva 1966). The republics were also granted the right to retain any above-plan revenues they could generate, to determine how revenues and expenditures would be divided among localities, and to set administrative boundaries for local governments under their jurisdiction (Okrostvaridze 1973; *Spravochnik partiinogo rabotnika* 1957:458–59). By 1957, the Sovnarkhoz reform turned economic administration over to 105 regional councils, 94 representing oblasti in the largest republics—the

RSFSR, Ukraine, Uzbekistan, and Kazakhstan—and one each in the other eleven republics.

In addition, the reforms under Khrushchev included several other major changes in planning and budgeting. The regime cut back on the number of indicators to be included in national economic plans, and simplified procedures for planning both costs and labor. Moscow also raised the cutoff point for "above-limit" investment projects. Before 1953, any new project of 1.5–10 million rubles or more (the exact limit depended on the sector involved) required specific approval from the center; under the new regime, the limits were raised to 5–25 million rubles (Davies 1958a).

The post-Stalin leadership also upgraded social welfare programs in the mid-1950s, and this too added to the programs and funds under regional administration. The pension system was revamped in 1956 and education was reorganized in 1958, with both measures pumping up regional expenditures. Agricultural investment climbed, and the increasing emphasis on consumer policies pushed republic expenditures even higher.

Altogether, these changes in federal organization and in priorities gave the Soviet republics a vastly increased share of the budget. Republic governments had accounted for only 6 percent of budgetary expenditures on industry in 1950; by 1958, their share had jumped to 76 percent. In agriculture, they had claimed only 26 percent of expenditures in 1950; but by 1958 they accounted for 95 percent (for sources, see appendix A). And by 1960, 94 percent of Soviet industrial output came from enterprises under republic or regional administration (*Narkhoz* 1960:214).

This is not to say that Moscow had given up its controls. On the contrary, the planning process was still centralized. Ministries had been dismantled, but many of their tasks had been absorbed by Gosplan and Gosbank, thus keeping control over the allocation of resources in central hands. Yet as the many criticisms of the Sovnarkhozy revealed, the reform did indeed allow regional officials more power—if only the power to evade or alter central priorities. Regional leaders were accused of hoarding resources and neglecting deliveries outside their own territory: since their primary obligation was to meet the local plan, machinery and supplies designated for export to other sovnarkhozy were diverted to local needs instead (Katsuk and Onipko 1961). Complaints of localism and of investment "fetishism" among regional officials thus began almost immediately after the Sovnarkhoz reform was adopted.

Sovnarkhoz officials were also subtly redefining national economic choices, diverting investment and budget funds from central priorities to local needs. Some were reprimanded for shifting resources into consumer goods and services, thereby taking funds and materials away from the more traditional priorities of heavy industry. The reprogramming of funds took on major proportions: in Karaganda, Sovnarkhoz officials siphoned 25 million rubles from heavy industry to build a circus, a theater, and sanatoria. Still more funds were diverted to build a vocational school, swimming pools, and a host of other public facilities.[2] Some local leaders, given the means, upgraded social benefits—a visible and surely popular means of responding to local needs.

Complaints arose too over the sheer administrative confusion that accompanied the Sovnarkhoz experiment. Top officials in the old ministries had been reassigned to Sovnarkhozy throughout the country, but many did not show up for their new assignments (Swearer 1959). Counting the ones who did, there were still too few people with the requisite expertise to fill all the key posts in 100-plus economic regions (Kosygin 1965).

The distortions introduced by the Sovnarkhoz system quickly prompted the consolidation of individual economic regions and the strengthening of controls at the top. By 1962, the original 105 sovnarkhozy had been amalgamated into 47; centralized state committees had assumed the responsibility for coordinating various branches of the economy from Moscow; and corresponding Gosplan departments had been expanded to provide more central control (Bergson 1964). The ultimate consolidation, of course, came in 1965 with the repeal of the Sovnarkhoz system and the return to branch administration.

Since then, territorial reorganizations have been less pronounced (see figure 2.1), and attention has focused more on restructuring the ministerial system. The two major efforts of the Brezhnev era—the Liberman and the ob"edinenie reform—both cut into the role previously accorded to regional leaders. The Liberman reforms, by emphasizing internal rather than budgetary financing in state enterprises, cut the total share of Soviet public expenditures passing through the state budget—thereby shifting some fiscal responsibilities from regional to enterprise or ministry control (Tulebaev 1973). The association reforms of the 1970s followed a different strategy but had similar effects on republic finances: given their emphasis on consolidation within and across different economic sectors, they resulted in the elimination of several republic branches from union-republic ministries. The reforms also complicated the process of integrating plans and solving problems between local factory management and local officials: with decision-making authority (and khozraschet status) pushed up the hierarchy to the level of an association, local officials now found themselves having to deal with a higher and more distant bureaucracy to resolve the same questions (Todorskii 1979). In addition, limits for new investment projects were lowered to give Moscow more direct control over funding, and the number of products to be planned directly by Moscow increased (Dyker 1983). The net result was an upward trend in the degree of centralization, as the division of budget funds between center and republics suggests. Nevertheless, the republics' share of the budget—and their share of responsibilities—is still larger than it was at any point in the Stalin era.

Sectoral Differences in Budgetary Centralization

Judging from the evidence of the budget, Soviet leaders have indeed lived up to the dictum that the federal system ought to be reorganized frequently. While the effect on the republics' share of total expenditures has been dramatic, it has also been far from uniform from one sector of the economy to another. These sectoral differences are tracked in figure 2.2, which shows the republics' share of the two major expenditure categories: economic development (in Soviet terminology, "financing the economy")—including investment grants and operating subsidies for industry, agriculture, construction, transport, communications, trade, housing, and municipal services; and social-cultural programs—including budget grants for "enlightenment" (education, science, and culture), health, and social security.

In the economic realm, the peaks and valleys follow much the same path as total expenditures: extreme centralization during the First FYP, the war, and the late Stalin period, coupled with a marked shift toward the republics during the 1950s and especially the Sovnarkhoz period. Yet the patterns vary across individual sectors: the republic share of industrial expenditures peaked during the Sovnarkhoz reform and then dropped radically, while republic involvement in agriculture continued at a much higher level even after the Sovnarkhoz experiment ended. The republic share of transport, communications, and trade expenditures also continued to increase well after 1965 (figure 2.2).[3]

FIGURE 2.2
Republic and Local Share of Soviet Budget, by Type of Expenditure

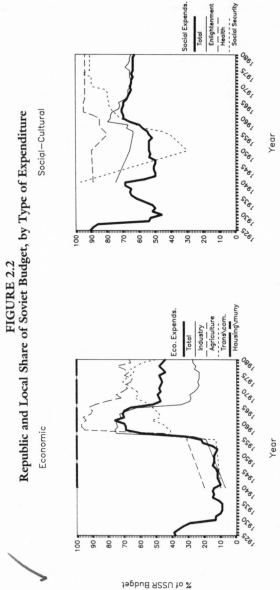

Industry includes construction; health includes physical education; enlightenment excludes science. Data between 1940 and 1950 are interpolated, as are data for 1951–54 on industry, agriculture, trans/com, enlightenment, health, and social security.
For sources, see appendix A.

Republic responsibility for social welfare programs has been more stable. Basic social services have consistently been provided by regional and local governments. The chief exception is in social security, where the central government's provision of veterans' and survivors' benefits after the war temporarily gave it the lion's share of expenditures. As war-related benefits diminished in importance and new social welfare programs came onto the agenda, the republics once again assumed the primary role in the social welfare budget.

Differences in Budgetary Centralization Among Republics

The budgetary turbulence illustrated in figure 2.2 has also had varying effects on different republics (Tulebaev 1973). Because of the dramatic changes in the allocation of industrial expenditures to different levels of government, predominantly industrial regions have experienced more fluctuations in their budgets than predominantly agricultural ones. The more the industry in the republic—especially major industry—the more the size of the republic budget has been influenced by the reorganizations described above.

In every republic, the devolution from 1953 onward inflated republic-level economic expenditures. Funds that each region had previously received through the central budget were now counted in republic budgets instead, and official statistics for republic economic expenditures tripled overnight.[4]

However, when the Sovnarkhoz reform was revoked, the impact varied from one republic to another, depending on the sectors dominating each region's economy. Since industry experienced the most dramatic recentralization (see figure 2.2), the most industrialized regions—such as Russia and the Ukraine—saw an absolute drop in republic economic expenditures (especially because heavy industry was now to be administered almost wholly by the central government).[5] These republics still received industrial funds from Moscow—in fact, their total investment allocations increased— but now the amount would be counted in the center's rather than the republic's budget. Other regions experienced far less of a change in their finances, since their economies concentrated more on sectors (such as light industry and agriculture) that continued to be relatively less centralized even after the return to ministerial administration.

The history of Soviet fiscal federalism is thus one of continual reorganizations, all in an effort to retain and yet modify Moscow's controls over the periphery. Recasting the administrative apparatus proved to be a substitute for more fundamental changes in economic priorities and planning.

This is not to say that the reorganizations have had no impact; certainly reforms in the economic structure of Soviet center-regional relations have had substantial effects on the role of governments outside Moscow. Indeed, the experience with the sovnarkhozy suggests that devolution may have worked only too well: given even a very limited increase in operational authority, regional leaders showed an inclination to siphon resources away from centrally defined priorities to local uses, some of them in the consumer sector. These local "deviations" suggest that from Moscow's vantage point, the risks of decentralization may go beyond the simple loss of direct political control over the periphery. Decentralization also threatens to undermine the Kremlin's fundamental economic priorities.

Revenues

Just as the republic share of Soviet expenditures has fluctuated over time, so too has the allocation of revenues between Moscow and the republics. Each transfer of programs between central and regional jurisdiction raises the question of funding sources for republics and localities, which have traditionally relied on less income-elastic taxes and fees. Moscow has claimed the more lucrative sources of budget revenue. Thus governments below the national level share the same predicament as their counterparts in the West: an imbalance between basic sources of revenue and demand for public services and programs.

The regional and local "revenue problem" has dogged Soviet leaders since the beginnings of the Bolshevik regime, prompting a good deal of experimentation with the tax system. The timing of these experiments corresponds closely to what was happening to central and regional expenditures (see figure 2.3).

During the 1920s, each level of government relied on different sources of revenue. For the center, the main sources of income were excises on consumer goods and taxes on industry, which grew apace as the economy recovered from the devastation of the Civil War and the NEP moved into full swing. In contrast, republic and local governments were allocated

FIGURE 2.3
Republic and Local revenues and Transfers Received, 1925–1980

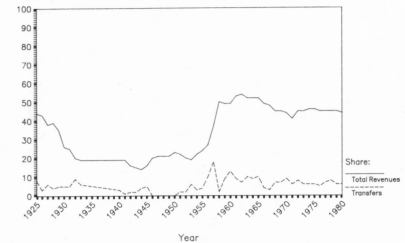

Year

Total revenues represent the republic and local share of USSR budget revenues. Transfers are calculated net, as a share of all republic and local revenues. Data for 1934–39 are interpolated, as are transfers for 1946–49.

For sources, see appendix A.

direct taxes on personal incomes and agriculture, and nontax revenues such as stump and license fees (Plotnikov 1954). These sources proved to be far more limited in raising budgetary income. Direct taxes on individuals appeared to be a political liability to the new regime, and at first were employed less as a means of raising income than as a device for regulating private economic activity (Millar and Bahry 1979). The literature on taxation was filled with references to tax policies as weapons in the struggle against the bourgeois class. And political imperatives aside, direct taxes were simply difficult to collect for a financial system lacking the organization and personnel needed to keep track of what people were earning and what they owed (D'iachenko 1978). Thus central revenues grew more rapidly than did republic and local ones during the 1920s, creating a budgetary shortfall at the republic and local level.

Moscow's initial solution was to provide central subsidies to the republics (and republic subsidies to the localities). But subsidies drew increasing fire for undermining fiscal responsibility: regional and local officials seemed to be more concerned with getting a larger subsidy than with exploiting their own sources of revenue (Okrostvaridze 1973). Consequently, Moscow turned to the principle of tax-sharing, giving both republic and local governments a fraction of national tax revenues collected in their territory. Regional and local officials now were to have a stake in seeing that national revenues were collected promptly and efficiently.

Yet in spite of the concern with fiscal responsibility in the periphery, promptness and efficiency were nearly impossible. There were simply too many taxes to monitor, and the organization of the financial system was still precarious at best in outlying regions. In the course of the NEP, Moscow adopted a profusion of new taxes on agriculture, industry, trade, incomes, and local property, with over 60 different taxes imposed on industry alone (D'iachenko 1978; Sabirov 1966). And these were to be collected by a Commissariat of Finance that was still barely organized in the periphery. The further one traveled from Moscow, the more difficult it was to find effective fiscal administration. Officials in Turkestan could not find enough qualified people to staff local finance departments, and Soviet accounts complain of disorganization and corruption. (Sabirov 1966). In the Caucasus, regional officials rarely were able to prepare a realistic budget until the fiscal year was over (Okrostvaridze 1973).

The disarray increased rapidly when the new five-year plan in 1928 multiplied revenue needs. Budget projections called for a dramatic increase in expenditures; but the revenue system, with its confused array of taxes, was slow and cumbersome in responding. The very process of tax collection proved costly: enterprises often needed special staffs on hand to decipher the welter of tax regulations and rates, and to keep accounts for each tax separately (D'iachenko 1978). The pressures led to a major reform of the tax system in 1930, with 61 taxes on industry and trade merged into 2— a turnover or excise tax chiefly on agricultural and consumer goods and extractive industries, and a profit tax on the proceeds of socialized industry (Plotnikov 1948).[6] Enterprises were to pay taxes to the level of government holding jurisdiction over them, and since Moscow now had direct jurisdiction over most of industry, agriculture, trade, transport, and communications, revenue collection became a highly centralized affair. It was now up to the national Commissariat of Finance to make sure that taxes were paid. Regional and local governments would no longer be responsible for the major work of the revenue system, and would instead receive subsidies to balance out the limited expenditures they were to make.

The reform unquestionably streamlined the revenue system, and thereby overcentralized it as well. The Finance Commissariat simply could not keep adequate and timely account of the tax obligations of all the enterprises and ministries now under central jurisdiction. Payments were frequently delayed and sometimes evaded altogether (Plotnikov 1948). Moreover, the Finance Commissariat's attempt to enlist republic and local assistance in checking on tax compliance at the local level met with little success, since—as financial authorities complained—regional and local officials had little incentive to help collect revenues that would flow to the central budget (Bescherevnykh 1960).

Together these difficulties prompted further reforms in 1931. Revenue collection was decentralized, with the republics now assigned to collect the turnover tax and allotted a percentage of the receipts collected within their borders, to give them an incentive for tracking down every ruble owed. In this connection, the tax offered central planners a key advantage over other revenue sources: it was essentially a fixed payment based on production or sale of goods and could be planned with relative ease (Millar and Bahry 1979).[7] That made it a useful source for shoring up republic revenues, and it became the main means of balancing republic budgets: the percentage retained in each region was recalculated each year to cover the gap between the expenditures planned for the republic and the available locally generated revenue sources. The percentage of the tax retained in each republic thus varied across regions and from year to year. The highest deductions went to the least developed republics, where other taxes such as agricultural and personal income taxes yielded too little to cover spending needs (Kudriashov 1962). And as table 2.1 shows, the same principle has continued to operate over time: the Central Asian republics keep almost 100 percent of the turnover tax revenues they collect, while more industrialized regions—such as the RSFSR, the Ukraine, Latvia—hand over roughly half of their turnover tax receipts to the all-union budget. In effect, the tax serves as a major device for redistributing revenues and financing economic development in less advanced regions.

The tax reforms of the 1930s thus affirmed several basic principles that would subsequently guide revenue allocations among different levels of government (Bescherevnykh 1976). Most direct taxes on the population and "local" revenues such as license and stump fees were to be left wholly to republic and local governments, where they could be spent visibly on local needs (Davies 1958a). In addition, profits from enterprises under

TABLE 2.1
Share of Turnover Taxes Retained by Republic Governments,
Selected Years[a]
(in percent)

	1950	1960	1970	1980
RSFSR	6.5	24.7	32.7	47.9
Ukraine	16.4	27.7	27.2	54.8
Belorussia	28.5	44.2	64.3	64
Uzbekistan	22	47.9	100	98.2
Kazakhstan	33.3	100	100	100
Georgia	27.8	63.6	75.7	67.2
Azerbaidzhan	19.9	59.1	79.5	52.6
Lithuania	39.8	61.6	75.2	91
Moldavia	54.8	22.1	37.8	54.1
Latvia	3.0	11.2	26	43.1
Kirgiziia	47.8	93.4	78.7	100
Tadzhikistan	48.6	80.1	100	91.1
Armenia	43.8	59.0	100	61.8
Turkmenia	35.3	99.8	98.6	100
Estonia	21.4	51.0	35.8	56.9

[a]Share of all turnover taxes collected in the territory of the republic. Percentages are from proposed budgets.

SOURCES: Zverev (1950); "Zakon SSSR o gosudarstvennom biudzhete SSSR na 1960 g.," in *Zasedaniia* (1960:690–92); "Zakon SSSR o gosudarstvennom biudzhete SSSR na 1970 g.," in *Pravda*, December 19, 1969, p. 2; "Zakon SSSR o gosudarstvennom biudzhete SSSR na 1980 g.," in *Pravda*, December 1, 1979, p. 2.

republic subordination were to go to republic budgets. Other taxes, especially the more lucrative ones such as turnover taxes, were to be shared by Moscow as it saw fit each year in order to balance republic budgets. Soviet budgetary law thus came to distinguish between "assigned" (*zakreplennye*) revenue sources—those that were collected by and left at a single level in the budget hierarchy—and "shared" (*reguliriuiushchie*) sources—those divided up among different levels (see table 2.2). This system was supposed to minimize the need for subsidies to the republics and to ensure their fiscal responsibility (Kudriashov 1962). They now kept a percentage of the revenues generated within their borders, and had a stake in seeing that every ruble was collected on time (Shirkevich 1972).

Since revenue sources were now to be divided according to the need to cover expenditures, republic shares of both revenues and expenditures came to be virtually identical. When central government spending climbed

TABLE 2.2
"Own" and "Shared" Revenues in Soviet Fiscal Federalism[a]

	Percent of all Budget
"Own" Revenues:	Revenues in 1980[b]
All-Union budget	
Profit payments of all-union subordinate enterprises and ministries	17.78
Customs revenue	n.a.
Union-Republic budget	
Profit payments of republic-subordinate enterprises and ministries	8.32
Forestry revenue	0.2
Local budget	
Profit payments of local-subordinate enterprises and ministries	3.58
"Local" taxes and fees (theater taxes, license and notary fees, fines, vehicle registration, and property taxes, among others)	0.4
"Shared" Revenues:	
Turnover tax	31.09
Personal income tax	7.58
Lottery bond revenue	0.2
Lottery revenue	0.1
Income taxes on kolkhozy and collectives	0.6
Agricultural tax	.08
Bachelor tax	.04
[Social insurance]	4.61

[a]"Own" *(zakreplennye)* revenues are those assigned to a single level of government; and "shared" revenues *(reguliruiushchie)* are divided among levels. Note, however, that the central and republic governments may allocate a portion of their "own" revenues (e.g., of enterprise profits) for use by lower budgets.

[b]Total budget revenue reported in 1980 was 302.7 billion rubles *(Gosbiudzhet* 1982:11–12, 46–47, 70–71). The totals in this column add up to considerably less than 100 percent, omitting customs duties, budgetary reserves, and other, more ambiguous categories (for more detail, see Birman 1982).

during the war, so too did the national share of tax revenues. Agricultural taxes were raised, and personal income taxes were increased and shifted from a local source to one shared by the center and the localities. Poll or head taxes were also imposed on able-bodied adults, as was an additional tax on bachelors and childless families, and these too were shared, though the bulk of the revenues went to the center (Allakhverdian et al. 1966).

The Sovnarkhoz experiment had the opposite effect. When economic administration was turned over to regional councils, agricultural taxes and

TABLE 2.3
Major Revenue Sources for Republic Budgets
(in percent)

Republic share of total USSR	1950	1960	1970	1980
Taxes and fees paid by individuals				
Individual income tax	50	49.5	50	54.1
Agricultural tax	50	100	100	100
Bachelor's tax	50	100	100	100
3% lottery bond	0	50	50	50
State lottery	—ᵃ	100	100	100
Taxes and fees paid by state enterprises				
Turnover tax	12.3	35.3	44.6	57.2
Profit payments	38.9	65.9	45.1	40.1

ᵃThe lottery was instituted in 1957–58.

SOURCES: Gosbiudzhet (1962:7–9, 66–69); Gosbiudzhet (1972:11–12, 75–78); Gosbiudzhet (1982:10–11, 46–48).

income taxes on cooperatives were transferred from the all-union to the republic budget, and republic deductions from bond revenues and from turnover and personal income taxes were raised to give the republics additional revenue (Bescherevnykh 1960).

Through all the changes, however, one thing has remained constant—Moscow's penchant for keeping the most lucrative revenue sources and assigning regional governments the bulk of taxes collected directly from the population (see table 2.3). Soviet leaders can therefore exploit the fact that most of the taxes paid by individuals are plowed back into the social welfare and cultural programs that republic and local governments provide. The "tax bite" gets softened by linking it directly to visible local benefits.

By relying on the turnover tax to balance republic budgets, Moscow has also left regional leaders highly dependent on a few key economic sectors for the bulk of their revenue (Dosymbekov 1971). The tax, which alone accounts for 40 percent of republic budget revenues, is collected primarily from the extraction of natural resources and from agricultural and consumer products (Vasilik 1982; Miroshchenko 1974). Other taxes on these same sectors provide an additional 20 percent of republic revenues: the bulk of the profit payments collected by republic budgets are derived from agricultural and consumer products, since these are the sectors predominantly under republic jurisdiction.[8]

A bad year on the farms or in the extraction of natural resources therefore cuts significantly into the short-term funds available to republic budgets—and thus into the means for financing social welfare, consumer services, and other social cultural programs funded by republic governments. Consequently, Soviet fiscal federalism links republic programs closely with the success of the primary sectors in the Soviet economy (Pavlenko 1983).

Intergovernmental Transfers

Given all the changes in the republic share of expenditures and in the revenue system, Soviet planners have had to rely on subsidies and transfers to the republics as something of an unfortunate necessity. For the most part, however, Moscow's revenue-sharing scheme has tended to keep the total amounts doled out to republic governments rather low.

Over the years, Moscow has used three types of transfers to help meet regional expenditure needs: "subventions" or grants-in-aid to cover operating expenditures; categorical grants (*dotatsii*) to finance specific projects such as public buildings, highways, etc.; and "means" (*sredstva*) to cover programs jointly financed by Moscow and the republics (such as elections) and to cover funding needs unforeseen at the start of the fiscal year. (Avetisian 1979; Kudriashov 1962).[9]

Each of these has played a somewhat different role at different times. Subventions were chiefly used during the 1920s and 1930s, to cover expenditures in less developed regions, where local revenue bases were so limited that even 100 percent deductions from all-union revenues were inadequate to balance the budget (Kudriashov 1962). In the mid-1920s for example, republic budgets in Turkmenia, Uzbekistan, and the Transcaucasus were all covered by subsidies from Moscow (Bescherevnykh 1976). These grants-in-aid to the republics were phased out as rapid development pushed economic tasks out of republic budgets and as tax bases expanded in outlying areas, bringing more revenues into republic coffers.

Additional grants (*dotatsii*) were also used in the 1920s and 1930s to help supplement regional budgets, providing capital for duly planned investment projects in outlying regions (Sabirov 1966).[10] These too have become less important with time, although they are still used on occasion to provide central assistance to republic governments on a project-by-project basis (Avetisian 1979; Tulebaev 1973).

In contrast, "means" have varied in importance, especially since the Stalin era. The reasons are not totally clear, because Soviet accounts do not provide any exhaustive breakdown of what this category represents. We do know, however, that it differs from subventions and subsidies, since it represents adjustments made after the plan and budget have already been adopted (Avetisian 1979). It includes some ad-hoc subsidies to cover emergencies, such as a revenue shortfall caused by a bad harvest, not anticipated in the annual plan or budget. It also covers finances for some joint union and republic government activities. In addition, "means" also represent a budget escrow account, including revenues from any enterprise that is transferred between central and republic jurisdiction after the fiscal year has started. Since revenue from the enterprise has already been built into the corresponding expenditure plan at the "old" level of government, it is kept there temporarily, but under the label of "means" rather than under regular budget accounts until a new plan and budget are drawn up the following year.

This use of "means" as an escrow account helps to explain the erratic pattern; transfers peaked as a share of republic revenues in 1957—the year that the Sovnarkhoz reform transferred economic programs and funds to the republics. And they dropped radically when the Sovnarkhoz reform was revoked. In fact, the net flow of "means" for several regions during 1966 and 1967 was negative: payments to the central budget exceeded transfers received—as we would expect at a time when economic responsibilities were being recentralized.[11] Thus to the extent that "means" simply count functions transferred between Moscow and republic governments, true subsidies from Moscow are used sparingly.[12]

Wherever possible, then, Soviet leaders have tried to avoid subsidies to the republics, in favor of tax-sharing schemes to give regional leaders the proper incentives to be fiscally responsible. In view of the fact that most planned transfer payments to the republics have been eliminated, the strategy has worked. Yet this very incentive to fiscal responsiblility is also a powerful inducement to lobby—not for a larger subsidy but for a stronger tax base. The greater the local industry, the more turnover taxes and profits potentially available for republic budgets (Piskotin 1971; Voluiskii 1970). Central Asia offers a case in point, with some economists arguing that their republics have been deprived of needed turnover tax revenue because local products are shipped to other (mostly European) republics for processing; turnover taxes on such products flow into the other republics' coffers, rather than the local republic budget (Tulaebev 1973; Iskanderov 1969; Ketebaev 1986). They have suggested that the processing ought to be done locally, thereby giving the local economy the revenue benefits and, not so incidentally, providing jobs for local workers.

The structure of the federal system also gives regional leaders reason for concern over the revenue potential of the primary sectors of the economy. Since so much republic budget revenue derives from agriculture and natural resources, republic leaders find themselves heavily dependent on these branches to keep funds flowing for other republic programs. And as chapter 3 explains, they figure prominently on regional agendas.

CHAPTER THREE

REGIONAL INFLUENCE AND SOVIET BUDGETARY DECISION MAKING

BY ANY MEASURE, the Soviet republics gained in political and economic status after Stalin. The local revolution after 1953 elevated more republic leaders to the Politburo; gave republic premiers permanent representation in the national cabinet; raised regional issues higher on the political agenda; and increased both the programs and funds under republic jurisdiction. During the Khruschev years, regional leaders also assumed greater responsibility for economic administration. Since then, their role has been more limited and the Soviet system has again become more centralized. Yet on balance they have acquired more responsibility since 1953—and with it, more problems. The programs they oversee demand increased resources, but as chapter 2 demonstrated, republic revenues continue to be dominated by less lucrative taxes and fees, and to be very much dependent on the state of agriculture and on natural resource development. The republics' enhanced role also demands greater center-regional coordination; but regional leaders have little of the political authority they need to make coordination work. Ironically, then, republic officials' complaints about their powerlessness multiplied while their political and economic status improved.

Judging from their complaints, it is tempting to conclude that republic officials exert no influence at all over decision-making in Moscow. Yet a careful examination of plan-and budget-making leads to the opposite conclusion: republic politicians are players in an elaborate bargaining process between center and periphery. They lobby constantly for more support from higher-ups, and they sometimes manage to win. Moscow's responses

vary, of course, depending on the request being made. And regional politicians rarely get all they request. Yet regional lobbying definitely pays.

This chapter explores regional leaders' appeals and their impact on the
planning and budgetary process. The emphasis is on the role that republic
leaders play in the creation of plans and budgets: on the scope of their
authority, their agendas, and the results of their lobbying efforts.

The Planning Process

The planning process begins with an assessment of the successes and
failures, bottlenecks and problems, of the last plan. As Birman (1978)
notes, new goals start from last year's, with a heavy bias toward incrementalism. Soviet accounts of the planning process emphasize the same
point, claiming that each new plan (and budget) derives primarily from
the last one (Kotov 1974; Vasilik 1980). F. V. Popov (*Pravda*, March 5,
1986, p. 6), first secretary of Altai krai, confirmed this in his address to
the Twenty-Seventh Party Congress, complaining that Moscow's reliance
on planning "from the achieved level" meant inadequate growth in his
region's investment funds.

With the results of the previous plan as a base, Gosplan prepares forecasts
of demand, capacity, and available resources, and methodological guidelines for ministries, regional and local governments, and individual factories, farms and other institutions to follow in compiling their own plans.
Much of the effort, of course, concentrates on five-year plans; but the
annual plan is really the operative one.

The process of setting priorities is described in much less detail in Soviet
sources.[1] Judging from the limited evidence available, Kremlin leaders plan
"by exception," concentrating chiefly on the largest projects and the most
serious bottlenecks.[2] Other projects and problems are left for the Council
of Ministers and Gosplan, which develop control figures translating the
party's goals into concrete targets for central ministries, the union republics, and certain key regions and cities.[3] Ministries and republics in turn
flesh out these assignments and transmit them downward to subordinate
institutions—associations, enterprises, factories, farms, local governments.
Plans and proposals from the local level also work their way back up the
hierarchy, with a constant stream of data and requests flowing between the
top and bottom rungs in the planning hierarchy (Cherkashin 1969). Each

ministry and each republic combines these proposals into draft plans which are then submitted to Gosplan (Kim 1975).

Gosplan examines them through standing commissions chaired by a deputy president and composed of representatives from its relevant branch or territorial departments. Since requests for funds and resources always exceed what is available, Gosplan's chief role at this stage seems to be to economize—to trim the fat from ministry and republic plans. When necessary, delegates from a ministry or from a republic gosplan are called upon to provide additional information or justification for a proposal (Maniushis 1978). For the most part, however, Gosplan apparently conducts its review internally, with participation by ministerial and regional officials limited primarily to documenting particular items in their proposed plans (Kutafin 1980). Coordination in the review process is provided by a general commission, chaired by Gosplan's first deputy president.

Once the various commissions have studied, cut, and combined ministry and republic draft plans, the results are sent to the Council of Ministers for approval. Here too specialized commissions examine the individual parts of the proposed plan, and recommend changes and corrections to the council Presidium (Kutafin 1980). The commissions also take up ministry and republic requests to reverse cuts imposed earlier. The Council of Ministers thus serves as a court of appeals for ministerial and regional leaders whose pet projects were rejected or ignored during Gosplan's deliberations (Dosymbekov 1974; Kotov 1974; Bescherevnykh 1976).

The plan also goes to the central party apparat for further study, with five-year plans submitted to party congresses as well. Unfortunately, descriptions of the planning process give little information about the review process in the Central Committee; but judging from the proceedings at party congresses since 1956, party bodies serve as still another forum for ministerial and regional appeals to amend the plan. Speakers at each congress typically stress problems and projects that Gosplan and other central officials have overlooked, and each congress appoints a commission to study their requests and ratify revisions to preliminary plan directives.

The amended plan directives ultimately go to the Supreme Soviet for still further review and amendment and then formal ratification. Sector-oriented standing commissions and subcommittees of the plan-budget commission in each chamber review both the Council of Ministers' draft and ministry and regional appeals for more assistance and resources (Khimicheva 1966; Vasilik 1982). The plan-budget commissions then compile a list of changes to be recommended when the plan and budget go to the floor of each chamber for ratification, subject to approval by Gosplan and the Ministry of Finance. Appeals and requests that cannot be resolved by the end of the Supreme Soviet's deliberations are returned to the Council of Ministers and to Gosplan for further study (Bescherevnykh 1976).

The basic steps in approving the Soviet budget are much the same, only it is the Ministry of Finance which plays the role of coordinator and budget-cutter, and the budget itself is contingent upon the plan. The same process of guidelines trickling down and draft budgets bubbling up takes place, with the Ministry of Finance checking to see that budget proposals from ministries and republic governments fit with the plan and with financial targets for the given year. After the Finance Ministry completes its review of the proposals, the budget too goes to the Council of Ministers and the party for review; and to the Supreme Soviet for final ratification.

The Role of Republic Governments

Formal approval of both the plan and budget flows from the top down: central party and government agencies determine basic plan targets and budget totals for the USSR as a whole, and then do the same for each republic. Moscow must approve production targets and new investment for republic-subordinate programs, total expenditures for each republic's budget, and subtotals for republic budgetary expenditures on the local economy, on social and cultural measures, and on administration (Okrostvaridze 1973). Central leaders also allocate budget revenues among republics, giving each region a share of all-union taxes and fees collected within its territory.

Within this framework, republic leaders can make marginal adjustments to their revenues and expenditures. One method is to adopt a somewhat larger budget than was specified by the Supreme Soviet, sometimes as much as 3 to 5 percent larger (See table 3.1.) Since republic planners rarely have all the data they need to finalize their budget projections until after the Supreme Soviet's deliberations are over, these changes represent corrections—made with central approval—to the preliminary republic figures originally submitted months earlier to the Ministry of Finance (Kim 1975; Bescherevnykh 1976).

The system also formally encourages republic leaders to make minor

TABLE 3.1
Republic Amendments to National Budget Decisions, Selected Republics[a] (in millions of rubles)

	RSFSR		Ukraine		Belorussia		Kazakhstan		Lithuania	
	(1)	(2)	(1)	(2)	(1)	(2)	(1)	(2)	(1)	(2)
1961	25,332	25,488	7,482	7,528	1,283	1,293	3,096	3,105	546	547
1962	26,412	26,503	7,616	7,653	1,345	1,351	3,379	3,395	580	583
1963	27,862	28,234	7,887	7,959	1,474	1,476	3,566	3,589	630	640
1964	29,163	29,293	8,292	8,325	1,532	1,532	3,913	3,916	693	715
1965	31,552	31,635	9,283	9,316	1,660	1,688	3,981	4,002	765	789
1966	32,986	33,191	9,871	9,912	1,842	1,963	3,990	4,027	839	890
1967	27,696	28,235	9,900	9,956	2,067	2,068	3,984	4,000	932	957
1968	28,736	29,007	10,296	10,426	2,211	2,229	4,240	4,279	1,022	1,047
1969	32,193	32,606	10,446	10,540	2,500	2,504	4,561	4,577	1,112	1,127
1970	34,204	35,313	10,959	11,027	2,673	2,744	4,682	4,692	1,186	1,210
1971	39,228	39,986	12,310	12,548	3,063	3,072	4,915	4,919	1,412	1,418
1972	42,373	43,420	13,163	13,263	3,354	3,424	5,410	5,510	1,608	1,617
1973	44,381	45,313	13,888	13,961	3,613	3,654	5,539	5,607	1,707	1,727
1974	NA	NA	NA	NA	NA	NA	NA	NA	NA	NA
1975	52,119	53,498	16,387	16,485	4,180	4,197	6,515	6,574	1,964	1,980

[a]Column (1): Total republic budget adopted by Supreme Soviet USSR.
Column (2): Total republic budget subsequently adopted by republic supreme soviet.
SOURCE: Bescherevnykh (1976:161).

adjustments in the course of the fiscal year: regions that manage to raise any revenue in excess of their budget targets or to economize on their expenditures are entitled to keep the extra funds for republic and local use (Tulebaev 1973; Dosymbekov 1974). However, this incentive to greater fiscal effort apparently turns into just another manifestation of the ratchet principle: when extra revenue is raised or expenditures are cut, Moscow adjusts republic budget targets upward the next year to absorb the slack (Liberman 1970).

Republic leaders have considerably more leeway with respect to local economic decisions. They ratify plan targets, investment projects, and revenue and expenditure totals for local programs under their jurisdiction (Zlobin 1975; Vasilik 1982). All these decisions must, of course, conform to central guidelines; but regional officials do put their own distinctive stamp onto local policies. They can, for instance, redistribute funds among subordinate local governments, and allow each locality a different percentage deduction from their own revenues (Tulebaev 1973). Their authority in these domains is evident from the public record of revenue allocations within different republics.[4] Some regions, like the Ukraine, have shared the profits of republic-subordinate industries with the localities. Others, like Kazakhstan, have relied on turnover taxes and direct taxes on the population to finance local government. And the mix of local revenues changes from year to year within each republic in ways that suggest little orchestration from Moscow.

As this top-down system suggests, the degree of centralization and the role of the republics both vary, depending on the level of subordination of a given program, on the issue to be decided, and on the sector of the economy that is involved. Predictably, republic leaders have the least influence in sectors under all-union subordination, and as table 3.2 reveals, these include most manufacturing industries in the USSR. Auto-making, medical equipment, chemicals, virtually all machine-building, and most other heavy industries are all administered directly from Moscow, giving republic leaders little if any contol over plans for key sectors of their own region's economy. They may propose new projects or register complaints over ministry decisions, and they have the responsibility for checking on enterprise performance—for seeing that the party's industrial policy is carried out (Dosymbekov 1971). However, they have an advisory role as far as plan formulation in all-union ministries is concerned (Tulebaev 1973; Zenchenko 1979; Kochumov 1982).

Regional leaders have more opportunities for input into sectors under joint union-republic subordination—such as agriculture, construction, natural resources, metallurgy, light and food-processing industries, and economic and social infrastructure. The corresponding union-level ministry normally runs the largest enterprises directly from Moscow and sets plan targets, new investment levels, and budgetary allocations for all the others, leaving operations in these latter enterprises to republic oversight. However, there are no standard rules governing the way powers are to be divided within union-republic ministries, and the setup thus varies from one ministry to another (Bisher 1973; Baianov 1977). Production ministries tend to be more centralized than service ones; and within these two groups, there are still more variations, depending on the individual ministry involved.[5]

The degree of cental control also varies even among sectors exclusively under republic jurisdiction, such as housing, consumer services, and what is labeled "local" industry (e.g., souvenirs, art supplies, dishes, musical instruments, and other items made from local raw materials). In "local" industry, for example, Gosplan and the national Council of Ministers set plan targets and appropriations for all production that uses inputs from other republics, while items produced entirely from local materials—about a tenth of the total (Panskov and Velichko 1986)—are planned by the republics (Baianov 1977). Regional officials appear to have more discretion in housing and consumer services, although even here they depend substantially on central ministries to provide funding (Dosymbekov 1971).

The differences can be gauged roughly by examining the current republic share of budget funds in major sectors (figure 3.1). As we would predict from the discussion thus far, industry is the most highly centralized, with Moscow accounting for the lion's share of industrial expenditures, while republic governments claim a larger share in agriculture, services, and social welfare.

The differences reflect the traditional priorities of the Soviet regime, with industry, the traditional benchmark of economic success, under closer central scrutiny than are the less favored branches of the economy. But there is also another logic to the varying degrees of centralization: the sectors wholly or partly under republic jurisdiction are the ones most heavily shaped by local variations in climate, geological conditions, and consumer needs and preferences. To use the language of economic location theory, these sectors depend most on orientation to materials and to markets. They are the ones where adaptation to local conditions is most crucial, where administrators on the spot must have some flexibility to cope with the problems created by unique local circumstances.

In addition to the differences among economic sectors, the degree of centralization also varies with the kind of issue to be decided. Output targets and inputs for industrial production—for all-union, union-republic, and even republic-level enterprises—come from above; the only exceptions appear to be "local" industries using locally supplied inputs ("Planirovanie i territorial'noe" 1977). The same holds for decisions involving new investment: central ministries and Gosplan must approve all the funds, though the amount of central scrutiny depends on the size of the appropriation involved (Dosymbekov 1974; Dyker 1983).

Finally, the degree of central control also varies in ways that are less easy to measure. Regional leaders have substantial de facto power that is

TABLE 3.2
The Soviet Federal Hierarchy:
All-Union, Union-Republic, and Republic Level Ministries[a]

All-Union	Union-Republic	Republic
Primary		
Natural gas industry	Geology	
Oil industry	Forestry/paper/lumber industry	
	Oil-refining/petrochemical industry	
	Coal industry	
	Ferrous metallurgy	
	Nonferrous metallurgy	
	Energy and electricity	
Manufacturing		
Aviation industry	Light industry	Local industry
Auto industry	Construction materials industry	
Machine-building		
Machine-bldg. for feed/ livestock		
Machine-bldg. for light/ food/consumer service industries		
Medical industry		
Defense industry		
General machine-building		
Mineral fertilizer industry		
Instrument-making		
Communications eq. industry		
Radio industry		
Medium machine-building		
Machine-press and instrument industry		
Construction/road-bldg. service eq. industry		
Ship-building		
Tractor/agr. machinery industry		
Heavy and transport machine-building		
Chemical/oil machinery industry		
Chemical industry		
Electronics industry		
Electrotechnical industry		
Energy machinery industry		

TABLE 3.2 (*continued*)

All-Union	Union-Republic	Republic
Agricultural/food processing		
	Agr. procurements.	
	Land reclamation/water supplies	
	Meat/dairy industry	
	Food-processing industry	
	Fruit/vegetable production	
	Fisheries	
	Agriculture	
Construction		
Const. in Far East/Baikal regions	Repair/special constr.	Housing/civil constr.
Oil/gas industry constr.	Industrial constr.	
Transport constr.	Agricultural constr.	
	Construction	
	Heavy industry constr.	
Economic infrastructure		
Civil aviation	Communications	Inland waterways
Merchant marine	Trade	Consumer services
Railroads		Highways/roads
Foreign trade		
Social infrastructure		
	Higher/secondary spec. education	Housing/muny services
	Health	Social security
	Culture	
	Enlightenment	
Other		
	Internal affairs	
	Justice	
	Foreign affairs	
	Finance	

*The list of republic-level ministries here was compiled from a Moscow city directory, and may not be complete.

SOURCES: *Ezhegodnik bol'shoi entsiklopedii* (1982:11–12); *Moskva 1973* (1973:passim).

rarely described in any Soviet administrative text; as we saw in chapter 2, they sometimes redirect central appropriations and rework Moscow's directives to serve local ends.[6] One time-honored strategy is to sneak in a new local investment project by underestimating costs or dividing the project into smaller components. As long as a given component is "below-

FIGURE 3.1
Republic and Local Shares of Soviet Budget Expenditures, 1980

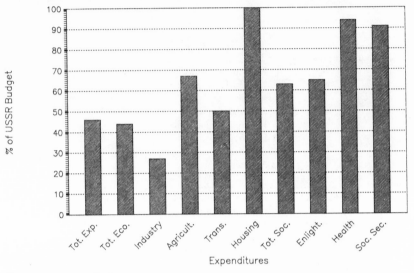

For sources, see appendix A.

limit," under a cost ceiling set by Moscow, it needs no direct central approval. Once started, it offers regional leaders substantial leverage in appealing for added funds, to ensure that the initial investment will not go to waste.[7] Similarly, new projects can also be initiated by labeling them as reconstruction or repair work, over which central controls have typically been less strict. Once again, having the the project on the books makes it easier to justify further appropriations.

The Dilemmas of Coordination

Thus centralization is far from uniform across the Soviet system (Jones 1981). Yet however much of a role republic governments play in different sectors, none of their programs operates in a vacuum: their economic well-being hinges directly or indirectly on the activities of union-subordinate enterprises and central ministries (D. L. Kartvelashvili, *Deviataia sessiia*, 1983:103–9). The very presence of centrally administered branches in each republic affects the use of local resources; the demand for labor, services, housing, and consumer goods; the need for infrastructure; and the flow of republic budget revenue. The republics have some leeway to make their own decisions in these areas, but regional *needs* are shaped by decisions made in Moscow. Coordination with central agencies is therefore essential if republic plans are to work.

Republic leaders are supposed to provide it by compiling two sets of plans and budgets, one covering only those programs under republic and local subordination and a second covering all the economic activity in their territory, including enterprises subordinate directly to Moscow (Ziiadullaev 1972b). Regions are the locus where grand central priorities and concrete local needs must be reconciled, and republic leaders are expected to help integrate them by drawing up "summary" (*svodnyi*) or "complex" plans and budgets encompassing all their republic's economy. They must review those portions of draft plans and budgets of central ministries that affect the region's economy and recommend changes that will bring national policies into line with local conditions (Tulebaev 1973). And central ministries are obliged to consult with regional officials over decisions that affect republic interests.

In practice, regional leaders find it nearly impossible to provide effective coordination. Even the simple act of securing data from Moscow poses a constant problem. Central ministries often turn over information only after projects and plans have already been approved on high, leaving few opportunities for meaningful input from below ("Planirovanie i territorial'noe" 1977). As both politicians and analysts in the republics complain, the data either arrive late or do not arrive at all (Ziiadullaev 1972b; Dosymbekov 1971; Avetisian 1979). What does arrive is sometimes so brief as to be only marginally useful in republic planning (Kokhonov 1977). And the problem is compounded by the frequent changes in plans that Gosplan and ministries adopt in the course of the year.

Some republic governments attempt more direct coordination by including the heads of all-union glavki or enterprises in the deliberations of the republic council of ministers (Maniushis 1978; Kochumov 1982); and of course directors of major enterprises are included in the central committees of republic parties and in supreme soviets as well as in local party and executive committees. But since major planning decisions are made in Moscow, such cooperation at the regional and local levels still does not provide republic officials with the timely and detailed information they need to develop comprehensive plans, or the support they need to implement local goals.[8]

Similar coordination problems arise even in programs under joint union-republic jurisdiction (Zenchenko 1979). Officials in the corresponding union-level ministries commit the same delays and oversights in providing data, draft budgets, and plans to their regional affiliates (Kim 1975). Republic leaders do find communications somewhat easier, since they have permanent delegates (*postpreds*) assigned to many union-republic ministries. These regional representatives collect copies of memos, letters, and instructions from individual ministries and the Council of Ministers and thus help to expedite the flow of information between Moscow and the other republic capitals (Tsikulin 1966). Postpreds also see that copies of republic complaints and proposals get sent to all the appropriate offices in Moscow, and monitor the course of republic appeals in different central agencies (Maniushis 1978).

Their presence undoubtedly helps to improve communications, but they still cannot overcome the coordination problems that plague republic leaders in dealing with Moscow (Kochumov 1982). For one thing, postpreds are primarily conduits—intermediaries between Moscow and the republics, whose chief role is to follow up on the initiatives of their government (Shafir 1968b). Having representation in a ministry does not guarantee that the initiatives will be approved or even that the republic will get the information it needs. Second, postpreds are assigned only to some union-republic ministries; all-union ministries have none. Third, their status is ambiguous: Soviet law confirms their right to be consulted, but does not specify when or on what issues. Such questions are normally left to each individual ministry to decide (Shafir 1968b; Al'peravichus 1971).

Thus communication between Moscow and republic capitals remains a problem, and republic officials find it nearly impossible to come up with realistic "summary" plans embracing the whole of their region's economy (Kutafin 1980; Kim 1975). They can compile plans only for the sectors under their jurisdiction, sectors that represent a limited share of republic economic activity (Bykovskii and Koliushin 1982).

Gosplan and the Ministry of Finance are supposed to help overcome this fragmentation between central and republic agencies; but they are oriented to branch rather than territorial concerns. Both are organized in a way that parallels the sectoral divisions in the economy, and their primary role is to compile sectoral plans and budgets (Chistiakov and Morozov 1971).[9] Regional issues are secondary. The official methodological guidelines for plan preparation (*Metodicheskie Ukazaniia* 1980) show where the priorities lie: out of 700 pages, a total of 8 are devoted to regional planning. In effect, the regional section of a national economic plan is simply the sum of the regional aspects of branch plans and is not binding on central ministries (Avetisian 1979). Moscow has, of course, targeted certain areas of the country for accelerated growth, but there is no real operative plan for regional development in the country as a whole (Dmitriev and Zenkovich 1980; Kistanov and Kostennikov 1966; Zenchenko 1979).

Given the structural biases in sectoral planning, the economic position of republic leaders is a difficult one: they have responsibility without power. They are expected to merge central and territorial interests in compiling budgets and plans, and their own region's economic success depends on effective coordination with Moscow, but they lack the formal authority to make cooperation work (Dosymbekov 1974). Georgia's Premier D. L. Kartvelashvili (*Deviataia sessiia* 1983:103–9) put the matter bluntly during 1983's budget deliberations in the Supreme Soviet: republic leaders must answer for the economic health of their region but are denied control over the key sectors that drive regional economic development.

Regional Lobbying

Their response is to look for other means of protecting regional interests, by appealing directly to the central government and party apparat. If a ministry or Gosplan fails to cooperate, regional leaders take their complaints higher: no CPSU congress or Supreme Soviet convocation is complete without addresses by regional leaders asking for better coordination and more funds. The list of requests is a long one. At the Twenty-Sixth Congress in 1981, Kazakhstan's party boss D. A. Kunaev (*XXVI S"ezd* 1981: 1:122–29) chided central ministries for failing to supply promised construction materials and pressed for the diversion of Siberian rivers to overcome his republic's water shortage. RSFSR premier M. S. Solomentsev (*XXVI S"ezd* 1981: 1:137–42) dwelt on local agricultural needs, asking for more funds to develop infrastructure and emphasizing the advantages of "complex development," a catchword for intersectoral coordination. Georgia's first secretary E. A. Shevardnadze (*XXVI S"ezd* 1981: 1:193–98) requested more funding for the local electric power industry, rail transport, and food processing plants. A similar list of problems and requests emerged during the 1981 budget debate in the Supreme Soviet: Turkmenia's G. Annamukhammedova (*Izvestiia*, November 21, 1981, p. 5) asked Gosplan to carry out promised irrigation measures and to appropriate funds for a new institute to train Russian language teachers; and Lithuania's premier V. I. Songaila (*Izvestiia*, November 20, 1981, p. 5) stressed his republic's need for more investment in municipal services. Given the opportunity to address a national forum, few regional leaders pass up the chance to highlight local problems and needs.

Their comments in these national political arenas represent just a fraction of the appeals that flow from the republics to the capital. Regional leaders take complaints and proposals directly to individual ministries, to Gosplan, and to the Council of Ministers as well as to party congresses and the legislature. And stenographic reports of Central Committee plenary sessions that Khrushchev allowed to be published reveal that here too regional and local leaders ask for more assistance and more resources from Moscow.[10] Regional requests also fill the growing literature on republic government and regional development: few books and articles are written without some recommendation on how to hasten local development or improve regional planning and center-regional relations.

In many cases the appeals simply involve a request that Gosplan and ministries in Moscow make good on projects already approved but yet to be completed. Other requests are bids to initiate new local projects—some relatively inexpensive, such as providing a day care center for workers in a Kazakh metallurgical combine, and some requiring massive investment, such as the diversion of northern and Siberian rivers to provide water for Central Asia (Dosymbekov 1974; Kunaev, *XXVI S"ezd* 1981: 1:122–29).[11] As we saw in chapter 2, republic spokesmen also focus on revenues— for example, on ways to alter the turnover tax.

Proposals that Moscow ease its economic controls also surface with surprising frequency: regional and local elites often ask for more power to coordinate planning in their territory. In 1965, for example, Moscow's mayor V. F. Promyslov and Leningrad oblispolkom president G. I. Kozlov told the Supreme Soviet that local governments needed more autonomy in budget decisions (*Zasedaniia* 1965:86–92, 111–16). In 1981, E. A. Shevardnadze recommended to the Twenty-Sixth Party Congress that rural raikoms needed more power to make decisions on the spot; Sverdlovsk obkom's V. P. Eltsin suggested that the 387 construction agencies operating in Sverdlovsk be amalgamated and put under oblast, rather than ministerial control (*XXVI S"ezd* 1981: 1:193–98). And many authors have advocated strengthening the role of the republics: they point out that given the departmentalism of branch ministries, only republic governments can provide the proper integration of branch and territorial concerns that the economy needs to function well (Maniushis 1978; Kochumov 1982; Khaburzaniia 1978).

Appeals thus run the gamut from speeding up central projects to proposing new ones; from complaints about central administration to suggestions for widening republic and local powers over the economy. Many of them seem motivated by the desire to deflect criticism for problems at home, to lay the blame on the center rather than on local administration. But leaders in republics and localities also engage in more than simple buck-passing—they propose adjustments in existing central programs and also initiate proposals. Given their revenue needs, and given the potential political rewards for expanding the local economy, they have incentives to press for new programs as well as for better implementation of old ones. Their input must of course be tailored to fit within Moscow's overall priorities; and as chapter 1 emphasized, a canny regional official will take great pains to stress how his proposal furthers central goals. Yet the fact that regional leaders make any such proposals suggests an important distinction between agenda-building and decision-making. Moscow unquestionably retains the power to allocate funds, but regional and local spokesmen offer their own suggestions on where and how such funds should be spent.

Mapping Regional Agendas

National discussion of the plan and budget offer a regular forum for appeals from below, a place where major local problems can be brought directly to the attention of central leaders. Thus deliberations at party congresses and in the Supreme Soviet should help us to identify the economic issues on regional agendas. To assess these agendas, all republic leaders' appeals on the plan and budget at each party congress since 1956 were coded issue by issue. (For an explanation of the coding procedure, see appendix B.) An "appeal" was defined as any concrete request involving resources—such as the following from the 1981 party congress (*XXVI S"ezd*, 1981: 1:146–50, 180–85, 302–6):

— Sharaf Rashidov contended that Brezhnev's Food Program would require new water sources for Uzbekistan, and this in turn demanded the diversion of northern and Siberian rivers to Central Asia; he also asked the Council of Ministers to study ways of improving mechanization in cotton-growing.

— Azerbaidzhan's Geidar Aliev complained that Azerbaidzhan was experiencing a deficit of electric power which all-union agencies would need to overcome in order for industry in the republic to grow.

— Moldavia's S. K. Grossu noted that economic infrastructure to support the food complex in his republic was underdeveloped; and he asked Gosplan and the Ministry of the Auto Industry to reequip a Tiraspol' auto factory to make refrigerated trucks.

And, as indicated above, other republic leaders voiced similar appeals.

An overview of their requests is presented in table 3.3. In addition, speeches by republic leaders in the Supreme Soviet's budget deliberations were also coded the same way, for selected years since 1955; and these results are in table 3.4. A total of 207 speeches was included. Since all republics normally have at least one delegate among the speakers at all these sessions, the data in tables 3.3 and 3.4 allow us to compare agendas among different regions and their leaders, and to compare the way agendas have evolved since the Khrushchev era.

However, such data do not represent all the appeals put forward by regional leaders. We are looking at only the tip of the iceberg, at speeches that are carefully orchestrated in Moscow. Each address must be cleared in advance on such occasions, and regional spokesmen typically follow a common format: praise for the current party leader and/or party policy in general; a few sentences on the party's foreign policies; a summary of the achievements and contributions of the speaker's home region; and a list of local problems and needs that require attention and resources from the national government. Given the need for prior clearance of each speech, the list of problems and needs is hardly spontaneous; it must pass Moscow's

TABLE 3.3
Republic Leaders' Economic Agendas at CPSU Congresses, 1956–1986ᵃ

Party Congress

	20th (1956)	21st (1959)	22nd (1961)	23rd (1966)	24th (1971)	25th (1976)	26th (1981)	27th (1986)
Total republic speakers:	16	16	15	19	17	15	15	17
Presenting appeals	12	13	13	14	13	8	11	16
Presenting no appeals	4	3	2	5	4	7	4	1
Number presenting appeals in:								
Agriculture, food-processing, water supplies	12	5	11	14	10	6	10	11
Energy, fuels, metals, minerals	7	9	10	9	6	4	8	11
Other industry	2	1	5	3	2	3	—	3
Light	2	—	—	2	—	1	—	3
Chemical	—	1	4	—	—	—	—	—
Infrastructure	4	2	2	2	3	1	2	3
Socialᵇ	4	—	1	2	3	—	1	3
Economicᶜ	—	2	1	1	—	1	1	1
Science, technology, research	1	—	—	—	1	—	—	2
Education	1	—	1	2	1	—	—	—
Construction equipment and materials	3	5	1	5	1	—	—	2
Employment, jobs	—	—	1	2	—	1	—	1

ᵃEach speech on plan directives by a republic leader was coded to identify the policy domains for which the speaker presented appeals. An "appeal" was defined as any direct request for concrete assistance from Moscow. The entries in the table represent the number of republic leaders who presented appeals in each policy domain. If a local delegate spoke on behalf of the entire republic, he was counted as a republic speaker.

ᵇIncluding health, welfare, culture, and housing.

ᶜIncluding trade, transport and communications.

For sources and an explanation of coding procedures, see appendix B.

approval. With all the controls, party congresses and Supreme Soviet convocations are as much command performances as genuine policy discussions.

Yet a careful reading of each regional leader's comments reveals more diversity and disagreement than we would expect to find if the speeches were merely dictated by the center. Leaders in the periphery typically put forward many more appeals than the central authorities can accommodate,

TABLE 3.4
Republic Leaders' Agendas
in Supreme Soviet Budget Sessions,
1955–1983[a]

	1955	1965	1975	1983
Total speakers:	18	28	17	16
Number presenting appeals in:				
Agriculture, food-processing, water supplies	12	14	10	8
Energy, fuels, minerals, metals	8	17	6	7
Other industry	3	6	4	5
Light	2	5	3	5
Chemical	–	1	–	–
Infrastructure (housing, services)	9	19	2	4
Social[b]	9	13	–	2
Economic[c]	1	13	–	2
Science, technology, research	1	2	1	–
Education	2	5	2	–
Construction equipment and materials	10	12	5	–
Employment, jobs	–	3	–	–

[a]Appeals are defined as in table 3.3.

[b]Including health, welfare, culture, and housing.

[c]Including trade, transport, and communications.

For sources and an explanation of coding procedures, see appendix B.

so that a good many get rejected. A central government that was orchestrating such lobbying efforts merely to show generosity would hardly give the losing requests so much national visibility. Nor would it allow the same appeal to be repeated again and again in subsequent congresses or Supreme Soviet budget debates. Moscow's public image is hardly enhanced by repeated complaints over unresolved problems. But appeals are repeated, often with a tone of frustration, by regional leaders who note that they had at best received only a partial solution—a compromise—in answer to prior requests. Equally important, many appeals implicitly challenge central policies, especially central cuts or inadequate appropriations that will adversely affect a given region's economy.[12]

These distinctions are admittedly subtle ones; but given the rules of esoteric communication, subtle differences in official rhetoric carry powerful messages. Moreover, the appeals that are raised reflect genuine local problems—inadequate supplies, labor imbalances, water shortages, and the like—that regional and local officials cannot solve alone. Thus while the acceptable range of issues that regional leaders may address is determined in Moscow, the issues themselves seem to represent genuine regional concerns.

The Content of Regional Economic Agendas

Out of all the regional appeals at party congresses and in the Supreme Soviet, one set of problems dominates the agenda. Requests concentrate overwhelmingly on agriculture and related areas such as food and textile processing, irrigation, land reclamation, and water supplies. In 1981, for example, ten of the fifteen republic leaders who addressed the Twenty-Sixth Congress stressed one or more of these issues. Their concerns ranged from problems with water shortages and inadequate farm machinery to agricultural infrastructure (see table 3.3). The same problems also dominate regional agendas in the Supreme Soviet (see table 3.4).

Three other issue clusters vie for second place. One is the development of energy, metals, and other natural resources. Another is the provision of economic and social infrastructure—railroads, highways, schools, housing, and the like. And the third cluster centers on the provision of construction equipment and materials. In many cases, these problems too tie into agricultural concerns, with appeals for increased electric power, construction materials, housing, and other resources linked to the development of rural areas.

What is equally striking is the marked lack of attention to other sectors of the economy—especially to major industry. There have been few republic appeals devoted to industries other than light, food, chemicals, and mining/metallurgy; and when such appeals do arise they focus primarily on the need to reequip existing facilities, or to build infrastructure to haul supplies and finished products, attract workers, and otherwise provide for "complex development."

Occasionally an issue gives rise to a "coalition" of republics, with a select group of regional leaders stressing their common needs. One of the most widely publicized cases was the proposal, mentioned earlier, to divert northern and Siberian rivers to Central Asia, which party bosses from Kazakhstan, Turkmenia, and Uzbekistan raised at the Twenty-Fifth Party Congress in 1976. Uzbek and Turkmen leaders also cited their joint water problems earlier, in 1966 (*XXIII S"ezd* 1966: 1: 164–73, 382–390); and

TABLE 3.5
Republic Lobbying at CPSU Congresses by Career Type,
1956–1981

	Natives[a]	Mixed Careers[b]	Imports[c]
Republic speakers:	93	15	5
Presenting appeals	68	12	4
Presenting no appeals	25	3	1
Number presenting appeals in:			
Agriculture, food-processing, water supplies	54	10	4
Energy, fuels, metals, minerals	42	10	1
Other industry	13	2	1
Light	3	1	1
Chemical	5	–	–
Infrastructure	13	2	1
Social	9	1	1
Economic	5	1	–
Science, technology, research	2	–	–
Education	4	1	–
Construction equipment and materials	12	2	1
Employment, jobs	3	1	–

[a]Republic leaders who spent their entire prior political career in the same republic.

[b]Republic leaders who spent part of their prior political career outside the republic.

[c]Republic leaders who spent their entire prior political career outside the republic.

For sources and an explanation of coding, see appendix B.

Azerbaidzhan's party boss, V. Iu. Akhundov (ibid.: 371–78) in a bid for more oil-drilling equipment, pointed to similar needs in other oil-producing regions that same year.

Most regional leaders, however, concentrate on their own republic's achievements and needs. And most do indeed press for some sort of support from higher-ups: all but a few of the republic leaders speaking at party congresses and in the Supreme Soviet since 1955 have lobbied for change, either in planning or in allocations to their republic.[13] It makes little difference whether the republic's leader is imported or homegrown; he confronts the same problems and tends to raise the same demands whether he is an outsider or a native. Thus, for example, when Leonid Brezhnev served as a party boss in Kazakhstan, he stressed the same local problems and put forward the same appeals as other local leaders—all of them Kazakhs.[14] Other "imports" have been equally likely to lobby on behalf of regional interests: as table 3.5 illustrates, there is little difference

TABLE 3.6
Republic Leaders' Agendas at CPSU Congresses and Politburo Status[a]

	In Politburo	Not in Politburo
Republic speakers:	38	75
Presenting appeals	27	57
Presenting no appeals	11	18
Number presenting appeals in:		
Agriculture, food-processing, water supplies	22	46
Energy, fuels, metals, minerals	19	34
Other industry	2	14
Light	–	5
Chemical	1	4
Infrastructure	4	12
Social	3	8
Economic	1	5
Science, technology, research	–	2
Education	1	4
Construction equipment and materials	6	9
Employment, jobs	–	4

[a]For congresses from 1956 through 1981. Includes both full and candidate members, counted only if they were in the Politburo at the time of their speech.

For sources, see table 1.1 and appendix B.

in the disposition to lobby among "natives" (those who have spent their entire careers within the same region), "mixed career" officials (those who have spent part of their careers outside the republic), and "imports" (those whose have spent their entire previous career outside the republic). Moreover, "mixed" and "imported" leaders focus on the same issues as do "natives." Their concerns, which are presented in table 3.5, are essentially no different from those raised by "native" officials. Leaders who are brought in from other areas face the same need to coordinate, and the same pressures to meet the plan, as officials whose careers have been made in only a single region.

It is equally difficult to find any substantial difference between regional leaders with Politburo rank and those without. As a group, republic politicians serving in the Politburo have focused just as much attention on local problems and needs as other regional leaders have (see table 3.6). And, as a group, they tended to concentrate on similar issues, as table 3.6

TABLE 3.7
Agendas of New and Old Republic Leaders
at the Twenty-Seventh CPSU Congress

	Appointed under Gorbachev	In office before Gorbachev
Republic speakers:	4	13
Presenting appeals	4	12
Presenting no appeals	0	1
Number presenting appeals in:		
Agriculture, food-processing, water supplies	3	8
Energy, fuels, Metals, Minerals	4	7
Other industry	–	4
Light	–	3
Chemical	–	–
Infrastructure (housing, services)	2	1
Social	2	1
Economic	0	1
Science, technology, research	–	2
Education	–	–
Construction equipment and materials	–	2
Employment, jobs	1	–

Data on new appointees were made available by Robert Blackwell. For sources and an explanation of coding, see appendix B.

makes clear. Again, the problems and dilemmas of central planning and regional coordination would seem to be the same, whatever the national political status of the republic's party boss (or, in the case of the RSFSR, of the premier).

The same conclusion holds for newly appointed republic leaders: their concerns appear to be much the same as their more experienced brethren. The Twenty-Seventh Congress offers a timely opportunity to test for the differences, with four new appointees among republic first secretaries in the eleven months between Gorbachev's succession and the beginning of the congress. Their speeches, when compared against those of "veteran" republic party bosses (and the RSFSR premier), reveal the same issue structure—a preoccupation with agriculture, food and water supplies, energy and mineral development, and social infrastructure (see table 3.7)

If we compare appeals by region rather than by leader, the inclination to lobby also differs little from one republic to another. Even if one leader does not put forward direct appeals, his colleagues usually will. Moreover, the requests tend to be very similar, whether they emanate from industrial or from agricultural regions. In 1983's budget deliberations, for example, leaders from the Ukraine to Moldavia and Uzbekistan all requested more funding for water supplies. Delegates from Russia, the Ukraine, and Estonia stressed local agriculture's need for more machinery and fertilizer; and politicians from Armenia and Azerbaidzhan to Kirgizia and Kazakhstan all emphasized demands for more fuels and energy. Specific appeals, of course, vary depending on local conditions: "energy development" is likely to mean shale oil in Estonia, coal or nuclear power in the Ukraine, and natural gas in Turkmenia.[15] Appeals on agriculture's behalf have centered on tea or viticulture in Georgia but on cotton in Uzbekistan. Nevertheless, what is most distinctive about regional agendas are the many common themes sounded by leaders from the Baltic to Central Asia.

The Trend over Time

The inclination to lobby and the content of regional agendas have also been remarkably consistent since 1956. Many of the same basic concerns recur at every party congress and Supreme Soviet budget convocation (tables 3.3 and 3.4). For regional leaders, the issues of the 1980s were also the issues of the 1970s, 1960s, and 1950s. Agriculture has dominated nearly all discussions of regional needs, and energy/natural resources, construction, and social-cultural needs have been right behind. Thus, for example, Kazakhstan's leaders have come to virtually every CPSU congress since 1952 with a request for more investment in water supplies to provide both irrigation and electric power.[16] At the Nineteenth Congress (*Current Soviet Policies* 1953: 156–58), it was party boss O. Shaiakhmetov who called attention to the problem. At the Twentieth Congress in 1956, it was Leonid Brezhnev, then head of the Kazakh party, and D. A. Kunaev, then Chairman of the Kazakh Council of Ministers (*XX S"ezd* 1956: 1: 213–20, 2:168–74). Kunaev, later promoted to head Kazakhstan's party, returned to the same issue at subsequent party congresses.[17] Kazakh leaders have also been persistent in their appeals for river diversion, raising the idea as early as 1965 during the Supreme Soviet's budget deliberations (*Zasedaniia* 1965:81–86).

The persistence carried over even into the Gorbachev era. Despite the rhetoric of radical change during the first year, the comments and complaints from below at Gorbachev's first party congress had a very familiar ring. The language proved to be more vehement than under Brezhnev's more collegial leadership, with a tone reminiscent of 1956. But as table 3.3 reveals, the substantive issues were much the same as at past congresses. Republic leaders in 1986 asked for more attention primarily to two groups of problems—agriculture/food-processing/water supplies, and fuels/energy/metals/minerals. Kazakhstan's Kunaev (*Pravda*, February 27, 1986, p. 4), for example, repeated his concerns about the need to improve water supplies, and highlighted the need for more electric power to fully develop the Ekibastuz fuel-energy complex; Turkmenia's new party boss S. A. Niiazov (*Pravda*, March 2, 1986, p. 5) reiterated his predecessors' concern with water supplies, and called on Moscow to respond to republic proposals to develop a natural-gas/chemical complex; and another new leader, Kirgizia's A. M. Masaliev (*Pravda*, March 1, 1986, p. 6) asked for more investment in electric power, coal and other minerals, and lamb and wool production. In addition, a "second tier" of requests focused on light industry, social and economic infrastructure, and construction. Thus the basic issues raised by republic leaders were much the same as at past congresses, even with the advent of younger and seemingly more vigorous leadership in the Kremlin. The structure of branch planning and of the federal budget system creates a continuity of local appeals even in the face of changing leadership at the national level.

This is not to say that regional agendas are absolutely identical from year to year. There are some notable differences over time. One of the most dramatic was mentioned in chapter 1: the tone and type of requests from below shifted from the Stalin to the post-Stalin era. Thus republic leaders in 1952 tended to focus on shortcomings within their own republics and party organizations.[18] If plans went unfulfilled or other problems loomed, regional officials took the blame on themselves. Although they mentioned inadequacies in central planning and even took individual ministers to task for ignoring duly approved regional projects, the bulk of their criticism was samokritika. In 1956, with decentralization and destalinization at full gallop and Nikita Khrushchev courting regional elites, republic leaders found more to criticize in the central government and more need for funding in their own regions. RSFSR Premier M. A. Yasnov's (*XX S"ezd* 1956: 2:67–74) comments reflected the new mood: he complained that in spite of the Kremlin's emphasis on devolution, some central ministries were loath to give up their petty tutelage of regional officials. They were still planning some industrial output in the republics down to the month, for industries under local as well as republic administration, in excruciating detail. In one case, the RSFSR had received directives from above on the number of bedroom slippers to be produced locally each month! According to Yasnov, this was a clear violation of the new emphasis on republic rights, and he appealed to Moscow to give republic governments more power.

Other shifts in regional agendas surfaced with the change in regime from Khrushchev to Brezhnev. After 1964, few regional leaders were quite so eloquent about the virtues of corn as they had been in Khrushchev's day—to their apparent relief. And many were critical of the "highhanded methods" and poor leadership that had plagued agriculture, without, of course, mentioning any names.[19]

More recently, changing economic and demographic conditions have pushed several other items higher on regional agendas. During the economic slowdown of the late 1970s and early 1980s, some republic leaders complained that industrial capacity was underutilized and that planned economic growth rates were too low to sustain employment and consumption goals.[20] They also came to feel the effects of labor imbalances more acutely. Deficit areas requested more capital-intensive production to free up labor, while surplus areas called for more labor-intensive industries.[21] Environmental protection too has emerged as a regional concern, though for the most part it is closely linked in regional appeals with an "old" issue—usable water supplies.[22] In contrast, construction problems dropped in importance (see tables 3.3 and 3.4), reflecting the deemphasis on new investment and the increasing concern with renovation and repair of existing capacity.

However, these changes in emphasis among regional demands constitute shifts within a remarkably stable agenda since the 1950s. Agriculture, energy/natural resources, and infrastructure have continued to top the list no matter who holds power in the Kremlin or in the republics. The sectors of most concern to regional leaders have been largely the same from Khrushchev to Brezhnev, Andropov, Chernenko, and Gorbachev, and largely the same despite changes in the top leaders' priorities.[23] Thus, for example, farm problems have been a key regional concern whether national leaders were pouring resources into agriculture, as in 1956, or taking them away, as in 1981. Similarly, energy, fuels, and natural resources were a major regional preoccupation long before the energy crisis of the 1970s pushed them higher on the national government's agenda.

Why these particular issues? Certainly they all represent chronic problem areas in the Soviet economy, and it should not surprise us that regional officials find much to criticize. But there is more to the story than that. The sectors that dominate regional agendas are precisely the areas where republic governments share jurisdiction with central ministries—areas where the republics' dilemma of "responsibility without power" is most acute. The sectors that regional politicians emphasize most in national policy arenas are exactly the ones over which they have some but not total authority; sectors where they are expected to produce economic results but where they are most dependent on coordination with Moscow. As the agendas in tables 3.3 and 3.4 show, the branches of the economy under joint union-republic jurisdiction head the list of regional demands.

These sectors are also the ones on which republic governments depend most for revenues. As chapter 2 explained, agriculture and the light, food, and extractive industries account for over half of all republic revenues. Poor performance or bottlenecks here threaten the budget funds available for housing, health, education, and other social programs financed from republic budgets. Thus the revenue system adds another powerful and continuing incentive for republic leaders to concentrate their appeals on these sectors.

Constraints on information add still another incentive. Leaders in the periphery find it easier to document the farming and natural resource potential in their area than to show their comparative advantage in standard manufactured goods. They may be able to argue for investment in wool or rice, coal or oil by surveying local reserves; but they lack the comparative data necessary to argue for other types of goods—such as radios or bicycles—whose production depends much less on the natural configuration of the locality. The best information at hand is about local conditions, and these are more likely to influence location-bound sectors of the economy.

The Impact of Regional Demands

Some of the requests from below yield positive results. In fact, Moscow has created elaborate procedures for handling regional appeals. When individual ministries prove uncooperative, republic leaders may take their case to Gosplan, the Presidium of the Council of Ministers, the Central Committee and, as we have seen, to party congresses and to the Supreme Soviet. They may even appeal to the Politburo, although a careful examination of the literature and of the Politburo's recent agendas suggests that individual regional requests rarely make it this far.

To ensure that resources will be available to make adjustments, planners at every level in the hierarchy hold back reserves during the early stages of plan formulation, and these are then used by Gosplan, the Council of Ministers, the Central Committee, and the Supreme Soviet to cover some of the appeals from ministries and from regional leaders. Each agency also has an incentive to inflate the targets it hands down to subordinates, creating a margin of safety for itself in case a subordinate organization fails to produce according to plan. Thus planners build in a layer of insulation against unexpected problems, and this small reserve can be used to correct bottlenecks and respond to problems voiced by regional leaders.

Most regional requests go first to central ministries, where day-to-day decisions are made and where coordination is most needed. The number of requests is not clear, since Soviet authors provide no full accounting. But given the scope and complexity of the planning process, there are obviously more demands than each ministry has the time or resources to fulfill—as the complaints of regional and local officials attest.

Yet a request can find a sympathetic audience, as one candid account from Lithuania illustrates. According to Maniushis (1978:80), Lithuania's Council of Ministers requested 44 million rubles from the Ministry of the Chemical Industry in the mid-1970s to increase synthetic fiber and chemical fertilizer production and to open a new plastics plant. The ministry responded with a compromise, a grant of 5 million rubles. Without more detail on the total number of appeals, it is difficult to determine how often such requests succeed. But judging from this and other examples (Dosymbekov 1974), some initiatives from republic leaders do indeed meet with at least partial success.

Still, as regional officials complain, many more proposals get buried in the vast reaches of ministerial bureaucracy. The same seems to be true of appeals to both Gosplan and the Ministry of Finance. Although the two agencies have formal review procedures to examine republic proposals, they are "budget-cutters," whose mission is to defend the public purse from unnecessary projects and expenditures. They seem less inclined to reinstate projects or increase allocations.

The Council of Ministers, party apparatus, and Supreme Soviet give regional appeals more attention. The council examines regional requests during the formulation of plans and budgets, and arbitrates conflicts between ministries, Gosplan, and regional and local governments by appointing a deputy president to review disputes.[24] As in the case of appeals to ministries, we have no way of knowing how many republic proposals and complaints are handled in this way. Again, we must rely on scattered evidence in books about republic planning, and these offer some examples of successful lobbying. When Kazakh leaders complained about the lack of appropriations for housing and day care at a new machine-building plant in Karaganda, the Council of Ministers responded with the funds (Dosymbekov 1974:50–61). And when Lithuania's government argued that local light industrial enterprises could not find workers unless they offered housing, the council provided the additional appropriations for housing construction. Lithuania also argued for and won more funds to finance municipal services, land reclamation, and civil construction (Maniushis 1978:82).

Central party and Supreme Soviet deliberations offer regional officials still more opportunites to present appeals.[25] At party congresses, the business of handling such requests is formally delegated to a commission to review "corrections and additions" to the party's draft plan directives for the upcoming five-year period. In fact, each one seems to be especially well suited as a forum for regional appeals. A look at the mix of commission members listed in table 3.8 will explain why: they typically include either the first secretary or the premier from all the republics (sometimes both), a few local party and government leaders, and a very specific subset of USSR ministers—from agriculture, water supplies, fuels, energy, natural resources, metallurgy, and services (infrastructure), *sectors where all-union and republic leaders share jurisdiction*. Party commissions thus unite regional leaders with the central ministers whose cooperation they need most.

Congresses, then, not only provide a forum for airing regional problems; they also help to bring together central and republic planners. And at least some regional appeals find support. Corrections to the plan directives published at the end of each congress often include funds to meet part of the requests put forward by regional leaders. Thus, for example, when the

TABLE 3.8
Composition of Commissions to Amend Plan Directives at CPSU Congresses, Selected Years

	1956[a]	1966	1976	1986[a]
Total membership	66	95	90	99
Republic leaders[b]	19	22	22	17
Local leaders	4	16	12	12
USSR Government Officials				
Council of Ministers	5	9	6	7
Gosplan	3	1	1	1
Ministries				
Agriculture	3	1	1	2
Light and food industries	–	1	2	1
Energy, fuels, metals, minerals	5	5	5	4
Construction	–	1	1	1
Social infrastructure[c]	3	1	3	3
Economic infrastructure[d]	1	3	–	1
Finance	1	–	1	1
Other	4	1	4	8
Other state committees	1	4	3	2
Supreme Soviet presidium	1	2	1	2
Central Committee CPSU	6	8	13	14
Others[e]	10	20	15	5

[a]There were four members in 1956 and 18 in 1986 for whom I was unable to find career data.

[b]Including deputy chairmen and department heads in the Central Committee Buro for the RSFSR.

[c]Including health, education, welfare, culture, and housing.

[d]Including trade, transport, and communications.

[e]Including enterprise directors, collective farm chairmen, workers, farmers, and others without an official position in the party or state apparatus. The number for 1986 may be much higher because identifying information on many of the "ordinary citizen" delegates is lacking, and they are included in the unidentified group described in note a.

SOURCES: *XX S"ezd* (1956); *XXIII S"ezd* (1966); *XXV S"ezd* (1976); *Pravda*, March 4, 1986, p. 1; *RL Research* (April 9 and 16, 1986), *Soviet Political Leaders* (July 1957); *Deputaty* (1959, 1970, 1979).

Georgian party asked to have output targets (and corresponding appropriations) for the local tea industry raised, and the Kazakh government asked to speed up local ore-processing for ferrous metallurgy, the final directives from the 1971 congress approved their requests.[26] When Central Asian leaders asked that the question of diverting Siberian rivers be included in plan directives "for further study," the directives for 1976–80 were amended accordingly. And plan directives adopted by the Twenty-Sixth Congress (1981) were altered to accommodate Kirghizia's request for bigger appropriations to finance irrigation. The final version of the plan in 1981 also added more funds for improving water supplies in the other Central Asian republics, for developing orchards and viticulture in Tadzhikistan, and for developing infrastructure and natural resources in the RSFSR—all of which corresponded to some, but not all, of the republic appeals presented at the congress.

This is not to say that such appeals are in any way spontaneous—they have been carefully constructed and reviewed in Moscow beforehand. And most of them are old requests that have been afloat for some time. Nor do party congresses decide on the spot whether to commit funds. The changes in plan directives normally represent authorizations rather than appropriations; they indicate formal central approval, subject to further study and amendment. And in many cases the final decision may be long delayed while Gosplan and the relevant central ministries grind through the inevitable paperwork. And the delays, in turn, prompt new appeals, with regional officials complaining that they received only partial satisfaction of their original request.

Regional complaints may also have a broader effect, by pinpointing national policies in need of change. Khrushchev's campaign to develop the chemical industry and especially fertilizer production is a case in point. The decision came after complaints at the Twenty-First and Twenty-Second congresses from regional leaders who found themselves unable to deliver promised increases in farm output—particularly Khrushchev's pet crop, corn—without increased supplies of fertilizer, herbicides, pesticides, and other chemical products.[27] The complaints, along with agriculture's poor showing during the late 1950s and early 1960s, seem to have persuaded Khrushchev to pour resources into the chemical industry. Collectively, then, regional demands can serve as an important barometer of problems that must be corrected if national policies are to succeed.

Along with the lobbying efforts at party congresses, appeals raised in the Supreme Soviet also prompt amendments to the state budget. The legislature's standing commissions each year ratify still more changes in national appropriations in response to regional problems. However, the process works differently than it does in party congresses. The Supreme Soviet's amendments typically concentrate more on health, education, welfare, culture, and municipal services rather than on industry or agriculture. Indeed, the projects that receive support resemble a classic pork-barrel bill, with the legislature doling out funds for civic improvement, new government buildings, and other public works. Weightier problems in productive sectors do get raised during the Supreme Soviet's deliberations (see table 3.4), but such appeals are typically left on the agenda "for further study"— by Gosplan and the Council of Ministers.[28] The Supreme Soviet has neither the power nor the time to make any major appropriations decisions. Its examination of the draft plan and budget at the end of the year is too late to allow any substantial changes. Amendments thus tend to be limited to marginal amounts—generally 1 percent or less of projected expenditures. Requests that would demand a bigger outlay of funds are deferred.

In keeping with the different focus, the Supreme Soviet also differs from party congresses in the composition of its appeals commissions. Whereas congress commissions tend to be dominated by regional leaders and union-republic ministers, the Supreme Soviet's plan-budget commissions reflect more of an emphasis on "common folk," with very few national ministers, more local leaders, and a great many more average citizens (farmers, workers, teachers, and the like—see table 3.9).

The membership roster fits well with the kinds of budget amendments adopted by the Supreme Soviet—added funding for day care, rural schools, municipal buildings, theaters, and so on. There is, then, a degree of functional specialization in the appeals process, with different institutions (at least the party and the Supreme Soviet) focusing on different types of regional demands.

Once again, it is important to note that this is not at all a spontaneous process: appeals are reviewed in advance, and decisions are made in advance about which ones to approve. When the plan-budget commissions report their recommendations to the full membership, the issue is already resolved before any formal vote is ever taken. But the appeals nevertheless represent genuine local problems, which leaders in the periphery bring to Moscow to solve; and the responses suggest an attempt—however modest and however far behind the scenes—to resolve them.

The Appeals Process and Regional Influence

The appeals process offers compelling evidence that national leaders take regional and local economic troubles seriously.[29] Moscow has created an intricate system of checkpoints in national agencies to ensure that problems in the periphery at least receive a hearing. Some of these checkpoints

TABLE 3.9
Composition of Plan-Budget Commissions in the Supreme Soviet,
1958, 1970, and 1979 Convocations[a]

	1958		1970		1979	
	N	U	N	U	N	U
Total membership	39	39	51	51	45	45
Republic leaders[b]	12	14	9	9	4	3
Local leaders	14	14	13	16	8	11
USSR Government Officials:						
Council of Ministers						
Gosplan						
Ministries:						
Agriculture						
Light and food industries						
Energy, fuels, metals, minerals						1
Construction						
Social infrastructure[c]						
Economic infrastructure[d]						
Finance						
Other		1	1	1	3	1
Other state committees	2					
Supreme Soviet Presidium						
Central Committee CPSU		1	1			1
Others[e]	11	9	27	24	30	28

[a]"N" and "U" stand for the councils of nationalities and of the union.

[b]Including deputy chairmen and department heads in the Central Committee Buro for the RSFSR.

[c]Includling health, education, welfare, culture, and housing.

[d]Including trade, transport, and communications.

[e]Including enterprise directors, collective farm chairmen, workers, farmers, and others without an official position in the party or state apparatus.

SOURCES: *Zasedaniia* (1958, 1970); *Pervaia sessiia* (1979); *Deputaty* (1959, 1970, 1979).

undoubtedly serve important symbolic functions, as in the Supreme So-viet's heavy emphasis on appeals to improve popular welfare. Yet others, which are less highly publicized, seem to be genuinely intended to gather feedback from below. In spite of the constraints on republic economic powers, regional leaders bring their problems to the capital and may go home with a bigger budget. Grassroots lobbying does indeed pay, if only by alerting Moscow to the obstacles in the way of implementing central policies.

However, it can take months and sometimes years to persuade higher-ups of the need for more funds. As we have seen, republic requests get directed first to central ministries, and ministries are slow to respond (if they respond at all). Regional leaders must prod them along by appealing to the Council of Ministers, the party apparat, or the Supreme Soviet. And even with prodding, these central agencies may still not agree among themselves on where and how to allocate resources. As some leaders in the periphery complain, requests that are approved by Gosplan do not always get carried out by the designated ministry; and appeals that are approved by the Council of Ministers or the Central Committee are sometimes ignored by Gosplan. Even the Politburo is not immune: resolutions passed down by the top leadership run into the same bureaucratic wall.[30] Problems at the regional and local level often become entangled in the many bureaucratic conflicts at the top.[31]

Thus few regional appeals ever seem to be adopted and implemented on the first try. On the other hand, few issues ever die: given the multiplicity of ministries and state committees, and of departments within Gosplan, the Council of Ministers, and the Central Committee—all of them with power to allocate some resources—a persistent regional official need only find one that is willing to support his request. And once he has even partial support, he has leverage for additional claims.

His request should, however, focus on the present. It rarely pays for republic leaders to anticipate future needs or problems. Appeals seem to be more successful when they grow out of current policy crises.[32] There are too many demands chasing too few funds to spend resources on problems that are still off on the horizon (Gustafson 1981). And even when top agencies do give their approval, projects may still drag on for years. The Council of Ministers and Central Committee seem always to approve more projects and proposals than Gosplan can actually fund.

Given the shortfall, regional leaders rarely get all they request. If Moscow responds, the result is usually a compromise, meeting appeals half-way with incremental increases. The Ukraine's Premier A. P. Liashko (*Pravda*, March 4, 1986, p. 7) offered a glimpse of the process during the Twenty-Seventh Congress's deliberations: he complained that a request for funds to expand local industry had been granted, but the ministry involved had given local officials only one-third of the amount that Gosplan had approved.

Small wonder, then, that the same issues crop up persistently on regional agendas. Consider the example of the Kazakh "water lobby." As we saw earlier in this chapter, every republic party boss since 1952 has lobbied for a bigger budget to finance water projects. And since 1952, the republic has indeed received more funds. But the increases have not kept pace with republic demand. With the emphasis on compromise, Kazakhstan got only some of the resources it had requested, and the issue thus continues to top the list of Kazakh demands. Efforts on behalf of the ambitious river diversion scheme suggest the same conclusion. National leaders agreed to study it in 1976, but have since leaned toward another compromise, improving the existing water system in Central Asia (Shabad 1983).

The success of any given appeal most likely depends on its scope, on the sector involved and its ranking among the prevailing national economic priorities, on the quality of the documentation and evidence that regional leaders present to make their case, and on the degree of slack in the national plan and budget. Success does not, however, necessarily depend on the region making the request: judging from the limited data available, there appear to be no systematic biases in favor of individual regions. The success rate for appeals in the Supreme Soviet is fairly even across republics, as table 3.10 shows.

No region has consistently fared better or worse in gaining extra appropriations (White 1982). Amendments adopted by party congresses also seem to be distributed evenly. Although congress proceedings do not indicate the total ruble amount of amendments made for each region they do list specific projects, and the "winners" include both large and small republics, both east and west, and republics with and without representation in the Politburo.

Thus Moscow does respond to regional appeals, albeit slowly and typically with less than is requested. Lobbying can pay—eventually. Central authorities unquestionably remain in control, but center and periphery are interdependent. Issues raised by republic leaders represent mutual problems that must be brought to Moscow's attention if national policies are to be carried out. Problems and requests do percolate upward, and the central government can dismiss them only at the risk of seeing its policies fail.

The total impact may be significant, even though the quantitative data we have on Supreme Soviet budget amendments represent only minor adjustments to Moscow's appropriations decisions. The Supreme Soviet is only one of many avenues for republic requests, and its marginal role

TABLE 3.10
Supreme Soviet Amendments to Proposed Republic Budgets, Selected Years

Budget increment adopted by Supreme Soviet[a]

	1961	1966	1971	1976
RSFSR	100.16	100.21	100.22	100.13
Ukraine	100.35	100.23	100.24	100.14
Belorussia	100.31	100.16	100.20	100.12
Uzbekistan	100.35	100.21	100.21	100.12
Kazakhstan	100.13	100.18	100.18	100.10
Georgia	100.28	100.20	100.15	100.17
Azerbaidzhan	100.15	100.20	100.30	100.18
Lithuania	100.18	100.12	100.14	100.10
Moldavia	100.31	100.17	100.24	100.16
Latvia	100.42	100.16	100.21	100.07
Kirgizia	100.24	100.17	100.12	100.17
Tadzhikistan	100.30	100.38	100.26	100.20
Armenia	100.27	100.16	100.23	100.08
Turkmenia	100.28	100.42	100.34	100.12
Estonia	100.31	100.23	100.16	100.12

[a]Adopted budget as a percentage of that proposed initially by the USSR Minister of Finance.

SOURCES: *Pravda*, December 23, 1960; December 11, 1970; and December 5, 1975; *Zasedaniia* (6-aia sessiia, 1961:40–64, 534–36). *Zasedaniia* (7-aia sessiia, 1966:37–59, 459–62). *Zasedaniia* (4-aia sessiia, 1976:31–50, 287–90).

in Soviet policy-making and the lateness of its deliberations inevitably limit the changes it can make. If all the successful regional appeals to individual ministries, the Council of Ministers, and the central party were added together, the sums won by regional officials would be larger, especially because they involve more expensive projects than those raised in the Supreme Soviet.

From Moscow's standpoint, the totals involved still amount to only a fraction of all appropriations. But the stakes for individual republics can be substantial. To return to the Lithuanian example mentioned earlier, the republic's request to the Ministry of the Chemical Industry netted a 3 percent increase in the budget for industrial development, for just one project.[33] Any single appeal may bring in only a small amount; but together, the sums at stake may add up to a goodly share of each region's appropriations. And with the many checkpoints in the process of compiling a plan and budget—from the ministries to Gosplan, the Council of Ministers, the party apparat, and the Supreme Soviet—a canny regional official has many potential sources to appeal to in his quest for resources.

The evidence of compromise suggests rather evenhanded treatment of requests from below. However, identifying the winners and losers in the competition over resources requires a more detailed examination of regional appropriations, and chapter 4 turns attention to how individual republics fare.

CHAPTER FOUR

POLITICS, REGIONAL COMPETITION, AND BUDGET POLICIES

THE OPPORTUNITY TO APPEAL surely helps to smooth the frictions between center and periphery, if only by providing a safety valve for the daily frustrations that regional leaders encounter in dealing with Moscow. Yet the process also confronts regional elites with contradictory pressures. On one hand, the more they focus attention on the same common issues, the greater their collective impact on Moscow is likely to be. A request for more chemical fertilizer production or for bigger outlays on irrigation will surely carry added weight when it is echoed by other regional leaders. On the other hand, having many voices in the chorus multiplies the competitors for the same finite economic benefits. Strength in numbers buttresses regional claims, but also heightens disagreements over where national funds ought to be distributed.

This chapter explores the competition and its outcomes. The major concern is to explain who gets what by examining regional appropriations from the 1950s onward. What are the key factors, both economic and political, that determine how funds are allocated and which regions receive the biggest funding increments?

As in any political system, such policy choices are likely to represent a mix of different goals and constraints. My object here is to unravel their effects—to weigh and compare rival explanations of Soviet policy. The discussion turns first to an overview of regional economic competition, then to an analysis of the factors that shape regional appropriations.

The Roots of Regional Economic Competition

Although the local revolution after 1953 added new fuel to the competing economic claims of different regions, the rivalry itself was hardly
new. Political battles over regional appropriations emerged as early as the
drafting as the First Five-Year Plan, when central and regional politicians
alike complained that early drafts slighted the issue of regional development and industrial location.[1] Planners corrected the omission with a
grandiose scheme to push eastward by developing the Ural-Kuznetsk combine. Ostensibly the move was meant to speed up economic growth by
exploiting the east's vast raw material reserves; but the decision had as
much to do with politics as with economics. Developing the east would
help to move the gravity center of Soviet industry away from vulnerable
western borders (Koropeckyj 1967; Davies 1974). The decision also reflected the political currents of the late 1920s and the shifting political
fortunes of the adherents of eastern vs. western development. Some advocates of the west appeared to be too cautious, forecasting relatively low
economic growth rates in a political climate that increasingly favored
higher—even if unrealistic—goals (Holubnychy 1965). Some were also
associated with the Left Opposition, and when the Left collapsed, so too
did the political footing of the "western lobby" (Holubnychy 1975; Koropeckyj 1971).

Thus with the adoption of the First FYP, the European part of the
USSR and especially the Ukraine were supposed to be downgraded in
Soviet economic development. Ukrainian leaders protested that economic
calculations showed higher returns in the west, where an industrial base
was already established; and one Ukrainian economist went so far as to
note the colonial overtones of the new investment strategy, but to no avail
(Volobuev 1928). Once the drive for rapid development gained momen-
tum, Moscow circumvented such republic complaints by further central-
izing economic administration (see chapter 2), revamping local
government, and thus fragmenting whatever power remained in the
republics.

Yet even in the highly restrictive atmosphere of the Stalin era, regional
leaders still complained about inattentive central ministries and inadequate
funds. One complaint was the "reverse provincialism" of central ministries:
top ministry officials, it seems, rarely set foot outside Moscow, and in-

dividual ministers were often criticized by name for ignoring unique local problems.[2] From the perspective of regional leaders, the center was also far too slow in carring out duly authorized plans. Many projects took two to three times as long as had been planned; others were approved but never got under way. References to the need to speed up or "force" the pace of development were common. At the Seventeenth Congress (*XVII S"ezd* 1934:436–39, 480–82), Uzbekistan's Khodzhaev claimed that energy needs in Tashkent and Samarkand demanded that the center force the completion of a new electric power plant; Kazakhstan's Isaev insisted that the goals of the current plan could not be met unless Moscow forced the construction of new mines in his region. Some comments from below also suggested local discontent with the pace and character of the rapid centralization during the first plan: Gorkii's Pakhomov (ibid:476–78) lamented that the process had centralized the profitable industries but left the unprofitable ones in local hands.

Regional officials also appealed outright for more funds. Then, as now, their requests were couched in the prevailing buzzwords; in the late 1920s and the 1930s, defense, nationality policy, and the wrongheadedness of the opposition were invoked to justify the need for greater investment in the periphery. And then, as now, appeals focused on agriculture, primary industries, and infrastructure. Isaev contended that mining, ore-processing and oil production in Kazakhstan required more central funding, as did agriculture and light industry and rail transport. Khodzhaev asked for more resources for Uzbek farms, rail transport, roadbuilding, water supplies, and energy. Belorussia's Goloded (*XVII S"ezd* 1934:441–42) asked that Moscow increase geological prospecting work so that his republic could exploit its natural resources.

However, the response was less than enthusiastic. Sergo Ordzhonikidze, then Commissar of Heavy Industry, scolded republic and local officials for their requests, noting that " if we tried to do everything that our oblasti and republics demand in the Second Five-Year Plan, it would take far more than five years" (*XVII S"ezd* 1934:435–36). But he also held out the promise of more funding as a carrot for current plan fulfillment: the only way more resources would be available for republic and local leaders to coax out of the center, he told the delegates, "depends on you, on all of us," in fulfilling the targets already laid down.

Two years later, Gosplan's vice-chairman, G. T. Grin'ko (1936:315) lamented that plan deliberations meant "endless discussions" betwen regional and central authorities and ongoing competition between regions. According to Grin'ko "the very structure of the Five-Year Plan is, to a certain degree, a result of the rivalry and conflicting claims among the individual economic regions and with the central authorities of the Soviet Union. . . . "

Judging from the deliberations of congresses and of the Supreme Soviet, central and regional leaders were also frequently at odds over the accuracy and legitimacy of requests from below. In 1938, the Chairman of the Soviet of Nationalities budget commission chided the central Finance Commissariat for overlooking requests from the republics. Finance Commissar A. G. Zverev acknowledged the criticism, admitting that his staff did not "make a thorough enough study of the claims of the republics." At the same time, both of them also challenged the data they received from outlying regions, scolding the Uzbek Finance Commissariat for concealing funds, and complaining that the union republics exaggerated their requests. According to Zverev, the Kirghiz SSR, which had a budget of 235 million rubles[3] for 1937, had requested 617 million for 1938, an increase of 263 percent.[4] Other republics were criticized for similar excesses, and for demanding a higher percentage of the turnover taxes they collected in order to fatten their budgets (*Second Session* 1938:114–15, 280–83, 362–65).

How much influence regional claims actually carried is not clear. But given the minor share of economic administration left to regional officials and the tone of self-criticism that characterized their public comments, the impact of their appeals seems to have been limited. The Supreme Soviet sometimes ignored their requests altogether in its budget deliberations: its budget commissions almost always proposed amendments to increase revenues to the state budget, but additions to regional appropriations were less frequent. Leaders asking for additional funds were often advised to find internal reserves.[5]

Budget deliberations for 1950 offer a case in point. The chairmen of the budget commissions in each chamber, I. S. Khokhlov and L. P. Korniets (*Zasedanie Verkhovnogo Soveta* 1950:65–74, 102–10) recommended adjustments increasing total budget revenues by 1,125 million rubles, but they proposed no increments for republic budget expenditures. As Korniets (ibid.:102–10) explained,

The leaders of some ministries and institutions, and also the Councils of Ministers of some union republics have given us requests for added funds.

We consider that the projects they are requesting can be carried out within the budget as already laid out, by economizing on expenditures and raising added revenues.

Similarly, party congresses designated commissions to study five-year plan directives and to recommend changes, but the changes did not conform to the requests put forward by regional and local leaders (as they were to do in the post-Stalin era).[6] Thus while regional lobbying continued between 1928 and 1953, there seems to have been less effort either publicly or behind the scenes to accede to requests from below.

With the appeals procedures implemented after 1953, and with Khrushchev's insistence on more equal treatment of different regions, economic competition became more visible. Leaders in the periphery began to refer to proposals which they had drawn up and submitted to central planners for developing new segments of the local economy.[7]

And any regional spokesman, it seemed, could now rationalize a request for added funds by highlighting some aspect of the local economy that fell below the USSR average (Khaburzaniia 1978; Iskanderov 1969; Udovenko 1968). Anastas Mikoyan (Perlo 1961:17–18) described the many frictions in an interview in the 1960s, reporting that investment planning

> is not a strictly peaceful process. Each struggles for his particular plans and plant—inside the All-Union Gosplan and the Gosplans of the Union Republics, until a decision is reached. Most issues can be smoothed out by argument and figures, but sometimes the Government must make a decision.

Occasionally some of the participants have even gone a step further, questioning the wisdom of appropriations or benefits to other regions.[8] And the issue of equal treatment at times emerges even more sharply: Tiumen's oblispolkom president, V. V. Nikitin (*Deviataia sessiia* 1983:187–92), complained to the Supreme Soviet in 1983 that ministries toe the line in providing housing, services, and infrastructure for Moscow, Leningrad, the Ukraine, and other regions, but he noted that for Tiumen, central government decisions on such matters are not enforced.

Publicly, of course, each regional politician glosses over the conflicts by reciting the benefits his region shares with the nation as a whole. But underneath the rhetoric of mutual assistance, each regional request is a bid for a larger share of a limited pie.

The race has become even more intense with economic slowdown of the 1970s and 1980s. From 1950 through the mid-1970s, a postwar investment boom brought every republic an increase in funding virtually every year; now, allocations for any given region may drop from one year to the next. In 1979, five republics (Kirgizia, Belorussia, Lithuania, Moldavia, and the Ukraine) saw their level of investment decline (*Narkhoz* 1979:373). Similarly, Tadzhikistan, Georgia, and the Ukraine experienced virtually no investment growth in 1981, while Estonia, Kirgizia, and Moldavia experienced a drop in funds (*Narkhoz* 1982:345). Others witnessed a modest increase, but at a rate much reduced from that of the 1950s and 1960s.

In response to this new era of stringency, plan directives increasingly call for limits on new investment in energy- and water-poor regions (i.e., the European part of the USSR) (*XXVI S"ezd* 1981:2:208–19). And as we saw in chapter 3, republic leaders worry about planned growth rates that are too low to sustain promised increases in income, employment, and consumption. Competition over bigger or smaller budget increases has given way to more fundamental conflict over growth versus decline.

The Dilemmas of Regional Planning

Faced with tightening economic constraints, Soviet planners have stepped up their search for a scientific approach to regional allocations and industrial location. Politicians and economists alike increasingly emphasize that correct regional development and national prosperity are intimately connected. The argument is stated best by N. N. Nekrasov (1975), one of the foremost Soviet regional economists: continued economic growth demands the right territorial proportions. Raising productivity hinges on the regional distribution of productive forces, and this, in turn, necessitates more sophisticated regional planning.

Judging from the burgeoning Soviet literature on regional development, much progress has already been made in advancing both theory and methods. Location theory, which blossomed in the 1920s and then languished under Stalin, has been reinvigorated and now boasts elaborate quantitative models of locational criteria and comparative advantage (V. V. Kotov 1980; Taaffe 1984). According to Nekrasov (1975), one such model generated a computer-based evaluation of 70 possible sites that eventually led to the construction of the Kama truck and Volga auto complexes.

Many republic governments are also experimenting with mathematical models of industrial location and the design of territorial production complexes, and both SOPS and several regional and local planning agencies have produced "perspective" plans (nonbinding guidelines spanning a decade or more) for long-term territorial development (Fedorenko 1984; Maniushis 1978; Nekrasov 1975). Some analysts have also begun to adopt the concepts of marginalism to improve assessments of investment options (Semina and Tatevosova 1980).

In addition, both planners and politicians place increasing emphasis on "complex development"—the integration of plans among different industries and among different sectors in each region. The 1979 reform decree made it a top priority, outlining several steps to be taken to balance (*sochetat'*) branch and territorial concerns (*KPSS v rezoliutsiiakh i Resheniiakh* 1981:13:405–51). As the enthusiasm for territorial production complexes (TPKs) attests, there is a growing realization that individual enterprises and sectors in a region cannot develop fully without coordination.

All told, progress in research on regional matters has been impressive. But it has not been matched by progress in day-to-day planning. Leaders at every level of government call for complex, integrated development, yet the planning system itself remains fragmented. Republic and local governments compile long-range plan guidelines, but they still lack timely information on the plans of central ministries, and their own plans are still subject to unexpected changes from above. Central planners, for their part, have elaborate quantitative models of regional allocations and industrial location, but the models typically embrace only a single branch of the economy and are often supported by only limited data. And planners in Moscow may endorse the notion of a territorial production complex, but they have been unwilling to endow such complexes with any real authority to coordinate or control economic activity.[9]

Thus despite the advances in regional theory, planners still confront formidable obstacles in their quest for the "right territorial proportions." One of the most difficult problems is simply to define priorities among the many diverse goals that regional plans are supposed to serve. Statements on Soviet regional policy, by individual leaders and in plan directives, present planners with a long list of competing objectives, all of which must be realized together. Moreover, each goal is itself subject to multiple and often conflicting interpretations. A consensus may exist in principle that regional policy ought to promote national defense or correct the imbalance of labor resources, but what these require in practice is not altogether clear. Part of the controversy arises from a lack of data: comparing strategies to employ labor reserves in Central Asia, for example, requires information not just on labor but on production possibilities and demand for the eventual products—and not just in Central Asia but across the USSR. Regional decisions should weigh opportunity costs as well as direct costs, but data on both continue to be all too limited. In addition, effective regional planning also requires administrative coordination, and as we saw in chapters 1 and 3, the structure of the Soviet state works against integration at the regional level.

The first and most important task for planners seems to be to determine the real objectives of regional policy, many of which are difficult enough to achieve singly, let alone in tandem. The list varies, depending on which sources one reads and the time period one examines. Yet several aims appear repeatedly in plan directives and in Soviet discussions of regional policy. These include:[10]

1) promoting economic growth in the nation as a whole;
2) promoting national defense;
3) guaranteeing the all-around development of each republic and region;
4) developing industries close to the site of raw materials;
5) developing industries close to the market for the finished product;
6) optimizing the use of natural resources;
7) promoting specialization and interdependence among regions;
8) promoting the complex development of each region;
9) protecting the environment;
10) increasing employment among the able-bodied;
11) eliminating the differences between town and country;
12) developing industry in labor-deficit areas;
13) speeding up the development of eastern regions; and
14) integrating all-union with local interests.

Not all these goals carry equal weight with Soviet leaders. Growth and defense surely rank highest on the list. Yet they cannot be divorced from the other aims of regional policy. For planners, the problem is not whether to promote national economic growth or to increase employment in labor-surplus areas; rather, it is how to achieve both, while promoting regional specialization, protecting the environment, and so on. As regional economist V. P. Evstigneev (1976) explains, the dilemma in regional planning is how to juggle the whole set of interdependent goals *simultaneously*.

The task is made all the more difficult by the competing and sometimes contradictory recommendations that attach to each goal. Even where aims themselves are unambiguous, planners are still faced with conflicting options. The ongoing debate over east versus west in regional planning provides a case in point. All the contenders agree that the choice should foster national economic growth. But does that require faster development of the east, or more rapid reindustrialization in the old "smokestack" regions of the west? Anyone predisposed to favor one or the other can find enough quantitative evidence to support either side. Indeed, the choice of evidence itself is a political choice (North 1972; Taaffe 1984). Advocates of western development stress the high cost of transporting raw materials and finished products in from the eastern regions to the major population centers in the European USSR.[11] On the other hand, advocates of eastern development make their case by concentrating on the sheer quantity of raw materials and lower extraction costs outside the European USSR.[12]

The labor shortages in the European USSR, Siberia, and the Far East offer a similar example of contradictory options. One argument emphasizes the need to develop capital-intensive industries in labor-deficit areas, using more machinery and fewer workers to generate growth (*Materialy XXVI S"ezd KPSS* 1981:279). Yet as Evstigneev (1976) argues, this strategy could backfire: capital-intensive industries may use relatively less labor than capital, but they require more total workers per enterprise than do other industries. Light industrial enterprises embody less capital per worker, and also require fewer and less skilled workers to be economically efficient. Thus "capital-intensive" industry may sound ideal as a solution to worker shortages, but it could ultimately put even more of a strain on already tight labor resources.

The issue of national defense poses a third example. No Soviet planner can overlook the importance of strategic needs in location decisions. Yet "defense considerations" could be interpreted to require any of three different patterns of regional development (Dyker 1983; Holubnychy 1975). One would concentrate key sectors inland, away from vulnerable borders, and thus create a buffer zone against attack. A second would follow the opposite logic, building up border areas in order to provide a deterrent.

Yet a third would emphasize dispersion, developing a network of linked but self-sufficient regions that could function independently even if other key territories were captured or destroyed.[13] Thus "defense needs" can be used to justify investment in the east and the west, in the heartland and in border regions; they can be invoked to support regional specialization or full, complex development of each separate region.[14] Virtually any regional policy recommendation can be draped with strategic significance, simply by choosing the corresponding interpretation of defense needs.

In theory at least, most such controversies could be resolved if only there were complete and accurate data on the costs and benefits of alternative choices. But information flows are still far from adequate. Academician N. P. Fedorenko (1984) complains, for example, that models for regional development and industrial location too often rely on oversimplified representations of the economy and on limited data. True costs and benefits are difficult to calculate, since prices do not accurately reflect relative costs and scarcities (Dienes 1972; Kistanov 1978). To add to the problems, the norms used to evaluate the effectiveness of investment vary across different sectors of industries and different regions (Dienes 1972, 1982; Jackson 1971; Dyker 1983). And estimates of transport costs are artificially low in some areas, making certain choices—such as investment in the eastern regions—appear to be far more attractive than they would normally be (North 1972; Taaffe 1984). The problems of data and method have proved so troublesome that when SOPS developed a general scheme for the future location of productive forces (in cooperation with a reported 560 other agencies), its proposals reportedly proved to be so crude and impractical that they were not implemented (Taaffe 1984; "Planirovanie i territorial'noe" 1977; Zenchenko 1979).

Of course, problems of inadequate data and suboptimal location are not unique to the USSR (Hoover 1948). Studies of Western countries suggest that location decisions "are rarely profit-maximizing" even in capitalist systems, since they are often "made very quickly, with only a few sites considered, and usually limited to one area" (Richardson 1973). And location is seldom the predominant criterion in investment decisions. The actual choice of location, then, often falls short of the ideal dictated by location theory (Bell and Lande 1982).

In the Soviet case, the problems are compounded by the sheer size of the country and by its geographic and ethnic diversity. Policies that work in one area might not succeed elsewhere, as regional and local officials are quick to point out. The problems stand out most clearly in agriculture, where natural variations in climate and land alone work against any uniform policy. The difficulties even extend down to equipment and machinery: tractors and harvesters that work well enough in the south break down in the northwest's relatively wet climate; locomotives that function in the European USSR stall when they reach Siberia's winter (A. A. Kokarev, *XXIII S"ezd* 1966: 1:554–61; G. I. Kozlov, *Zasedaniia* 1965:86–91).

Subnational leaders are in the best position to recognize such problems; they confront them every day. But regional and local officials suffer from tunnel vision. They are only too aware of the problems and needs in their own area, but they lack the data needed to compare economic options across regions (Hough 1969). They seldom if ever have the kind of comprehensive, detailed estimates needed to assess the true costs and benefits of alternative regional choices. Hence their heavy emphasis on agricultural and natural resource development when they appeal to Moscow: local advantages and capabilities in these sectors are inherent in the locality and can be documented through local sources. In contrast, production of most manufactured goods—for example, buses or television sets—is much less location-bound, and therefore regional and local leaders find it more difecult to "prove" that they have any comparative advantage unless they already have related enterprises in place.

Their problems are futher compounded, as we saw in earlier chapters, by the administrative structure of the Soviet state. Republic and local officials have the unenviable task of trying to coordinate decisions among central agencies over which they exercise little influence. And central agencies—Gosplan, central ministries—find it difficult to integrate plans by region. Indeed, they find it difficult to integrate plans among their own internal departments.[15]

The ministerial system also creates other problems for republic and local agencies. Ministries, faced with constant overextension of resources, lean toward urban, developed areas in their location strategies so as to economize on support expenditures. Investing in industrialized areas provides instant transport, housing, communications, markets, consumer services—agglomeration economies—that help reduce startup costs for a new or expanded enterprise. Ministries thus become free riders, using the benefits of existing collective goods without having to pay the full price for their development. Even in the face of strict limits on new investment in major urban centers, ministry officials still find ways to bend the rules (Botvin, *Zasedaniia* 1976:101–7; Maniushis 1978). As Soviet authors complain, this has created something of an anti-eastern bias in investment allocations, with industrial ministries tugging funds toward more developed sites in the west (Zenchenko 1979). And regional and local officials bear the costs, with overburdened infrastructure and services in developed areas and a dearth of services in less developed ones.

Political Influences and Regional Choices

All told, regional decisions never correspond perfectly to the dictates of theory. There is never enough timely information to weigh all the costs and benefits of regional decisions, or to factor in all the relevant variables. Nor does the methodology for making regional decisions permit a full comparison of all the alternative uses of national resources. Such decisions often stem from politics as much as economics, and even the choice of empirical data to evaluate regional options frequently becomes a political choice. Thus despite the renewed Soviet concern with location theory and the heightened emphasis on scientific regional planning, regional development continues to be very much a political question.

To say this, however, does not tell us which political factors exert the most influence, or which regions gain or lose in the process. Given the economic competition, how do individual regions fare, and what determines their success?

As chapter 1 explained, Western analysts offer a variety of competing political theories. One emphasizes the likely impact of political inequalities among regions: since some republic leaders have more clout and better connections than others, they are also assumed to be more successful regional lobbyists. In a system so wedded to hierarchy, regional politicians with direct access to top leaders in Moscow, direct access to the Politburo, should be better at winning additional attention and funds for problems at home. After all, they are in a privileged position to review preliminary plan targets and to discuss the outlines of future economic policies—an ideal vantage point for protecting local interests. And as we saw in chapter 3, they can be just as vocal in their lobbying as any other republic politicians.

Political insiders may also have another, less direct advantage in regional competition: an ability to open doors for their colleagues in republic government who need information or assistance from the center. Since information and assistance are so difficult to obtain for politicians outside Moscow, having a "friend at court" ought to be of enormous value in republic lobbying efforts. Thus if our theories about the importance of connections in the Soviet system hold true, those republic leaders with seats in the Politburo should have an inside edge in the regional competition for funds. If connections count, then "Politburo republics" under Khrushchev and Brezhnev—the RSFSR, Ukraine, Belorussia, Uzbekistan, Kazakhstan, Georgia, and Azerbaidzhan—ought to show larger-than-average annual increases in appropriations and a larger share of total national appropriations after their top leaders acquired Politburo rank.

Other political cleavages among the republics also figure prominently in Western assessments of regional influence. Moscow seems to differentiate among non-Russian regions, with some ruled almost exclusively by native leaders and others subject to monitoring and supervision by nonnatives, usually Russian or Ukrainian, brought in from outside. Reliance on natives, as Western scholars contend, reflects Moscow's greater trust in local leaders (Miller 1977). Such native-ruled or "self-administered" (Bialer 1980) regions presumably command more influence with the centeral government than those controlled by outsiders. They should therefore have a measurable advantage in coaxing more funds out of higher agencies.

Finally, one other political distincton may also count in regional leaders' ability to sway appropriations decisions in their favor. Some Western research suggests that newly appointed regional leaders may be more dynamic and more inclined to innovate, perhaps having a fuller agenda, more energy, or more support to pursue new funds for local development (Bunce 1979). If so, we should expect to find republics with a new party boss registering greater changes than other regions in the budgetary competition.

These arguments can be persuasive. They reflect some of our most basic assumptions about policy-making in the USSR: the importance of being an insider, the advantages of native rule, the impact of new leaders. They also assume that some regions are systematically and persistently favored in Soviet appropriations policies because of specific political advantages.

Yet as chapter 1 demonstrated, leaders from Khrushchev onward have promised "all-around" or complex development for all regions. The need to invoke ideological formulas demands at least lip service to regional and ethnic equality. But surely the political advantages do not go unnoticed in the Kremlin. Pledges of fair treatment and even development are a politically expedient—and conservative—means of appealing to regional and local elites.

This emphasis on equality suggests substantial political benefits for national leaders who pursue a functional logrolling strategy. Rather than favoring only their own political cronies, national leaders would find it more advantageous to be evenhanded, as in Khrushchev's convenient idea of equalizing per capita spending among regions, or Brezhnev's insistence on protecting the interests of all the republics. Their budgetary policies would thus include at least modest payoffs and benefits to as a large a number of regional claimants as possible.

Equally important, Kremlin leaders could find it unprofitable to tie economic benefits too closely to regional political privilege. Whatever the political relationship between the Kremlin and the leaders in a given republic, the center nonetheless must depend on the proper functioning of the republic's economy. Each region is one element in an increasingly interdependent whole. It could be extremely costly in these circumstances to deny funds to regions without direct political representation in Moscow, or without predominantly native leadership. Moscow needs high output and efficiency from all regions.

Central leaders also face other political dilemmas in allocating funds. Consider, for example, the problem of distributing expenditures to reinforce nationality policies. A persuasive case can be made that native-ruled regions ought to do better in the economic arena, because of their political trustworthiness. But an equally good case can be made that funds should be concentrated in *less* trusted areas, where loyalties presumably most need to be reinforced.

The appointment of a new republic leader, especially after the ouster of an incumbent, raises much the same dilemma. A new leader brought in to correct past mistakes in a republic might be given preference in appeals for appropriations; but Moscow would also benefit by raising appropriations to "old" leaders in other republics who continue to perform well. Indeed, handing over added funds to a newly appointed republic party boss would reward a republic for the poor record of the last incumbent.

The politics of regional allocations would thus seem to be far more complex than our standard notions would imply. In fact, Kremlin leaders are likely to benefit more from broader-based logrolling. We would expect national funds to be parceled out among a variety of different regional interests, to bolster the position of national leaders. Regional appropriations policies could thus depend very little on the political cleavages and inequalities among the republics.

Of course, none of these various political forces operates in a vacuum. Decisions are also shaped by sectoral priorities and economic constraints, by what has happened in the past, by available resources, and by other givens that limit the regional options of any leader. Soviet research on regional development suggests, for example, that the availability of labor—especially skilled labor—has been one of the most important factors shaping the allocation of new investment in the post-Stalin era (Mazanova 1974; Maniushis 1978). According to some authors, the availability of raw materials has also been a key determinant—though this argument is far more controversial (Mazanova 1974; Runova 1976). Varied levels of development have also been cited as important determinants of investment allocations, though this too is a controversial point (Dienes 1972; I. S. Koropeckyj, Koropeckyj and Schroeder 1981; Gillulla 1981). And, as we have seen, budget and investment policies are also subject to incrementalism, since decisions proceed "from the achieved level." Each of these influences must be accounted for and controlled before we can say anything meaningful about political influences on regional appropriations. The analysis that follows thus offers a multivariate analysis to compare the relative impact of political and economic/contextual factors.

Moreover, the impact of both politics and economic constraints may well vary depending on the policy domain under examination. For that reason, the analysis here explores appropriations policies in three domains: capital investment, enlightenment, and health care. Investment funds are, of course, the major prize of regional competition. As Dienes (1972) explains, the allocation of capital grants spurs a perennial battle among regional leaders, and investment policies are a key target of regional lobbying efforts. However, investment funds are also the most strictly controlled from Moscow, and regional politicians may therefore find it somewhat easier to influence appropriations in fields more directly under their own jurisdiction, such as enlightenment and health care.

Regional Appropriations and Political Privilege

INVESTMENT

How have investment funds been allocated among the Soviet republics since the Stalin years? The data offer some surprising answers: investment allocations grew more equal after Stalin, and annual investment growth rates too became more alike across the republics between 1950 and 1981. Within these broad outlines, *there is little evidence that the political status of any republic's leader affected its success in the investment arena*. Republic leaders in the Politburo have been only as successful as any others in the economic competition: annual increases in investment funds are virtually identical for republics with Politburo representation and for republics without it.

Similarly, investment has increased at the same rate for both native-ruled regions and for those with outsiders in key republic posts. And changes in funding have been the same for regions with old and with new party bosses. Political inequalities—representation in the Politburo, native rule, the appointment of a new republic party leader—have no impact on regional appropriations.

Using coefficients of variation to measure the interregional dispersion of investment, figure 4.1 shows the trend since 1950: the gap narrowed most under Khrushchev, widening slightly in the mid–1970s and then leveling off. Rates of investment growth also converged. In 1958, for example, republic increases over the previous year ranged from 8.0 to 30.8 percent; by 1981, the changes ran from −1.0 to 11.4 percent over 1980.

Regions on the low end of the economic scale thus had slightly higher rates of investment than we would predict on their level of economic development alone. The narrowed gap in funding created a mild form of redistribution from more to less developed areas, although the degree of redistribution diminished somewhat by the end of the 1970s (Gillulla 1979; Wagener 1973)

While the overall trend narrowed investment differences among the republics, some regions did benefit more than others. The Baltic, Central Asia, Belorussia, and Moldavia all experienced a modest net increase in

FIGURE 4.1
Inequality in Republic and Local Expenditures

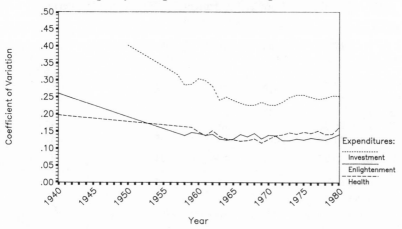

Coefficients of variation are unweighted.

Capital investment includes both budgetary and nonbudgetary expenditures. Data for 1940 exclude the Baltic and Moldavia. Enlightment and health care include budgetary expenditures only. Health care excludes physical education after 1975, and apparently includes expenditures for the 1980 Olympics. Data on investment between 1950 and 1958, and on enlightenment and health between 1940 and 1958, are interpolated.

For sources, see appendix A.

their share of total USSR investment between the Fourth and Tenth Five-Year Plans (see table 4.1).

These increases stemmed at least partially from several other economic choices: the dispersion of several industries such as textiles and food processing; the growth of agricultural investment from the 1950s through the middle of the 1970s; and, for western border regions, the increase in CMEA and in East-West trade (Gillulla 1981; Shabad 1980). Among the individual republics, the biggest gains went to Armenia, Belorussia, and Lithuania, where increases in skilled labor were among the highest in the country.[16]

Other regions fared differently: the RSFSR share of total USSR investment dipped and then recovered with the new emphasis in the 1970s on the non–Black Earth regions in agriculture and on energy and fuels under Brezhnev; the Ukraine, Georgia, and Azerbaidzhan did well early on but then lost ground because of their aging industries. However, Azerbaidzhan and Georgia recovered somewhat in the late 1970s as the energy crisis brought new investment into the oil industry.

TABLE 4.1
Regional Shares of Soviet Investment, By Five-Year Plan Periods
(in percent)

	RSFSR	Ukraine	"West"[a]	Baltic	Caucasus	Central Asia
1946–50	61.23	19.35	3.36	1.29	5.27	8.64
1951–55	64.25	16.52	2.83	1.33	4.70	9.46
1956–60	63.37	16.98	3.03	1.44	3.49	10.99
1961–65	62.39	17.63	3.70	1.90	3.77	13.39
1966–70	58.92	16.49	4.19	2.04	3.82	13.39
1971–75	60.26	15.93	4.51	3.11	3.45	12.68
1976–80	61.90	14.78	4.48	2.85	2.89[b]	12.34
1981–84[c]	62.25	13.84	4.46	2.84	3.96	12.50

[a]Belorussia and Moldavia.

[b]Excludes Armenia.

[c]Data were available only for 1981–84 at the time of this writing. The figures in this row may not be strictly comparable with the preceding ones.

For sources and a description of the data, see appendix A.

The relatively low share of investment in the Ukraine and Georgia is especially noteworthy, given their political preeminence. Both republics experienced a decline in their slice of the pie, even though the Ukrainian first secretary has been included in the Politburo almost without interruption since the 1920s; and Georgia's party boss was a candidate member from 1957 to 1972. Despite their political clout in comparison with other republic leaders, neither V. V. Shcherbitsky nor V. P. Mzhavanadze was able to neutralize the decline of their republics' investment. In the Georgian case, investment growth did pick up in the late 1970s with the reinvigoration of the oil industry in the Caucasus. However, the upswing occurred during 1974–77, when no Georgian party leader was included in the Politburo.

Other examples also suggest that Politburo representation offers little advantage in appropriations battles. The Kazakh share of investment actually dropped after the republic first secretary, D. A. Kunaev, was named a candidate member of the Politburo in 1966. Equally important, two of the regions that experienced the biggest gains from the mid–1950s to the 1980s, Armenia and Lithuania, had no republic spokesman in the party's ruling circle.

The impact of having a regional leader in the Politburo can be assessed more fully by comparing annual increases in investment among regions with and without representation. The data, in table 4.2, show no systematic bias in either direction: in some years, regions with representation do better, and in some years they do worse. A slight change in this pattern did emerge in the mid–1970s when Georgia's Mzhavanadze retired and left his republic without a spokesman in the Politburo. Since Georgia had been a low-investment region, the simple act of dropping it out of the group automatically raised the average for the remaining Politburo republics. But there is no evidence that membership in the Politburo itself confers any economic advantage.

Table 4.2 also extends the analysis by comparing investment growth in regions with new and "old" party heads, and native and nonnative leadership. In all cases, the conclusion is the same—privileged republics, with a new leader or with all-native elites in the top political jobs, do neither better nor worse than any other regions. "Old" leaders keep pace with the new ones, and nonnative leaders do as well as natives.

One could argue that the impact of political privilege is more subtle: it might come into play by raising appropriations in a republic above what they would otherwise be, given the region's level of economic development, natural resources, and labor force. Put simply, privileged regions could well have even lower increases in investment were it not for their political advantages. Thus to determine how such advantages really work, we would have to control for the economic differences among regions.

However, the results of the regression analysis presented in table 4.3 reveal that even when the economic differences among the republics are added in, privileged and nonprivileged regions still fare the same. If anything, regions with a representative in the Politburo or a new leader apparently did slightly worse in the competition for investment under Khrushchev.

Other factors carry much more weight in explaining where investment funds were allocated. As the significant constant term in table 4.3 reveals, one of the most important was incrementalism:[17] annual changes in each region's investment tended to be very stable—as Soviet officials themselves admit. But the consistency from year to year seems to have declined under Brezhnev, as changes in investment increasingly fluctuated from positive to negative.[18] The availability of skilled labor also shaped allocations under Brezhnev, bearing out the assessments by Mazanova (1974) and Maniushis (1978). Finally, regional investment in the Brezhnev era also corresponded

TABLE 4.2
Political Status and Investment Among Soviet Republics, 1958–1981
(in percent)

| | Annual increase in investment among republics with: | | | | | |
	Politburo Membership[a]		Succession[b]		Native Leadership[c]	
	Yes	No	Yes	No	Yes	No
1958	17.6	20.2	17.2	20.4	19.7	19.8
1959	12.6	17.2	12.6	16.5	14.4	17.3
1960	11.5	12.0	10.1	12.3	13.5	10.4
1961	6.8	12.8	11.6	11.1	8.8	12.4
1962	6.1	7.9	7.0	7.4	5.1	8.4
1963	9.4	7.8	5.1	8.8	10.0	7.5
1964	12.1	13.3	10.5	13.1	13.0	12.9
1965	11.6	13.1	12.8	12.6	11.7	13.0
1966	12.2	7.8	15.5	8.8	14.0	6.8
1967	9.6	9.3	8.2	9.6	8.9	9.7
1968	7.1	9.2	–	8.4	7.1	9.0
1969	1.6	3.6	–	2.8	0.4	4.0
1970	12.3	11.2	11.8	11.6	14.1	10.5
1971	5.9	6.1	–	6.0	6.8	5.6
1972	6.7	5.4	7.5	5.8	8.7	4.9
1973	4.5	5.5	1.6	5.6		
1974	6.8	6.8	–	6.8		
1975	6.8	5.8	8.7	5.8		
1976	4.7	2.4	–	3.2		
1977	6.9	4.2	–	5.3		
1978	5.1	4.0	–	4.4		
1979	2.0	2.0	5.6	1.7		
1980	1.7	1.2	–	1.5		
1981	6.1	3.8	4.3	4.9		

[a]Politburo membership here includes all full or candidate members who also held republic office, during the previous year.

[b]Succession refers to a change in the first secretary (or, in the RSFSR, of the premier) during the previous year. A dash indicates that no succession occurred.

[c]"Native" leadership here refers to instances where the first and second secretary of the republic party, and the premier and deputy premier were all of the indigenous republic nationality. The RSFSR is excluded from this column. Data on such leaders were taken from Hodnett and Ogareff (1973),which runs only up to 1972.

For sources and an explanation of the data, see appendix A.

TABLE 4.3
Political and Economic Determinants of Republic Investment, 1957–1981[a]

| | Multiple Regression Results:[b] | | | |
| | 1957–64 | | 1965–81 | |
	Incl. RSFSR	Excl. RSFSR	Incl. RSFSR	Excl. RSFSR
Independent variables:				
Intercept	.077*	.076*	.029*	.025*
Level of economic development	.581*	.571*	.127*	.126*
Population size	−.238	−.251	.200*	.205*
Skill of labor force	.189	.207	.251*	.245*
Comparative natural resource endowment	−.002	.004	−.005	−.006
Representation in Politburo	−.017	−.015	.009	.009
Succession	−.032*	−.038*	.020	.021
R^2	.296	.290	.060	.064

[a]The dependent variable is the annual change in investment for each republic during the given period. Coefficients significant at $p \le .05$ are marked with an asterisk. A measure of "native" leadership (see the definition in table 4.2) was also included in the model but only for the years up through 1972. The coefficients for it were −.021 for 1957–64 and .028 for 1965–72 (for the fourteen non-Russian republics). Neither was statistically significant.

[b]Results are based on a general linear model, using standardized data.

For a description of the variables and sources, see appendix A.

more closely to the size of a republic's population. In contrast, under Khrushchev the level of a republic's economic development proved more influential.

At first glance, this would seem to contradict the finding that inequality in regional appropriations diminished under Khrushchev. But the two conclusions are not really at odds: the coefficients of variation reveal how large or small the interregional gap is, while the regression results explain allocations among different regions within that gap. In other words, a redistributive policy can reduce the inequality of investment among regions, granting more to less developed regions than they would otherwise have available given the level of their economies. But even a small degree of inequality may still yield the regression results in table 4.3, since they are independent of the size of the gap itself.

It might also be argued that the results may be distorted by the very different size and economic weight of the RSFSR versus other Soviet regions. But this argument is not supported by the evidence: if the RSFSR is excluded from the analysis, the results of the regression analysis turn out to be virtually identical (see table 4.3).

The data in tables 4.2 and 4.3 thus confirm that appropriations have been much more diffuse than any simple model of political favoritism among regions would allow. Regions with the highest representation at the center (the Ukraine, Georgia) have done poorly; while regions with few such political resources have done remarkably well. There is no link between the national standing of a regional leader and the increases in investment for his republic.

Instead, the politics of regional investment seems to be a politics of compromise, with funds dispersed among a variety of regional contenders, politically privileged or not. For confirmation one need only look at discussions of five-year plan directives: these guidelines on developing the economy read like quintessential political platforms where regional issues are concerned. They advocate development in small and medium-sized towns, but also call for improving production and services in large cities. They typically call for more development in the eastern regions, but also for renewal in western areas too. They have the look of documents authored by committee.

Thus when Khrushchev (1959:30–31) reported on the the targets for the plan directives adopted in 1959, he made a special point of emphasizing the needs of both the eastern and the western regions of the country: "While developing the productive forces of our country's eastern areas to the utmost, we must utilize to the full the potentialities for increasing production in the European part of the USSR."

This strategy included developing raw materials, power resources, and chemical production in the European section of the USSR. Similarly, plan directives for 1966–70 stressed fuel development in the east but also envisioned the development of new and labor-intensive industries in the west (*XXIII S"ezd* 1966: 2:362). And directives for 1971–75 listed a long series of goals for complex development in Siberia, Central Asia, and the Far East, but also advocated "maximal use" of western regions' energy resources—such as atomic power (*Gosudarstvennyi piatiletnyi plan* 1972:245–49).

The economic problems of the late 1970s and early 1980s have made this kind of accommodation more difficult, and preliminary plan directives for 1981–85 included a ban on the development of new energy- and water-intensive production in the European USSR. Yet the final directives adopted by the Twenty-Sixth Congress softened this prohibition, by providing that "as a rule," such industries should be excluded from the European regions (*Current Digest of the Soviet Press,* May 20, 1981, 33:24). The final directives also advocated funding for the European USSR to expand, upgrade, and reequip existing productive facilities, with more emphasis on nuclear power stations and on exploring the possibility of river diversion to mitigate water shortages in the west. Directives for 1986–90 also called for limits on the building of new enterprises in major cities, except in cases of consumer industries, but still fell short of a total prohibition (*Pravda,* March 9, 1986, p. 5).[19] Even in the face of tighter economic constraints, plans still suggest an effort to touch all major bases. Partisans of both eastern and western development can usually find some support in the national plan (Taaffe 1984). In Boris Rumer's words "for every thesis in the plan there is an antithesis" (Rumer 1982a:1–2).

This is not to deny the greater *fanfare* given to some issues, such as the development of the eastern regions. Every set of plan directives since 1928 has described the new frontier in glowing terms. But words alone are not necessarily an indication of government priorities. As the late Soviet geographer A. A. Mints (1976) revealed, the allocation of funds between east and west has been much more even than the official rhetoric would suggest (see also Granberg 1986). The shift in funding has been exaggerated in the Soviet literature on regional development. Between 1951 and 1975, each new set of five-year plan directives offered verbal support for more rapid eastern development, but the actual share of investment going to Siberia and the Far East was virtually constant, between 15 and 17 percent of the total; it did not reach 20 percent until the beginning of the 1980s (see table 4.4). And this was not appreciably higher than it had been in the 1930s.[20] Supporters of the west—a coalition of regional interests and central economic ministries—have in fact managed to hold their own in spite of the verbal emphasis given to opening up the east.

The compromises over competing regional demands suggest that there is no comprehensive and internally consistent plan for regional development in the USSR (Rodgers 1974; Abouchar 1976). There simply is no single grand strategy for regional growth. The Soviet Union is too large, and its natural and human goegraphy is too diverse, for a single goal to

TABLE 4.4
Share of Soviet Investment to Siberia and the Far East, 1918–1975
(in percent)

	Total	W. Siberia	E. Siberia	Far East
1918–1928	14.8	3.9	4.5	6.3
1928/29–1932	13.5	4.4	4.2	4.8
1933–1937	13.3	4.0	3.5	5.7
1938–6/1941	15.0	3.7	3.8	7.6
6/1941–1945	18.0	6.1	4.1	7.8
1946–1950	13.0	4.4	4.1	4.5
1951–1955	15.2	5.7	4.8	4.8
1956–1960	15.7	6.2	5.6	3.9
1961–1965	15.7	5.9	5.4	4.4
1966–1970	16.3	6.5	5.1	4.7
1971–1975	16.2	7.1	4.6	4.5

SOURCE: Rumer (1984:68–69).

predominate. Nor do the data or methods currently in use allow full and effective regional planning.

Even if they did, appropriations would still be dispersed, because of the countervailing advantages that obtain in different regions: the northwest's highly skilled labor, more advanced industry, and infrastructure, versus the Far East's natural resources, versus the South's natural resources and abundant labor supply. Given these complementary capabilities, and the process of planning by compromise, regional allocations thus result in a patchwork of investment policies, with some areas gaining from some decisions and losing on others. Indeed, the compromises are sometimes quite explicit. As republic spokesmen themselves point out, an appeal from below may gain support in Moscow—but typically it is only partial support and partial funding, given the number of proposals that get submitted and the difficulty of evaluating them all fully. The results therefore confirm Bialer's (1980) prediction: the outcome of regional economic competition has largely been a draw.

ENLIGHTENMENT AND HEALTH APPROPRIATIONS

The same conclusions also apply to spending for enlightenment and health care, where decisions have explicitly been tied since the Stalin years to a standard of equal per capita spending (Bescherevnykh 1976). Differences in per capita outlays have been extremely modest (see figure 4.1) since Khrushchev proposed to base republic budgets on the size of their populations. Moreover, average increases in funding have been essentially similar, whether republics had representation in the Politburo or not, whether they had an all-native top leadership or not, and whether they had a new or an "old" party boss (see table 4.5).

Controlling for the differences in economic conditions adds even stronger confirmation: once we add in variables capturing the differences in level of economic development and population among regions, the political attributes of a republic still show no correlation with success in the battle for funds (table 4.6). Regions with a seat on the Politburo did about the same as other regions in gaining appropriations for enlightment and health; and areas with a new party boss or natives in all four republic leadership posts did neither better nor worse than any others.

Expenditure policies have not, of course, been perfectly uniform since the beginning of the Khrushchev era.[21] Appropriations for enlightenment were highly incremental under Khrushchev (see the significant intercept term in table 4.6) and geared toward areas with fewer of their own educational resources. Under Brezhnev, appropriations again proved to be incremental, but were geared to larger and somewhat more prosperous regions. As figure 4.1 indicates, however, the extent of this shift was quite modest; and it may represent less an explicit change in allocational criteria than a change in emphasis from public to higher education. While elementary and secondary schools must generally be built where there are students, universities and institutes tend to be situated in large cities and regions, closer to employment prospects. Given these differences, the shifting policies from Khrushchev to Brezhnev may reflect a difference in the level of education receiving emphasis.

In health care, the two regimes reflect a similar pattern of appropriations: slightly higher expenditures in more developed regions (and in the Brezhnev period, even more for nonagricultural regions). However, only the Khrushchev era was characterized by an incremental spending policy—the Brezhnev years witnessed a less stable rate of change.

The evidence on regional investment, health, and enlightenment expenditures thus meshes well with the analysis of individual appeals in chapter 3. Appropriations have been rather evenly distributed regardless of the political makeup of a republic's top leadership and regardless of the leadership's access to the Politburo. Political favoritism clearly appears to

TABLE 4.5
Political Status and Expenditures on Enlightenment and Health Care Among Soviet Republics, 1958–1980
(in percent)

	Politburo Membership[b]		Succession[c]		Native Leadership[d]	
	Yes	No	Yes	No	Yes	No
	Annual increase in enlightenment expenditures among republics[a]					
1958	3.3	6.2	5.7	5.6	6.1	5.2
1959	25.4	23.7	26.2	23.9	23.0	25.3
1960	8.7	9.7	7.9	9.8	9.1	9.7
1961	9.1	9.4	10.0	9.2	9.2	9.5
1962	8.9	10.2	10.3	9.6	9.3	10.0
1963	6.7	8.0	5.9	7.8	6.9	7.8
1964	7.5	10.1	5.8	9.5	9.0	9.4
1965	19.6	21.3	23.2	20.6	21.0	20.6
1966	4.2	6.7	4.1	6.0	4.9	6.3
1967	6.2	9.1	10.3	7.6	5.9	8.9
1968	9.5	8.9	–	9.1	9.0	9.2
1969	6.8	8.1	–	7.5	7.1	7.8
1970	4.5	5.7	5.1	5.2	5.0	5.3
1971	7.1	7.8	–	7.5	6.7	7.9
1972	6.9	7.5	5.8	7.4	7.5	7.2
1973	8.4	9.0	7.8	8.9		
1974	7.4	7.3	–	7.3		
1975	5.2	5.7	5.8	5.5		
1976	4.6	4.3	–	4.4		
1977	3.5	4.1	–	3.4		
1978	5.0	5.5	–	5.3		
1979	3.2	4.3	8.3	3.5		
1980	4.4	5.5	–	5.0		

play less of a role than logrolling and compromise in decisions about where government funds are to be spent. The appropriations process seems to be one of constant adjustments at the margins, and these lead to a diffusion of funds among different contenders.

This suggests a need to reconceptualize the impact of political status and connections for regional leaders out to defend local interests. As many veterans of the process emphasize, these are valuable assets in the competition for funding. But given the sheer number of central agencies in-

TABLE 4.5 (*continued*)
Political Status and Expenditures on Enlightenment and Health Care Among Soviet Republics, 1958–1980
(in percent)

	Politburo Membership[b]		Succession[c]		Native Leadership[d]	
	Yes	No	Yes	No	Yes	No
	Annual increase in health care expenditures among republics[a]					
1958	6.6	9.6	9.8	8.8	9.2	8.9
1959	8.1	10.6	11.0	9.7	10.3	9.6
1960	9.6	8.8	9.2	9.0	11.0	7.4
1961	8.1	8.7	8.3	8.7	8.2	8.8
1962	5.5	6.8	8.3	5.9	5.4	6.9
1963	6.1	6.9	7.5	6.6	6.1	7.0
1964	7.7	9.5	4.9	9.2	7.6	9.5
1965	19.6	19.1	23.6	18.9	19.8	18.9
1966	6.1	6.7	4.1	6.7	6.4	6.6
1967	5.5	5.2	5.1	5.3	5.6	5.2
1968	9.7	9.5	–	9.6	9.9	9.4
1969	5.1	6.1	–	5.7	4.7	6.2
1970	9.4	8.3	7.0	9.0	9.5	8.4
1971	4.0	4.5	–	4.3	4.3	4.3
1972	4.4	5.5	4.5	5.1	4.9	5.1
1973	7.7	4.8	4.9	6.1		
1974	1.8	4.9	–	3.9		
1975	4.9	5.6	7.6	5.0		
1976	5.0	6.3	–	5.9		
1977	3.8	4.9	–	4.5		
1978	9.8	10.3	–	10.1		
1979	4.4	5.6	7.0	4.9		
1980	7.3	7.0	–	7.1		

[a]Expenditures are in current prices and are not comparable with the constant-price investment data in table 4.2.

[b]Politburo membership here includes all full or candidate members who also held republic office, during the previous year.

[c]Succession refers to a change in the first secretary (or, in the RSFSR, of the premier) during the previous year.

[d]"Native" leadership here refers to instances where the first and second secretary of the republic party and the premier and deputy premier were all of the indigenous republic nationality. The RSFSR is excluded from this column.

For sources and an explanation of the data, see appendix A.

volved, each with its own reserve of funds to allocate, persistent regional officials have more than one option in their quest for resources from above.

TABLE 4.6
Political and Economic Determinants of Republic Budget Expenditures for Enlightenment and Health Care, 1957–1975[a]

| | Multiple Regression Results[b] Enlightenment | | | |
| | 1957–64 | | 1965–75 | |
	Incl. RSFSR	Excl. RSFSR	Incl. RSFSR	Excl. RSFSR
Independent Variables:				
Intercept	.134*	.135*	.036*	.038*
Population size	.100	.120	.742*	.700*
Agricultural output	.093	.072	.025	.030
Level of economic development	.262	.273	.224*	.207*
Skill of labor force	−.482*	−.474*	.069	.071
Representation in Politburo	−.016	−.024	−.001	.00
Succession	−.010	−.026	.003	.003
R²	.089	.118	.241	.212
		Health Care		
Independent variables:				
Intercept	.072*	.072*	.012	.012
Population size	−.010	−.012	.385	.407
Agricultural output	−.021	−.020	−.080*	−.084*
Level of economic development	.211*	.215	.379*	.374*
Skill of labor force	−.035	−.038	.165	.164
Representation in Politburo	−.011	−.011	.004	.003
Succession	.003	.004	−.00	.001
R²	.124	.116	.170	.168

[a]The dependent variables are the annual changes in budget expenditures for enlightenment and health care for each republic during the given period.

Coefficients significant at $p \leq .05$ are marked with an asterisk.

A measure of "native" leadership (see the definition in table 4.2) was also included in the model but only for the years up through 1972. The coefficients for it (for the fourteen non-Russian republics) were: enlightenment: .003 for 1957–64 and −.004 for 1965–72; and health care: −.010 for 1957–64 and −.008 for 1965–72. Neither was statistically significant.

[b]Results are based on a general linear model, using standardized data.

For a description of the variables and sources, see appendix A.

Those without connections in higher party agencies may still have one in Gosplan; and those without a friend in Gosplan may have several in different ministries and their myriad subdivisions. Moscow's policy of building multiple checkpoints and controls into the planning system also means multiple avenues and sources of reserve funds for an appeal from below.

Politics matters—but it is a different kind of politics than any model of political privilege alone would imply. Republics whose leadership boasts ties in high places do not do markedly better than other republics; they sometimes actually do worse. And other regions do much better than average even without the political resources of Politburo representation, new leadership, or native rule. This suggests that different regions have offsetting advantages and political resources that result in a rather even allocation of funds. Appropriations decisions are indeed highly politicized, even down to the kinds of information regional leaders present to support their case. But the impact is to blunt, rather than sharpen, differences in regional spending.

CHAPTER FIVE

LOCAL AGENDAS
AND
LOCAL BUDGETS

IN MANY WAYS, local leaders face even more pressure than republic officials do. They are the ones who deliver goods and services—schooling, health care, public transportation, trade, and housing—to local residents. They are also the ones to whom citizens complain when goods and services fall short. They must answer for problems in the factories and farms in their territory, guarantee that plans are met on time, and cope with the chronic imbalances created by disparate growth rates in industry and agriculture, on one hand, and in social and economic infrastructure on the other.

At the same time, they labor under yet another layer of slow and cumbersome bureaucracy—at the republic level;[1] and they have even less direct control over the resources that flow into their area. Not only must local leaders capture the attention of distant offices in Moscow; they also suffer from the departmentalism and delays that arise in republic agencies. They accuse the republics of precisely the same kinds of neglect that republic leaders face in their own dealings with the center (Dmitriev and Zenkovich 1980:73–74). Even after a 1981 reform to enhance the economic role of local soviets (*Izvestiia*, March 29, 1981, p. 1), local officials still complain that their input is often ignored.[2] Thus, for example, V. V. Nikitin, president of Tiumen's oblispolkom (*Deviataia sessiia* 1983:191), told the Supreme Soviet in 1983 that

> our proposals for changes in the draft plans of union- and republic-subordinate enterprises are considered by the glavki and industrial associations in

our oblast, but they do not always receive support in some ministries or even in the departments of Gosplan.... the oblispolkom is supposed to approve the list of new construction projects (*titul'nyi spisok*), but even when it does not approve, the list is still adopted.[3]

The constraints on local power show all too clearly in the budgetary process. As chapter 3 explained, the "top-down" system gives republic governments the last word on local finances. The republics approve revenue plans and redistribute revenue sources (and thus expenditures) for subordinate localities; and they must also approve projected outlays by subordinate governments for industry, agriculture, transport, and other domains.

The local share of these expenditures is modest and declining, as shown in figure 5.1. Local governments, which outspent the republics from the 1920s to the mid–1950s, now account for the smallest share (14.4%) of the Soviet budget (Panskov and Velichko 1986). The deconcentration after Stalin (see chapter 2) thus had much more of an impact on the republics than on local governments. The repeated public campaigns for greater initiative and responsibility at the local level (Hill 1983) have been accompanied by a real decline in the budgetary, and hence administrative role of local governments.

But the impact has varied among different sectors of the economy. Among productive sectors, local governments have—and have always had—very little industry directly under their own jurisdiction; they account for a miniscule share (less than 5 percent) of Soviet budgetary outlays on industrial development (see figure 5.2). In agriculture, they command a somewhat larger share, but one that has declined since the height of the Sovnarkhoz reform. In transport and communications, the trend has been just the opposite, with the local percentage of the budget climbing during the 1970s. The local role has been much more substantial in the social realm, especially in housing and municipal services (which in Soviet terminology are technically counted among the productive sectors) and health.

Even in housing, health, and social services, however, investments by productive ministries to service their own workers leave local officials only a limited share of the resources that flow to their area. In Leningrad, local authorities controlled only 78 percent of all hospital beds, 65 percent of all doctors, 64 percent of nursery facilities, and 70 percent of all housing in the 1970s (Mezhevich 1978:113; Tarasenko 1980:76). And Leningrad

FIGURE 5.1
Republic Versus Local Shares of Soviet Budget Expenditures, 1924–1980

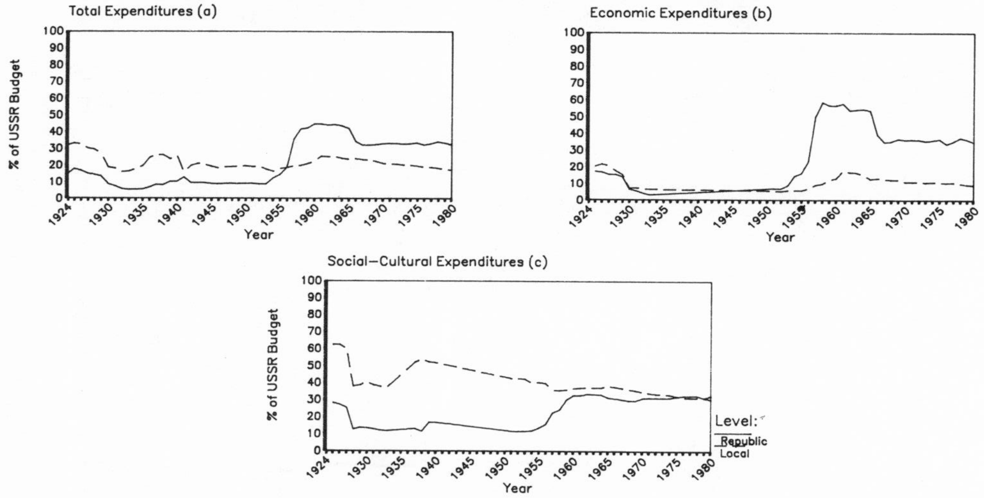

Total expenditures exclude reported defense expenditures.

Economic expenditures include industry, construction, agriculture, transport, communication, housing, trade, and other economic services.

Social-cultural expenditures include education, culture, health, physical education, and social security.

FIGURE 5.2
Local Share of Soviet Budget by Type of Expenditure

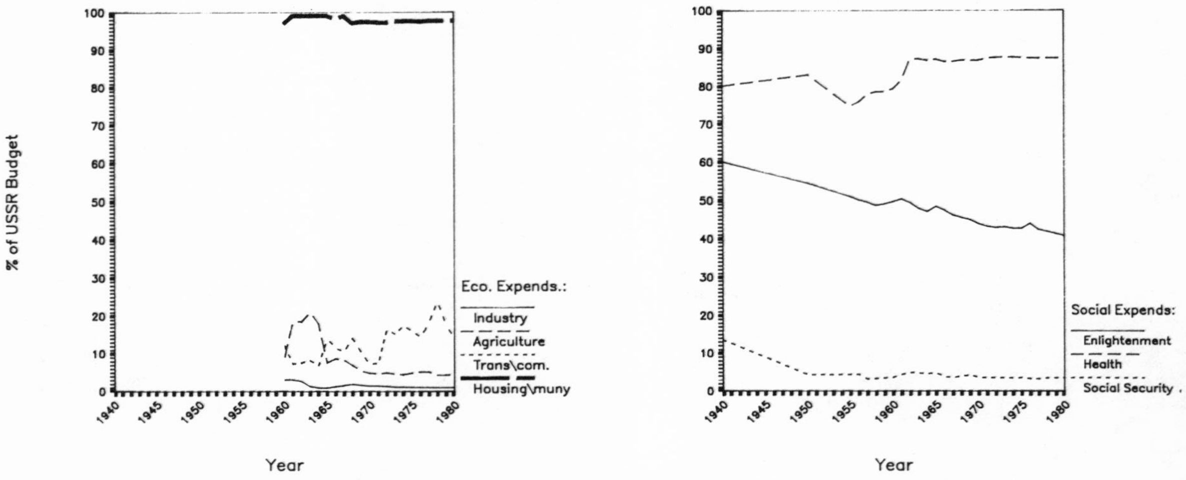

% of USSR Budget

Year

Year

Eco. Expends.:
Industry
Agriculture
Trans\com.
Housing\muny

Social Expends:
Enlightenment
Health
Social Security

Data on enlightenment, health, and social security between 1940 and 1950, and also between 1950 and 1955, are interpolated.
For sources, see appendix A.

had relatively more control over local services than did other Soviet cities; Mezhevich (1978) reports that in the RSFSR as a whole, city and workers' settlement soviets could claim only 35 percent of the housing in their communities. The local government share of housing investment is even lower in some areas.[4]

One remedy for this diffusion of funds has been to pool resources from different enterprises and ministries, making local soviets the coordinators (*zakazchiki*) of new investment in housing and services. Yet this solution still poses problems for local leaders, since enterprises and ministries often renege on their commitments to joint projects (Tarasenko 1980).[5] Efforts to transfer existing housing stock to local soviets have also met with only limited success: enterprises and ministries are reluctant to lose control over desirable space, and thus have been more likely to turn over buildings in need of renovation or repair; local soviets have been reluctant beneficiaries, lacking the funds, supplies, and labor to shoulder a larger and costlier housing stock (Morton 1983; Derzhavin 1986). Similar obstacles have characterized an attempt since 1971 to transfer retail trade establishments to local jurisdiction (Cattell 1983).

Even if enterprises and ministries cooperate, local governments are not always in the best position to provide economic leadership: except for the largest cities, few of the USSR's 40,000-plus localities have all the planning staff, expertise, or data necessary to formulate comprehensive and workable plans for local development (Azovkin and Sheremet 1985:147–49; Kutafin 1980).[6] Local governments have been caught between the need to coordinate more sectors and more production, on one hand, and pressure from above to limit administrative overhead and contain the growth of the payroll on the other.

Those who are on the payroll often lack detailed and uniform guidelines or indicators for developing summary or complex plans (Koliushin 1979).[7] Some local soviets merely compile a list of the indicators provided by relevant enterprises. Yet adding these together does not yield a coordinated strategy for local development (ibid.) Labeling such documents "complex plans" may create an image of coordination, but the lack of personnel, of consistent guidelines, and of information work against it (Bykovskii and Koliushin 1982). The targets that are drawn up therefore tend to focus almost exclusively on the sectors under local jurisdiction, and as figure 5.2 illustrated, that embraces only a small portion of the economic activity in each community.

The constraints on local economic power are matched by relatively limited political representation at the national level. Despite the fact that several republic leaders gained seats in the Politburo under Khrushchev and Brezhnev, there were but two "local seats"—for Moscow and Leningrad, the only two cities not formally subordinate to a union republic. Only union republics have direct representation in the Council of Ministers (ex officio) and in union-republic ministries; and just one local government, the Yakut ASSR, is formally represented in Moscow by a postpred.[8] Local representation is significant only in the Central Committee and the Supreme Soviet. Moreover, when Soviet sources discuss the process of compiling and approving national plans and coping with republic appeals, they do not mention direct participation by local officials except for the few whose plans are approved directly by the Council of Ministers and Gosplan (see, e.g., Kutafin 1980).

Still, local leaders confront the same problems that republic officials do. They too depend on the primary sectors of the economy for the bulk of their revenues, and these should figure just as prominently in local agendas as they do at the republic level.[9] Local leaders too are expected to help coordinate plans and production among different sectors, and they face the same obstacles in attempting to integrate local plans among ministries, associations, enterprises, and the like. As Moscow State University's O. E. Kutafin (1976:137) explains, local officials often find it difficult even to get information from superior agencies. Many ministries which are supposed to provide plans and data to local governments submit the materials well after the year has already started; some provide too little to be of use in compiling local plans (Tulebaev 1973; Mezhevich 1978).

The localities, like the republics, have the obligation but not the power to integrate plans for local development. The result is an inability to fully coordinate or control where and how the local economy will grow (Bykovskii and Koliushin 1982).

Thus in spite of the economic and political differences between republics and localities, economic agendas ought to be similar at both levels. This chapter compares them, by assessing local agendas at the same Party congresses and Supreme Soviet convocations analyzed in chapter 3. All speeches by oblast, ASSR, or other local leaders dealing with plan directives have been tabulated and coded in the same way, to examine the economic requests that local leaders put forward. A total of 208 speeches was coded, covering all party congresses from 1956 to 1986 and covering Supreme Soviet budget sessions for 1955, 1965, 1975, and 1983.

This chapter also extends the quantitative analysis with data on intrarepublic investment from selected regions. The results should, however, be considered as provisional until there are more and better data on expenditures below the republic level. Budget figures are published regularly, but they are woefully incomplete in coverage; investment data offer better coverage but contain year-to-year gaps and inconsistencies. As figures 5.1 and 5.2 show, local budgets capture too little of the government's spending to be of any use in assessing how much the government spends in each oblast, city, or raion. On average, the local budget represents only one-twentieth of the funds spent in the locality for industrial development, and only one-tenth of what local governments receive to support agriculture.

Investment data are more complete in this respect, since they include funds spent in the locality from all sources, budgetary and nonbudgetary; central, republic, and local. But they have been published only for some oblasti and cities in selected years, and have not been published at all for RSFSR oblasti after 1975. What has been published often cannot be compared either over time or across republics, for several reasons. One is that oblast boundaries change from year to year, making it difficult to know what was spent where. A second is that the rules defining which items to include or omit in investment data change too. In some years, funding for collective farms and for individual housing construction have been left out, and these add up to a sizable omission in heavily agricultural areas. Thus the data are rarely comparable even within the same republic over time, let alone among different republics.

In view of these limitations, the analysis of appropriations at the end of this chapter focuses on within-republic investment in two regions representing different levels of development and cultural/political traditions, from the Soviet east and west—the Ukraine and Uzbekistan. While the two do not provide a complete overview of intrarepublic trends, they can be instructive about the differences and similarities in republic experiences.

Local Spokesmen and Local Agendas

One thing quickly becomes clear in assessing local agendas: while all republics virtually always have at least one spokesman on the roster at Supreme Soviet budget convocations and at party congresses, only a small percentage of local leaders ever address such national bodies. And each

TABLE 5.1
Local Speakers on Plan Directives at CPSU Congresses, 1956–1986[a]

Party Congress

RSFSR	20th (1956)	21st (1959)	22nd (1961)	23rd (1966)	24th (1971)	25th (1976)	26th (1981)	27th (1986)
Moscow								
city	1	1	2	2	1	1	1	1
oblast		1	1	1	1	1	1	1
Leningrad oblast	1	1	1	1	1	1	1	1
Bashkir ASSR	1	1	1	1	1	1	1	1
Gorkii oblast	1	1	1	1	1	1	1	1
Krasnodar krai	1	1	1	1	1	1	1	1
Sverdlovsk oblast	1	1	1	1	1	1	1	1
Tatar ASSR	1	1	1	1	1	1	1	1
Krasnoiarsk krai	1	1		1	1	1	1	1
Altai krai	1			1	1	1	1	1
Rostov oblast	1	1		1		1	1	1
Saratov oblast	1	1		1	1	1		
Novosibirsk oblast				1	1	1	1	1
Primorskii krai		1		1	1	1		1
Volgagrad oblast	1	1	1		1			1
Kemerovo oblast				1	1		1	1
Cheliabinsk oblast	1		1					1
Dagestani ASSR	1					1		1
Orenburg oblast					1	1	1	
Voronezh oblast	1	1						1
Yakut ASSR		1				1		1
Belgorod oblast				1		1		
Khabarovsk krai		1					1	
Kuibyshev oblast	1	1						
Omsk oblast		1						1
Riazan oblast	1	1						
Stavropol krai	1	1						
Tiumen oblast							1	1
Ulianovsk oblast				1				1
Buriat ASSR						1		
Irkutsk oblast								1
Ivanovo oblast	1							
Kalinin oblast	1							
Kaliningrad oblast	1							
Karelian ASSR	1							
Mari ASSR				1				
Penza oblast						1		
Perm oblast				1				
Smolensk oblast	1							

TABLE 5.1 (*continued*)
Local Speakers on Plan Directives at CPSU Congresses, 1956–1986[a]

	Party Congress							
	20th (1956)	21st (1959)	22nd (1961)	23rd (1966)	24th (1971)	25th (1976)	26th (1981)	27th (1986)
Ukraine								
Kharkov oblast	1							1
Kiev oblast	1							
Dnepropetrovsk oblast	1		1		1			
Donetsk oblast	1			1		1		
Belorussia								
Grodnensk raikom					1			
Uzbekistan								
Fergana oblast	1							
Kazakhstan								
Kokchetav oblast								1
Komsomol raion				1				

[a]Includes all officials of krais, oblasti, cities, and raions who spoke at each Congress. Local officials speaking on behalf of their entire republic are counted as *republic* representatives. Other "local" delegates, such as collective farm chairmen, teachers, and the like, are not counted.

For sources, see appendix B.

national forum has distinctive criteria for the selection of local speakers. At party congresses, the very largest cities, oblasti, and kraia predominate (see table 5.1). Seven localities had a delegate on the podium at every congress between 1956 and 1986—Moscow, Leningrad, Gorkii, Sverdlovsk, Krasnodar, and the Bashkir and Tatar ASSRs—seven of the eight most populous areas in the country.[10] Similarly, the next largest localities (Rostov and Saratov oblasti, Altai and Krasnoiarsk kraia) form a second tier, with speakers at six or seven of the congresses during the same period. In the third tier are localities represented at only some of the congresses: a group also skewed toward larger cities and oblasti, but one in which population size seems to play somewhat less of a role. The segmented roster bears out Mary McAuley's (1974) observation that Moscow's selection process serves a mix of goals.[11] These yield a list of local speakers with a heavily Russian/Ukrainian cast: only 4 out of 208 between 1956 and 1986 came from outside the RSFSR and Ukraine (see table 5.1), even though local membership in the CPSU Central Committee is far more balanced geographically.

TABLE 5.2
Local Speakers at Supreme Soviet Budget Sessions,
1955, 1965, 1975, and 1983[a]

	1955	1965	1975	1983
RSFSR				
Moscow				
city	1	1	1	
oblast				
Leningrad				
city				
oblast		1		
Bashkir ASSR	1	1		
Kalinin oblast		1	1	
Karelian ASSR		1	1	
Tatar ASSR	1	1		
Balashov oblast	1			
Buriat ASSR	1			
Dagestani ASSR		1		
Irkutsk oblast			1	
Kabardinian ASSR	1			
Kaliningrad oblast		1		
Kalmyk ASSR		1		
Kamchatka oblast		1		
Krasnoiarsk krai		1		
Kurgan oblast		1		
Mari ASSR	1			
Mordvinian ASSR		1		
Murmansk oblast		1		
Omsk oblast		1		
Perm oblast		1		
Sakhalin oblast				1
Tambov oblast		1		
Tiumen oblast				1
Tuva oblast			1	
Udmurt ASSR		1		

In the Supreme Soviet, the list of speakers reflects somewhat more diversity, with size of population less important in determining who will speak. Russian and Ukrainian delegates still predominate, but the roster also includes a few more representatives from non-Slavic areas. Thus, for example, all five Central Asian republics have had at least one local delegate on the podium for the sessions analyzed here—but few have ever had a

TABLE 5.2 (*continued*)
Local Speakers at Supreme Soviet Budget Sessions,
1955, 1965, 1975, and 1983[a]

	1955	1965	1975	1983
Ukraine				
Kiev city		1	1	
Dnepropetrovsk oblast		1		
Kharkov oblast				1
Uzbekistan				
Bukhara oblast	1			
Karakalpak ASSR			1	
Surkhandar oblast				1
Kazakhstan				
Kustanai oblast	1			
Kzyl-orda oblast				1
Kirgizia				
Osh oblast			1	
Tadzhikistan				
Gorno-Badakshan oblast			1	
Turkmenia				
Tashauz oblast				1

[a]Includes all officials of krais, oblasti, cities, and raions who spoke at each convocation. Local officials speaking on behalf of their entire republic are counted as *republic* representatives. Other "local" delegates, such as collective farm chairmen, teachers and the like, are not counted as local officials.

For sources, see appendix B.

local speaker address a party congress on behalf of his locality (see tables 5.1 and 5.2). Supreme Soviet convocations also include fewer "repeats" from one convocation to the next: as table 5.2 reveals, different localities are spotlighted at each session.

The broader geographical focus in the Supreme Soviet fits with the aura of representativeness that is supposed to characterize the deputies, especially the ones from outlying regions. But it also reflects the differences in agendas between party congresses and Supreme Soviet convocations: congresses review five-year plan directives for national economic development, with reactions from the regional and local delegates on whom the plans depend most for success. Local speakers would seem to be chosen in large part with an eye to their area's importance in fulfilling national economic targets. In contrast, the Supreme Soviet concentrates more closely on the state budget, with its emphasis on "nonproductive" sectors such as housing and services, and thus has a more universal focus.

The Concerns on Local Agendas

Given the high percentage of speakers from urban, industrial localities in both national arenas, we would expect local delegates to concentrate on industry's needs, simply because the list of local representatives is skewed in that direction. This is borne out in local appeals: requests on behalf of industrial enterprises account for a major share of all requests from local leaders (see tables 5.3 and 5.4). In 1986, for example, I. K. Polozkov of Krasnodar complained that his region received only 75 percent of the electric power it needed, and he asked that the new five-year plan be altered to include construction of a new atomic power station (*Pravda*, March 1, 1986, p. 2). At the Twenty-Sixth Congress, Kemerovo obkom's L. A. Gorshkov asked Gosplan and the Ministry of the Coal Industry to work with his oblast in building new coal mines and reequipping old ones (*XXVI S"ezd* 1981: 2:41–47). The Tatar ASSR's R. M. Musin asked for help in speeding up construction of an atomic power station and in providing regular supplies and new equipment for his area's lagging oil industry (ibid.: 1: 367–71). Earlier, at the Twentieth Congress, Rostov's N. V. Kiselev raised a proposal to open 10–15 new coal mines; and Stavropol's I. P. Boitsov complained that the industrial ministries and Gosplan had not fully recognized his region's potential for developing a local oil and gas industry—which could open the door to major new industrial development in Stavropol' (*XX S"ezd* 1956: 1:173–80, 187–93).

However, local spokesmen are selective in the types of industries they emphasize. The bulk of their requests concentrate on sectors under at least partial republic and local jurisdiction—the light and food industries, forestry, electric power, fuel and mineral extraction, metallurgy. Once again, these are sectors where regional and local leaders are more directly involved with planning and implementation, and also sectors on which governments below the national level depend for a sizable portion of their budget revenues. And, once again, they are the industries for which local leaders find it easiest to "prove" local capabilities. Other industries—from autos

TABLE 5.3
Local Leaders' Economic Agendas
at CPSU Congresses,
1956–1986[a]

	20th (1956)	21st (1959)	22nd (1961)	23rd (1966)	24th (1971)	25th (1976)	26th (1981)	27th (1986)
Total local speakers on plan *directives*	23	24	12	21	18	22	18	25
Number presenting appeals in:								
Agriculture, food-processing, water supplies	15	4	3	10	6	12	6	7
Energy, fuels, metals, minerals	15	14	4	9	5	5	8	13
Other industry	15	9	6	7	5	6	3	6
Light	1	1	–	2	1	1	1	3
Chemical	5	5	1	2	–	–	1	1
Infrastructure (housing, services)	8	4	3	8	8	5	8	13
Social[b]	3	–	1	5	2	–	3	9
Economic[c]	4	4	–	2	4	–	2	5
Science, technology, research	2	5	–	–	–	–	2	3
Education	3	1	–	2	1	1	1	–
Construction equipment and materials	10	2	–	–	3	2	3	3
Employment, jobs	1	2	1	1	4	–	–	3

[a]Each speech by a local leader was coded to identify the policy domains for which local spokesmen presented demands. An "appeal" was defined as any direct request for assistance from Moscow. The entries in the table represent the number of local leaders who presented appeals in the corresponding policy domain. For an explanation of coding procedures, see appendix B.

[b]Health, housing, welfare, and consumer services.

[c]Transport, trade and communications.

For sources, see appendix B.

to machine-building, medical instruments to electronics—crop up less frequently in local appeals.

Not only do local leaders focus more attention on selected branches of industry; they also tailor different types of appeals to each branch. For mining, fuels, metallurgy, forestry, and the light and food industries, local requests run the gamut from speeding up construction projects and plans already under way to proposals for new factories, mines, and energy sources. For other industries, especially those under all-union subordi-

TABLE 5.4
Local Leaders' Agendas at Supreme
Soviet Budget Sessions,
Selected Years[a]

	1955	1965	1975	1983
Total local speakers	10	20	9	6
Number presenting appeals in:				
Agriculture, food-processing, water supplies	5	12	1	3
Energy, fuels, metals, minerals	3	12	5	2
Other industry	2	13	4	3
Light	1	6	2	1
Chemical	1	1	–	–
Infrastructure (housing, services)	8	15	6	3
Social[b]	6	12	3	3
Economic[c]	2	8	6	–
Science, technology, research	–	–	1	–
Education	–	1	–	–
Construction equipment and materials	4	7	4	–
Employment, jobs	–	6	1	2

[a]Each speech by a local leader was coded to identify the policy domain for which local spokesmen presented appeals. An "appeal" was defined as any direct request for assistance from Moscow. The entries in the table represent the number of local leaders who presented appeals in the corresponding policy demain. For an explanation of coding procedures, see appendix B.

[b]Health, housing, welfare, and consumer services.

[c]Transport, trade, and communications.

For sources, see appendix B.

nation, local appeals typically highlight modernization of or planning or supply problems in existing industries. Local leaders seldom propose new facilities in sectors directly subordinate to Moscow.

Agriculture also holds pride of place on local agendas, even though local spokesmen in both national forums come chiefly from industrial areas. N. V. Kiselev, in reciting Rostov's needs to the Twentieth Congress, included funding for irrigation among his requests; L. A. Gorshkov's appeals to the Twenty-Sixth Congress included both more coal mines and more funding for Kemerovo's agricultural waste disposal. Concern with farm problems extends even to the most urban of regions: Moscow oblast first secretary G. G. Abramov told the Twenty-Second Congress that Moscow

TABLE 5.5
Local Lobbying at CPSU Congresses
by Career Background, 1956–1981[a]

	Natives[b]	Mixed Careers[c]	Imports[d]
Total local speakers	59	15	37
Presenting appeals	51	13	33
Presenting no appeals	8	2	4

[a]Includes only those local leaders for whom data were available on prior careers, for the Twentieth (1956) through the Twenty-Sixth (1981) Congress.

[b]Local leaders whose entire political career prior to the Congress was spent in the same locality.

[c]Local leaders who spent part of their political career prior to the Congress in a different locality.

[d]Local leaders whose entire political career prior to their current position was spent in a different locality.

For sources, see appendix B.

needed more specialization in agriculture (*XXII S"ezd* 1961: 2:243–52); and V. I. Konotop later requested greater agro-industrial integration, more support for vegetable farming, and more agricultural equipment for Moscow at the Twenty-Fourth and Twenty-Fifth Congresses (*XXIV S"ezd* 1971: 1:435–42; *XXV S"ezd* 1976: 1:386–92).

Local appeals also reflect a preoccupation with transportation, schools, health care, housing, and other types of infrastructure. Many focus on the gap between industrial versus infrastructure growth, and its impact on the ability to find and keep good workers. Kharkov obkom's first secretary V. S. Mysnichenko explained his oblast's experience to the Supreme Soviet in 1983 (*Deviataia sessia* 1983:73–77): investment in local tractor factories had grown nearly twice as fast as funding for housing and consumer services—leaving the factories with labor shortages and correspondingly low productivity. Other comments by regional and local officials indicate even sharper disproportions in the east.

The career background of each speaker seems to make little difference in the issues he raises: as at the republic level, appeals differ very little between native, mixed, and imported leaders (table 5.5). All three career types lobby energetically on behalf of local problems; and all three show concern for the same basic issues. The leadership of Rostov oblast offers a case in point. The first secretary in 1966, M. S. Solomentsev, came to the oblast after a career of party and government posts in Cheliabinsk, Karaganda, and the

Kazakh SSR, while the first secretary a decade later, I. A. Bondarenko, had built his career locally. Yet the issues they raised were quite similar—Solomentsev concentrated in 1966 on the need to increase agricultural machinery and to expand irrigation (*XXIII S"ezd* 1966: 1:518–25); Bondarenko focused in 1976 on renovation in local agricultural machinery production and on river diversion to provide irrigation (*XXV S"ezd* 1976: 1:336–40). And in 1981, Bondarenko again went back to the issue of agricultural machinery (*XXVI S"ezd* 1981: 1:158–62).

As we would expect, the proportion of natives to imports has varied, from the predominance of outsiders under Khrushchev's revolving-door personnel policies, to the emphasis on local recruitment under Brezhnev's "stability of cadres" (see table 5.6). Still, in spite of the shift in recruitment strategies, career type seems to have little effect on the substance of the economic appeals that local leaders present in Moscow. The common issues they raise suggest the pressures of overseeing the local economy, and local agendas tend to be similar whatever the career paths of local officialdom.

The impact of a local leader's status in national politics is more difficult to judge. Since virtually every local speaker at party congresses is a member of the Central Committee, and virtually every one takes the opportunity to ask for attention or assistance from higher-ups, there is too little variance to allow any conclusions about the impact of membership. On the other hand, the few local delegates to the Politburo have differed considerably in their willingness to lobby; but the sample remains so small (Moscow's V. V. Grishin and B. N. El'tsin, Leningrad's G. V. Romanov and Iu. F. Solov'ev) as to defy easy generalizations. Romanov bid for central support several times during his tenure as first secretary of Leningrad obkom and Solov'ev continued the tradition in 1986; on the other hand, Grishin never made any public requests for support, and El'tsin devoted his first congress appearance as Moscow party boss to the deficiencies of party leadership at all levels.[12] But the heads of Moscow's other government and party agencies have compensated by presenting a full list of appeals even when the city party boss did not.

THE CONTINUITY OF LOCAL APPEALS

Many of the issues on local agendas resurface from year to year, since appeals must often be repeated. The same local problems, the same bottlenecks, persist over time, lending a degree of continuity to a region's

TABLE 5.6
Local Leaders' Economic Agendas at CPSU Congresses by Career Background, 1956–1981[a]

Party Congress

	20th (1956)			21st (1959)			22nd (1961)			23rd (1966)			24th (1971)			25th (1976)			26th (1981)		
	L	M	I[b]	L	M	I	L	M	I	L	M	I	L	M	I	L	M	I	L	M	I
Number of local leaders presenting appeals:	3	3	7	5	4	5	4	1	4	8	3	8	10	—	5	7	2	4	14	—	—
Number presenting appeals in:																					
Agriculture, food-processing, water supplies	3	1	—	—	—	1	1	1	1	3	1	5	4	—	3	4	1	3	6	—	—
Energy, fuels, metals, minerals	1	1	—	4	1	4	2	1	1	5	1	3	3	—	3	4	2	—	8	—	—
Other industry	1	1	—	3	3	3	3	1	2	2	1	4	3	—	1	1	—	2	4	—	—
Light	—	—	—	—	—	—	1	—	—	—	1	1	1	—	—	—	—	—	1	—	—
Chemical	—	—	—	1	—	1	—	—	—	1	1	1	1	—	—	—	—	—	1	—	—
Infrastructure (housing, services)	1	1	—	2	2	—	1	1	1	3	1	2	4	—	1	3	—	1	8	—	—
Social[c]	—	—	—	1	—	—	—	1	—	2	1	2	1	—	1	—	—	1	3	—	—
Economic[d]	1	1	—	1	—	1	—	—	—	1	1	—	3	—	—	2	—	—	4	—	—
Science, technology, research	—	—	—	—	—	—	—	—	—	—	—	—	—	—	—	—	—	—	—	—	—
Education	—	1	—	—	1	—	—	—	—	1	—	1	1	—	—	1	—	—	1	—	—
Construction and construction materials	—	1	—	1	—	—	—	—	—	—	—	—	—	—	3	1	—	1	2	—	—
Employment, jobs	—	—	—	—	—	—	—	—	—	1	—	1	2	—	2	—	—	—	1	—	—

[a] Includes only local leaders for whom career data could be found.

[b] "Locals" (L) include leaders whose entire political career prior to the Congress was spent in the same locality. "Mixed careers" (M) indicate those leaders who spent part of their political career prior to the Congress in another locality. And "imports" (I) are local leaders who spent their entire previous political career outside their current locality.

[c] Health, welfare, housing, and consumer services.

[d] Trade, transport, and communications.

For sources, see appendix B.

requests even under different party bosses. Thus, for example, Rostov party leaders from N. V. Kiselev in the 1950s through M. S. Solomentsev in the 1960s and I. A. Bondarenko in the 1980s all pressed for more funding to expand irrigation; and Bondarenko went on record in support of river diversion to solve Rostov's water problems. In Leningrad, party leaders from Frol Kozlov and I. V. Spiridonov in the 1950s to Romanov and Solov'ev in the 1980s focused national attention on Leningrad's activities in research and development and in science education.

Moreover, there is a striking degree of continuity even in the highly charged atmosphere of the Gorbachev era. From Kemerovo, L. A. Gorshkov complained in 1981 about the lag in developing the local coal industry—as he noted, the last new mine had been built twenty years earlier, and renovation was creeping along at a snail's pace (*XXVI S"ezd* 1981: 2:41–47). In 1986, his successor N. S. Ermakov told the Twenty-Seventh Congress that central authorities were unjustifiably neglecting the local coal industry, where no new mines had been built and where renovation was creeping along at a snail's pace (*Pravda*, March 5, 1986, p. 3). From Novosibirsk, A. P. Filatov voiced the same problem in 1981 and 1986: researchers in Novosibirsk faced enterprise resistance and overwhelming bureaucratic obstacles in their attempts to introduce new industrial technology (*XXVI S"ezd* 1981: 2:147–52; and *Pravda*, March 3, 1986, pp. 5–6).

We might contend, of course, that the repetition of local appeals simply reflects the immobilism of the late Brezhnev era and the transition to Gorbachev. But a glance at table 5.3 suggests that the continuity has deeper roots—the issues on local agendas in 1986 differed surprisingly little from those of earlier years.

This is not to say that successive local leaders have identical agendas; the mix of issues varies a good deal from year to year and leader to leader *within the same locality*. The specific problems mentioned and the way in which appeals are presented do change, if only because the urgency of different problems varies from year to year. Moreover, each speaker's comments are tailored to fit the prevailing political climate. A request on agriculture's behalf in 1961 would refer to the party's long-term program; in 1981 or 1986, the same request would be justified by referring to the Food Program. Discussion of water supplies and irrigation might concentrate in 1956 on farmers' problems with water shortages; thirty years later the same issue might be couched in terms of broader ecological concerns. Yet the underlying local problems are much the same.

As a result, requests must often be repeated time and again, much to the dismay of local leaders. Sakhalin oblast's P. I. Tretiakov gave vent to the frustration during the 1983 budget session in the Supreme Soviet (*Deviataia sessia* 1983:206–11) when he asked "Why must we in the localities point to the same problems over and over, even ones that have already been decided?" Moscow's El'tsin took up the same theme three years later: "Why, from congress to congress, do we raise a series of the same problems?" (*Pravda*, February 27, 1986, pp. 2–3). And Bashkiria's M. Z. Shakirov suggested that the rapid rise of Gorbachev did little to break through the logjam: the new regime's 1985 decree on developing nonferrous metallurgy (part of it in Bashkiria) had not even begun to be implemented months after its adoption (*Pravda*, March 1, 1986, p. 2).

These complaints suggest that the problems brought to Moscow are problems that cannot be solved easily or quickly, arising from the very structure of sectoral planning. And Moscow's response of compromising among varied sectoral and regional interests prolongs the process still further, breeding a perennial overcommitment of resources that offers partial funding to many but enough funding only to the highest priority projects.

SHARED ISSUES ON REPUBLIC AND LOCAL AGENDAS

As a comparison with chapter 3 reveals, local leaders stress many of the same issues that republic officials do when they come to Moscow. They confront the same dilemmas and share the same need to smooth over the distortions created by sectoral planning. Moreover, their input is not independent; local leaders take their appeals to republic agencies, and this input surely feeds into republic agendas.

Some indirect evidence on this score can be gained by comparing appeals at both levels in the same republic. Since two leaders may use different wording to voice the same request, the exact degree of overlap is difficult to measure. Local officials are more likely to offer specifics—the name of a farm or plant in need, the kinds of tools required for agriculture, etc.— while republic officials seem to speak in more general terms about feed or agricultural machinery or renovation in a given industry. Yet a review of their comments suggests that they sometimes raise the same basic requests, and the similarities offer a rough index of the joint appeals on republic and local agendas. At the Twentieth Congress, RSFSR Premier M. A. Yasnov presented an appeal for agricultural machinery that matched requests from Altai krai and Voronezh oblast (*XX S"ezd* 1956: 2:67–74). His successor, D. M. Poliansky, reiterated a request from Krasnodar krai for more electric power in agriculture (*XXI S"ezd* 1959: 1:137–45) and a Leningrad complaint about waste and underutilization of capacity in metalworking (*XXII S"ezd* 1961: 1:283–90). More recently, M. S. Solomentsev, in his tenure as RSFSR Premier, supported appeals from Altai krai, Rostov, and Moscow for more agricultural equipment, and appeals from Moscow, Sverdlovsk, and Altai for social infrastructure (*XXV S"ezd* 1976: 1:160–66; *XXVI S"ezd* 1981: 1:137–42). And at the 1986 congress, both Shcherbitskii and Vorotnikov mentioned some of the same issues as their local counterparts. Shcherbitskii and Kharkov's V. P. Mysnichenko both played up the advantages of cooperation with CMEA countries, and the need to renovate plant and equipment in the food-processing industry (*Pravda*, March 3, 1986, pp. 4–5 and February 27, 1986, p. 2). And Vorotnikov put forward requests that echoed those from several oblasti, including Moscow and Gorkii, Voronezh and Krasnoiarsk (see appendix B for sources to table 5.3).

Republic leaders reiterate some but by no means all of the requests put forward by their local leadership.[13] And their choice of which local appeals to support does not appear to be wholly disinterested: Poliansky's earlier career had been in Krasnodar, Solomentsev's, in Rostov, and Vorotnikov's, in Kuibyshev and Voronezh.

The Response to Local Appeals

Local requests also evoke much the same responses from above that republic appeals do, a series of slow and partial steps that yield some but rarely enough assistance to the locality. Local leaders must, of course, follow the correct channels, appealing to republic agencies where appropriate before taking a request higher.[14] Given their subordination to republic governments, they appear to have somewhat less recourse to central agencies unless their appeal touches on a key central priority. And when they do approach Moscow, their requests are reportedly left to the final decision of the individual ministry, rather than Gosplan or the Council of Ministers (Todorskii 1982:121).[15]

Thus there are fewer individual examples of successful local requests to Moscow, but enough to demonstrate how such issues are resolved. Party congress proceedings reveal that a handful of local appeals have been incorporated into the final drafts of plan directives—for instance, granting funds for water resources to Donetsk in the Sixth Five-Year Plan (1956–60) and to Altai krai in the Tenth (1971–75), for electric power development to Donetsk in the Tenth Plan and to Dnepropetrovsk for iron ore processing in the Eleventh (1976–80). These were, of course, agreed upon in advance of each congress; but they nevertheless represent serious issues for the localities.

The comments of local officials themselves are more telling about the fate of specific requests. Time after time, leaders from the periphery come back to Moscow to protest that they received some satisfaction of previous appeals—a compromise—but not enough to complete the projects they originally proposed. Primorsk krai's V. E. Chernyshev lamented to the Twenty-Third Congress (*XXIII S"ezd* 1966: 1:247–54) that local leaders had proposed a new irrigation system to cover 100,000 hectares; but Gosplan had only granted resources to cover 30,000, too little to support local farmers' needs. Kzyl-Orda oblast first secretary T. Esetov sounded a similar complaint in the Supreme Soviet's 1983 budget convocation (*Deviataia sessia* 1983:144–48), noting that Gosplan had approved a request for irrigation in 1982, but the Ministries of Agriculture and of Melioration and Water Resources were only partially implementing it.

The proceedings from Gorbachev's congress suggest that little had changed by the spring of 1986. Krasnodar's I. K. Polozkov commented, for instance, that local proposals to alter the the crop mix and requests for corresponding resources had received some but not enough support from the center (*Pravda*, March 1, 1986, p. 2). And Omsk oblast's S. I. Maniakhin (ibid., p. 7) lamented that Omsk had requested and received a plastics plant which was to be the base for a petrochemical complex; but the proposal, submitted sixteen years earlier, resulted in a plant that was still not fully equipped and was not to be finished even in the new plan.

Local leaders thus admit that Moscow grants at least a small part of the funding they request. The compromises help to satisfy some of the pressing

FIGURE 5.3
Inequality in Oblast Investment, Ukraine and Uzbekistan[a]

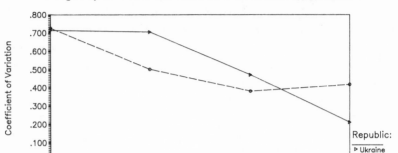

Year

[a]Unweighted coefficients of variation for per capita investment. Data points are 1950, 1960, 1970, and 1983 only, and all but the 1983 Ukraine data exclude kolkhoz and private investment. For data, see table 5.7.

needs from below, but they also put local officials on a treadmill of appeals to secure the resources that will allow them to finish the job.

LOCAL APPROPRIATIONS

The quantitative evidence on appropriations to the localities in the Ukraine and Uzbekistan supports the same conclusion; investment data bear the stamp of compromises over competing demands. Per capita investment has been diffused among different localities, as we would expect in a system of functional logrolling, creating a pattern of mild redistribution and gradual equalization within both areas (figure 5.3).

But the trend has not been even: Ukrainian oblasti experienced a drop in the intrarepublic investment gap, while Uzbekistan witnessed somewhat less change and a less even trend. The coefficient of variation within the Ukraine drops from .705 to .213 in between 1950 and 1983; for Uzbekistan, the coefficient drops from .726 in 1950 to .420 in 1983—but with several upward and downward shifts in the intervening years. The difference may reflect the unequal levels of development of the two republics: the Ukraine's old industrialized areas are more "saturated" with industry and its attendant problems than are Uzbek cities, putting more pressure on the Ukraine to diffuse investment away from the most developed oblasti. The result is a mild form of redistribution, providing poorer areas with more funds than they would otherwise be able to raise. Part of the difference between the republics for 1983 also reflects the inclusion of collective farm investment in the Ukrainian data.[16]

While yearly investment data for other republics is too limited to extend the comparisons, data aggregated by five-year plan periods from 1956–60 to 1971–75 support the same conclusion for other parts of the USSR. The coefficient of variation on investment per worker declined for all oblasti in the USSR as a whole and for oblasti within the RSFSR and the Ukraine as well (Liebowitz 1984). Trends in industrial employment offer a similar picture, with more rapid growth in less industrialized areas and what Sagers (1984a:167) calls a "striking diffusion of industrial employment from the country's major industrial nodes between 1940 and 1975."

With the gradual dispersion of investment, an oblast's political advantages have done little to increase its allocations. Oblasti with greater political status such as representation in the Central Committee or a new party boss have fared about the same as all the others in their quest for funding (see table 5.7). If anything, Ukrainian oblasti with Central Committee status have typically fared worse than others, since it is the larger and older industrial areas (e.g., Donetsk, Dnepropetrovsk) that tend to have representation but the smaller and less developed oblasti that have received larger increases in investment. The same seems to be true of Uzbekistan during the late 1950s and 1960s: the first secretary of the most populous oblast—Tashkent—belonged to the central committee, but his home base experienced a rate of investment growth below the average for Uzbekistan as a whole. The picture did change somewhat after 1970, with first secretaries from Samarkand and the Karakalpak ASSR gaining additional Central Committee seats. Given the higher average rate of investment growth in these two areas, adding them to the group raised the average for regions with Central Committee status. Yet representation alone seems to have done little to boost their fortunes in the appropriations process.

Similarly, oblasti with new party bosses have usually fared neither better nor worse than those with "old" leaders (table 5.7). The one exception seems to be during the first 3–4 years of the Sovnarkhoz era, when increases in investment for both the Ukraine and Uzbekistan were consistently

TABLE 5.7
Political Status and Oblast Investments,
Ukraine and Uzbekistan[a]

	Central Committee[b]	Non-Central Committee	Succession[c]	No Succession
		Ukraine		
1957	19.11	17.90	4.75	19.66
1958	9.62	11.32	17.38	11.35
1959	6.80	18.70	17.60	16.70
1960	9.15	15.76	17.90	14.26
1961	1.40	9.54	8.25	7.86
1962	9.53	5.57	7.68	6.86
1963	8.83	6.37	8.20	7.00
1964	9.70	12.59	13.83	13.94
1965	4.96	5.12	4.77	5.88
1966				
1967	7.42	9.45	6.53	8.94
1968	7.54	8.02	10.83	7.57
1969	4.51	4.25	7.50	4.16
1970	5.89	12.60	−0.30	9.44
1971	8.75	7.65	3.10	8.12
1972	8.24	10.68	9.25	9.53
1973	2.64	4.15	6.74	2.60
1974	7.71	6.45	11.75	5.81
1975	8.19	8.01	–	–
1976	1.56	2.28	2.80	2.00
1977	3.01	4.94	5.50	3.93
1978	6.66	12.21	11.65	9.48
1979				
1980				
1981	−1.02	3.72	−1.38	2.50

higher for oblasti with a newly appointed first secretary. The increases in spending may be either cause or effect: the product of new leaders under a system with slightly greater local autonomy, or—as is more likely—a reflection of personnel policies that sent new leaders into regions slated for more rapid economic growth (as in the example of Brezhnev's assignment to Kazakhstan). In either case, the pattern seems to have dissipated by the early 1960s, with no consistent differential in investment growth for regions with either new or old party bosses.

TABLE 5.7 (*continued*)
Political Status and Oblast Investments,
Ukraine and Uzbekistan[a]

	Central Committee[b]	Non–Central Committee	Uzbekistan Succession[c]	No Succession
1957	–	–	7.96	–4.55
1958	–	–	31.43	23.98
1959	–	–		
1960	–	–	36.10	21.80
1961	–	–	20.00	19.24
1962	21.90	13.12	17.93	13.51
1963	17.05	34.71	14.50	37.88
1964	3.00	49.17	24.22	62.27
1965	33.70	18.95	35.90	18.73
1966	8.40	17.83	29.57	12.87
1967	3.50	8.59	–3.60	7.05
1968	6.50	14.36	–	–
1969	–38.60	3.29	1.70	–1.81
1970	0.30	18.60	15.30	17.24
1971	–	–	0.50	3.73
1972	14.10	6.25	19.30	8.34
1973	13.85	8.66	–	–
1974	18.10	16.45	7.90	18.30
1975				
1976	14.30	5.83	–	–
1977	6.03	5.18	–2.00	6.94
1978	9.17	2.98	4.05	4.47
1979				
1980				
1981	9.05	7.09	–	–

[a]Average annual percent change in investment among all oblasti and capital cities. Horizontal lines indicate a break in the time series, so that the data are not comparable above and below the line. A blank indicates that no data were available; a dash (–) that there were no Central Committee members/successions for the year. Data on the Ukraine for 1957–65 and on Uzbekistan for 1957–74 exclude investment in kolkhozy and in private housing.

[b]Average change in investment for oblasti represented in the Central Committee during the previous year.

[c]Average change in investment for oblasti with a new first secretary in the previous year.

TABLE 5.7 (continued)

SOURCES: Ukraine:

1956–63 *Narodne gospodarstvo Ukr. RSR* (1963:418–19).
1964–65 *Narodne gospodarstvo Ukr. RSR* (1965:442).
1967–70 *Narodne gospodarstvo Ukr. RSR* (1970:350).
1971–75 *Narkhoz Ukr. SSR* (1975:330).
1976–78 *Narkhoz Ukr. SSR* (1978:191).
1981   *Narkhoz Ukr. SSR* (1983:209).

Uzbekistan:

1957–58 *Narkhoz Uzbek SSR* (1958:140).
1959–65 *Narkhoz Uzbek SSR* (1965:242).
1966–69 *Narkhoz Uzbek SSR* (1969:201).
1970   *Narkhoz Uzbek SSR* (1970:189).
1971–74 *Narkhoz Uzbek SSR* (1974:231).
1976–78 *Narkhoz Uzbek SSR* (1978:190).
1981   *Narkhoz Uzbek SSR za 60 let* (1984:216).

Central committee data were taken from the lists provided in each set of CPSU party congress proceedings. Data on leadership changes in the oblasti are from *USSR Facts and Figures Annual* (1983:52–54, 1982:65–71).

The impact of native rule on local appropriations is much more difficult to assess. The requisite names and biographies are available primarily for first secretaries, who were so predominantly of the local nationality in the Ukraine and Uzbekistan between 1956 and 1980 that any comparison with nonnatives leaves too few cases to be meaningful. More variance would of course emerge if we were to include the first and second secretary and the chairman and first deputy chairman of the local ispolkom—but there simply are not enough biographical data to allow us to compare these four top leaders among different oblasti from year to year.

Conclusions

The beginning of this chapter described the many constraints on local control over economic development—subordination to an additional layer of bureaucracy and jurisdiction over only a small portion of industry, agriculture, and even public goods and services. And as the data in figures 5.1 and 5.2 suggest, the constraints may have become tighter as pressures for coordination have grown while the share of budget funds channeled through local administration has declined. The rediscovery of politics outside Moscow has in fact put more programs and funds into republic rather than local hands. Local officials are left with a smaller piece of the budget, with admonitions to coordinate increasingly complex local development but also to contain or even cut the number of planners and administrators they employ.

Even though local governments have gained less than the republics have from the local revolution, both the economic concerns expressed by local leaders and the response to their appeals are fundamentally similar to those at the republic level. The same problems are created by ministerial planning and by revenue needs. The same process of slow and piecemeal responses also comes into play, providing local officials with partial solutions that legitimize their quest but keep them on a continual search for additional support. And the same offsetting advantages seem to be at work, giving rise to a pattern of appropriations that proves mildly redistributive among localities.

To a degree, the effects ought to vary with the size and importance of the locality. Minsk or Novosibirsk cannot claim Moscow and Leningrad's direct subordination to central rather than republic planners, their historical and international significance, or their political standing. Yet in spite of the privileges Moscow and Leningrad enjoy, they also suffer from the imbalances created by sectoral plans; even with their close physical proximity to the central government, they still find it difficult to mesh central plans with local needs (Taubman 1973). Moreover, the fragmented data on big city investment also hint at a process of dispersion, with Moscow at the top of the heap, but with a slowly diminishing gap in per capita spending across big cities.[17]

For the localities, as for the republics, politics matters—but it is a politics of compromises and slow (often glacial) adaptations that breed a constant round of fresh problems and fresh appeals.

CHAPTER SIX

RETHINKING POLITICS
BELOW THE NATIONAL LEVEL

THE EVIDENCE IN THIS STUDY suggests that the local revolution in
the USSR enhanced the role of politicians outside Moscow but also
saddled them with more—and perhaps more intractable—problems. With
the larger share of the budget, the expanded social and consumer programs,
and the increased political visibility have come greater pressures to correct
disjointed economic development and improve living standards for the
local population. With the predominance of sectoral over regional planning, officials in the periphery are denied the power and even the information necessary to plan and control the local economy.

Yet the growth of interdependence between central and regional/local
organs, the regularization of feedback through structured appeals procedures, and the balkanization of the central bureaucracy all afford republic
and local leaders a few political resources in this one-sided contest. The
party's domestic programs depend on implementation at the grassroots,
and local problems thus become national concerns. Central goals hinge
on regional and local leaders' ability to carry them out, and appeals from
the periphery skillfully exploit the connection in order to highlight local
needs. The most recent, and intriguing, evidence is the way in which
republic and local officials have used the new buzzwords of social justice
and responsibility of cadres under Gorbachev to sanctify prior requests.
New goals and rhetoric are grafted onto old appeals in ways that will
(hopefully) strengthen the local case.

The effects of national dependence on local implementation are intensified by the growing horizontal integration across regions and localities.
The emphasis that party leaders since Khrushchev have accorded to

strengthening regional interdependence may not yield greater efficiency, but it almost certainly means that local problems have more and more extralocal consequences. The labor glut in Central Asia, the energy short-age in the west, and the inadequate infrastructure in Siberia reverberate far beyond local borders.

The need for feedback on such problems offers leaders in the periphery their opportunity to promote local interests. The elaborate system of ad-ministrative checks on Soviet bureaucracy has given rise to appeals pro-cedures that allow the most urgent requests from below to gain a hearing in central organs. And the natural tendency for agencies at each level to build in reserves, to insulate themselves from unforeseen problems, pro-vides multiple small pockets that can be tapped to meet requests for added funds or revised plan targets.[1]

With so many players in this game, republic and local officials have a variety of sources to ply in hopes of gaining support. It goes without saying that some count much more heavily than others; having the ear of a Politburo member can hardly be equated with inside ties to a Gosplan department or a deputy minister. But the inequality in political connections is offset by their accessibility. The vast array of ministries, glavki, associ-ations, Gosplan and Gossnab departments, all with some part of the pie to distribute to lower agencies, multiplies the odds that an official outside Moscow will at least get an audience. In contrast, the top figures in the central party apparat have so little time and staff and so much to oversee that they are only likely to consider appeals after "lower" channels (min-istries, Gosplan, Gossnab) have already been approached and have proved unable to help.

Thus we should have no doubt about the importance of political con-nections and influence in coaxing resources out of higher-ups. But given the size of the bureaucracy, and the system of multiple overlapping agencies that share decisions and keep each other in check, there are a great many connections who can be helpful in responding to a request from below. The fragmentation of policy-making, the administrative redundancy built into plan procedures, are in one sense a bureaucratic nightmare for republic and local leaders, yet these very features of the central administration also multiply the opportunities for pressing a local claim. The failure of Pol-itburo and Central Committee membership to yield significantly higher regional or local appropriations (chapters 4 and 5) therefore reflects not

the uselessness of connections but the fact that there are so many connections that can be of use.

This conclusion fits well with Gustafson's (1981:51–52) observation
that opportunities to appeal are fragile and contingent, less a manifestation
of interest-group politics than of "waiting for the open window." He
suggests too that the growing number and complexity of national leaders'
goals, and the profusion of and rivalry among central ministries, departments, et al., create a multitude of windows—and the "art of being a
successful advocate in Soviet politics is to find them."

From Moscow's vantage point, the dilemma of responding to such
appeals is a tidal wave of input from below. Problems often get shunted
to higher levels, so that officials in the periphery can protect themselves
before embarking on any new decision. Party leaders have decried this as
a "lack of initiative" (El'tsin, *Pravda*, February 27, 1986, pp. 2–3) complaining that, even with the insistence on appeals proceeding through the
proper lower channels, the Central Committee still faces a constant stream
of requests that ought to have been resolved lower in the political hierarchy.
And the requests are undoubtedly exaggerated, padded with enough fat
to keep projects alive even after the center has made the obligatory cuts.

From the local perspective, intervention from above holds the prospect
of funds to help further local goals. A positive response to any one problem
is likely to involve only a tiny share of all the resources available to Soviet
planners, but it may mean stagnation or growth for the local economy.
Lobbying from below can yield results, however modest and however
slowly, that add up to substantial long-run support for local needs.

Centralization and Center-Periphery Relations

To say that politicians below the national level have varied political
resources in their quest for support from higher-ups is not to say that the
system is in any sense "decentralized." The reforms of the post-Stalin era
did succeed in giving local and especially republic leaders more responsibilities and somewhat more administrative latitude, if only by giving
them more funds to divert. Still, their comments reveal how much real
decision-making authority remains in central hands. They turn to Moscow
for funding of everything from projects that would change the face of

Siberia (river diversion) to a day care center for the children of industrial workers in Karaganda. The very fact of their appeals, coming after plans are compiled, underscores how little control they have over the regular channels of planning and budgeting. Center-periphery relations have evolved dramatically since Stalin, but remain overwhelmingly one-sided. The interesting question is not whether the system is centralized but how leaders in the periphery cope with central controls. Fainsod (1958, 1963) offered a compelling answer by describing local officials' remarkable capacity for evasion—using family circles to insulate themselves against administrative checks, attempting to scale down the plans they receive to manageable proportions. The picture he presented is surely accurate; but the evidence in this book reveals that there is much more to republic and local politics. How else to explain the long-term and intense Central Asian lobbying for river diversion, or the enthusiasm of republic and local leaders for building new oil and gas complexes, new mines, new power stations?

Politicians outside Moscow rarely lack for suggestions on new projects that the center should fund (Hough 1969, 1971), justifying proposals by cloaking them in the most favorable evidence and by weaving them in with broader national goals. Of course, proposals that do not already fit in some way with national goals are not likely to see the light of day; republic and local leaders are clearly circumscribed in the types of projects they may put forward. And much of what they propose is often a reaction to the problems already created by previous central plans. Yet their constant stream of complaints and requests help to define the issues that the central leadership must address.

Political Context and the Structure of Economic Agendas

These issues, in turn, speak volumes about the formulation of economic agendas below the national level. Requests have a logic and a coherence that transcend changes in local leadership and even changes in regime. From 1956 to 1986 (and even before), officials at both the republic and the local levels, from industrial as well as farm areas, have attempted to focus the attention of central planners on a few key sectors of the economy. Requests and complaints have dwelt repeatedly on agriculture and related questions of water supplies, land use, food processing, and chemical fertilizers and pesticides; electric power, fuels, minerals, and metallurgy; social and economic infrastructure; and construction. Few other sectors, and few other industries, have received nearly as much emphasis in appeals from below.

Previous studies of local politics have noted the preoccupation with agricultural matters, explaining it in terms of chronic low farm productivity, a relative lack of skilled personnel in the countryside, and intense pressures from above (Hough 1969; Stewart 1968; Moses 1974; Biddulph 1983). This book suggests that the explanation also lies deeper: republic and local agendas are shaped as much or more by structural factors. The areas of primary concern to politicians outside Moscow are the ones most sensitive to specific local conditions—the most location-bound. And it seems to be no accident that they are also the sectors where Moscow has divided responsibilities between all-union and republic ministries (see chapter 3). Central taxation policies further reinforce republic and local interest in these same branches, since revenues below the national level derive so heavily from agriculture, consumer goods, and extractive industries. The tax reforms of the early 1930s have had a powerful if unintended effect on center-periphery relations from Stalin to Gorbachev.

Compartmentalization of data also influences the choice of issues on agendas below the national level, by depriving officials in the periphery of the information they would need to demonstrate true comparative advantages in most manufactured goods. They possess much more data on the capabilities inherent in the locality, in sectors such as farming and natural resource development—the capabilities they highlight in their quest for more funds.

These structural variables lend a continuity to republic and local agendas despite the changing of the guard either at home or at the center. The sectors that have dominated appeals from below under leaders from Khrushchev to Gorbachev have held sway even in the face of major shifts in national budgetary priorities. Within this persistent set of issues, the nature of the requests themselves does change with the current political winds: increasing agricultural investment breeds a crop of appeals for farm expansion; a drop in the priority of farm investment (as in the latter part of the Brezhnev years) brings complaints about the problems of undercapitalization. Politicians outside Moscow carefully tailor their requests to fit with prevailing campaigns (as in the Food Program of the 1980s), but the underlying issues they bring to Moscow have been consistent.

Equally striking is the similarity of agendas among both old and new local leaders, natives and imports, with high political connections and without. Neither the revolving door nor stability of cadres has fundamentally altered the litany. The "exchange of cadres" across republic and local lines and the distinction between native versus imported leadership seem to have little effect on the basic economic problems that confront leaders in the periphery. The dilemmas of unbalanced growth and uncoordinated sectoral planning haunt republic and local officials regardless of their newness on the job, ethnic origins, or network of political ties.

Surely each republic and local leader views such problems differently; his unique combination of background experiences gives him a different conception of what is necessary and perhaps what is possible. The character and effectiveness of local leadership may be a critical component in how a locality responds to the problems of local development (Ruble 1982). But the agenda seems to be shaped by structural features that supersede the individual characteristics of local elites. Context—in this case, a combination of locational constraints, administrative structure, and revenue policies—thus proves to be an important variable in explaining the highly select set of issues that preoccupy leaders below the national level.

The Policy Process

The myriad appeals from below, and the procedures that allow them a hearing, suggest that feedback from outside Moscow is more extensive than any directed society model seems to allow. Some of the responses, highly visible at party congresses and in the Supreme Soviet, reflect a calculated, prearranged public ritual to showcase central concern for local problems. But there are more appeals, and more responses, behind the scenes, indicating that the carefully choreographed public show is only the surface of a much larger and genuine process of collecting data on and resolving local bottlenecks. Complaints and proposals offer an essential corrective for distant central bureaucracies in the quest to implement national policy. They also yield political advantages to national party leaders, for whom "protecting the interests of all republics and regions" has come to be an oft-repeated phrase. The courtship seems to have been most intense under Khrushchev; but it is intriguing to note similar overtones even under Gorbachev and Ryzhkov.

Complaints by republic and local officials also provide a candid picture of the diffusion and wrangling at the center. The broad array of requests submitted directly to ministries and to Gosplan reveals indirectly the enormous influence each of these central organs wields over appropriations decisions. And it reveals how often they ignore or subtly rework the directives of the Council of Ministers and even of the central party apparat.[2] Complaints show too the range of bureaucratic battles—among ministries, with Gosplan, and even among different departments within each of these organizations.

Ironically, the proliferation of central controls has led to an erosion of control. The elaborate cross-checks on the powers of the central bureaucracy create multiple decision centers, each with the power to withhold or redirect funds, and each with the "unassailable" weight of expertise behind its decisions. Sverdlovsk's Iu. V. Petrov (*Pravda*, March 2, 1986, p. 6) described a case in point in the construction industry: controlling organs are so numerous that the chief controller, the Ministry of Finance, doesn't know who they all are—and therefore no one assumes final responsibility.

The effort to find common ground among these competing organizations yields a series of compromises and ongoing adjustments (Jones 1984), with relatively few projects receiving all the necessary resources for timely completion, and with many more projects begun than the economy can sustain at one time.[3] As one Central Asian economist (Moldokulov 1978:31–32) laments, planners in Moscow seem unable to choose priorities or to concentrate resources effectively. There are too few resources chasing too many projects—the familiar problem of overinvestment or "raspylenie."

More funds are authorized than are appropriated, an effort to juggle more economic goals and work more compromises than the actual size of the pie will allow. Surely this reflects the sheer complexity of the economy—an inability to account for every ruble at every moment, to structure the tradeoffs among multiple and competing economic goals, or to reconcile conflicting proposals even when priorities are clearly defined (see chapter 4). The limited and often selective information presented to justify new projects can only make the process more difficult.[4]

But the authorization-appropriation gap may also be intentional: a nod of approval even without full funding allows central planners to show a modicum of responsiveness to local problems. More important, by granting authorization but only minimal funding, Moscow creates a powerful incentive for officials in the periphery to hunt for their own additional resources, to engage in the familiar search for "reserves" thought to be hidden in every organization. Overauthorization may be a bureaucratic device to counteract all too common hoarding of materials and labor.[5] And it certainly serves the political ends of the center by sustaining at least the image of central support for local development.

Plan directives and expenditure patterns both bear out this interpretation. Five-year plan directives, as noted in chapter 4, read like documents written by committee, with multiple targets to satisfy rival bureaucratic interests. And even when the language of the plan highlights a particular goal above all others, as in the case of developing the east, other goals receive endorsement too.

The same evidence of compromise characterizes the responses to appeals at party congresses and Supreme Soviet budget convocations. A small reserve is made available to meet a few of the requests submitted by republic and local leaders—a process of adjusting plans and budgets at the margins to cope with local needs. In the Supreme Soviet, these adjustments have all the earmarks of classic pork-barrel legislation, providing modest funds for public works to a large "coalition" of regional and local officials. In both national forums, the extra authorizations are distributed rather evenly across republics, with no region receiving an undue share of funds.

Certainly Soviet leaders have a vested interest in appearing to be even-handed in such national rallies of the faithful, and one might wonder whether the compromises and adjustments reflect merely good theater rather than real appropriations. But all the other data on expenditure decisions behind the scenes point to precisely the same process of compromise, to an ongoing series of adjustments. The subsequent comments of the participants themselves are eloquent testimony, in none too appreciative a tone. Republic and local politicians from Belorussia's Mazurov in 1956 to Altai krai's Popov in 1986 have complained about repeated compromises and split-the-difference decisions that provide some but rarely enough resources for local projects. The fact that they must raise the same issues again and again suggests that their comments—and their frustrations—are genuine.

Aggregate data on investment allocations to republics and oblasti support the same conclusion. Appropriations reflect the diffusion that arises from bureaucratic decision-making. The result has been a mild form of redistribution, allotting slightly more to less developed regions than would otherwise be the case, even after Brezhnev's claim in the early 1970s that the main task of regional equalization had been met. Offsetting economic advantages, coupled with offsetting political resources, have provided funding even to regions without any of the more obvious signs of political privilege.

The slow pace has led Western analysts to question whether Soviet leaders have in fact pursued a policy of equalization among republics and regions. While the term "policy" may be too strong (implying a more systematic approach than really exists), Khrushchev and Brezhnev supported the concept of equalization, and appropriations policies in their time were indeed redistributive. The most plausible explanation seems to be that equality has been one of several competing goals in shaping regional policy (see chapter 4). Since the planning process follows branch principles first, questions of regional equity come in at the margins, as adjustments to plans laid out by sector.

The impact of appropriations is a different question. Given the different levels of productivity, economic profiles, labor forces, and other economic characteristics in each region, the same amount invested will yield unequal returns (Bahry and Nechemias 1981). Hence the data presented here tell us little about the effectiveness of investment or about its impact on the living standards of the resident population.[6]

Republic and Local Political Privilege

The findings presented in this study suggest that both the budgetary process and center-periphery relations are intensely politicized, but they involve subtle varieties of politics that cannot be explained only by the careers, personal backgrounds, or high-level connections of leaders outside Moscow. Despite the obvious importance that both Soviet and Western sources ascribe to friends in high places, regions and localities with the highest connections seldom curry the most economic favor. The Ukraine, Georgia, and Kazakhstan bear witness to the low levels of investment growth that can befall republics with first secretaries in the Politburo; Donetsk, Dnepropetrovsk, and Tashkent oblasti suggest the same conclusion for localities with representation in the All-Union Central Committee. And the high rates of investment growth for regions *without* obvious political clout (e.g., Lithuania, Armenia) suggest that officials in the periphery have other political resources to use in their quest for funds.

Economic and political advantages are more diffuse, and so too are the "windows" or decision points where republic and local leaders can present an appeal.

A similar conclusion applies in the case of native leadership and of newly appointed party bosses. If "self-government" and succession are political resources, they are only two among many others that republic and local leaders can bring to bear in supporting their case. Regions with nonnative and/or "old" leaders fare just as well as any others, perhaps because the old and the imported have had the opportunity to develop their own skill in pressing local claims and their own network of contacts. Otherwise their chances for political survival would seem to be rather limited.

Republic and local agendas also challenge traditional assumptions about the impact of career backgrounds on the behavior of political leaders outside Moscow. If the tendency to lobby signifies identification with local economic problems, then identification is just as high among officials brought in from outside as it is among natives. Leaders with both types of background concentrate on much the same set of issues, whether new or old, recruited locally or sent in from outside the republic or oblast. The common causes among this diverse set of politicians reveal, once again, the influence of economic structure and context. But they also highlight the incentives in operation for politicans below the national level. As Armstrong (1959) suggested, leaders in the periphery have a keen awareness that their jobs and potential promotions hinge on the economic well-being of their assigned territory. Even though Moscow may "exchange" cadres as a way of damping down identification with the locality, the economic pressures of local office seem to reward those who defend local interests. Hence a Brezhnev arriving in Kazakhstan takes up some of the same economic issues as a Kunaev; a Solomentsev arriving in Rostov argues for some of the same causes as a Bondarenko.[7] Their styles and strategies may differ, but the problems they confront are similar in spite of the varied backgrounds they bring to office.

Politics Outside Moscow and Post-Brezhnev Economic Reforms

Analysis of the substantive appeals by republic and local leaders at the Twenty-Seventh Congress suggests that the structure of economic agendas below the national level had changed very little by 1986, in spite of the "large-scale economic experiment" under way since 1983 and the political housecleaning in Gorbachev's first year. There were, however, more appeals for reorganization than at any time since 1956, and the content of the reforms revealed an acute recognition of both the need to reshape incentives and the dilemmas of branch versus territorial planning.

Thus far, the economic experiment in industry and services has included ministries ranging from the All-Union Ministry of Instrument-Making to the Estonian Ministry of Consumer Services, and republics ranging from the Baltic to the Caucasus, with plans to implement the reform package union-wide (and a similar set of reforms under way in agriculture). The primary goals seem to be to streamline and enhance central planning, by:

1) reducing the number of plan targets for enterprises and associations to fulfill and replacing them with "normatives" to guide the allocation of resources;

2) emphasizing fulfillment of planned output sales (based on contracts) rather than simply planned output, in order to reinforce the connections between producers and their clients;

3) fixing plan targets and normatives for the duration of the plan period, in order to create stable expectations among producers;

4) fostering labor-savings by allowing enterprises and associations to dismiss workers but keep the wages saved for use in rewarding the remaining labor force;

5) providing other incentives to managers and workers by increasing opportunities to earn bonuses and tying the rewards more closely to increases in output and productivity and reductions in costs (e.g., by allowing greater deductions from profits for social-cultural and material incentive funds);

6) offering managers more discretion over capital repair, reequipment, and research and development expenditures; and

7) lowering the level of independent financial accounting to the "brigade" level within enterprises, so that rewards can be more closely calibrated with individual output.

To strengthen territorial planning, construction has been reorganized to replace the union-wide ministries in different branches with ministries demarcated by region (i.e., for construction in the north and west, in the south, in the Urals and West Siberia, and in the east). Republic ministries of construction are to be removed from union subordination and put instead under their republic council of ministers (except in the case of the RSFSR, where construction will be managed by all-union ministries) (*Pravda* August 20, 1986, p. 2, and September 13, 1986, pp. 1–2).

The reform package also gives republic and local governments wider powers to coordinate economic infrastructure, social welfare, consumer goods and services, and environmental protection in their area. As of 1987, they are required to compile both one- and five-year territory-wide plans for economic and social development (i.e., including the growth of the economy as a whole, the development of social and economic infrastructure, and labor resources) for submission to higher agencies. Ministries, for their part, are required to gain local approval of branch plans before submission to Gosplan. And governments below the national level are now empowered to create their own production associations or cooperative enterprises in consumer goods and services using local materials. They may also use up to 1 percent of the output of union and republic-subordinate enterprises for equipment and automation in local industry "where production capacity permits," and reallocate unused materials or productive capacity among all enterprises in their area ("O merakh po dal'neishemy" 1986:5–13). As a further spur to the consumer sector, certain types of limited private production and services have been legalized, but with a prohibition against the hiring of other people (*New York Times*, November 20, 1986, p. 17)

To give local authorities more incentives for coordination, local governments are to receive all turnover taxes from "local" industry, consumer services, and consumer cooperatives (Pabat 1985); half of above-plan profits and temporary markups on consumer "goods of improved quality" produced by union and republic-subordinate enterprises (Panskov and Velichko 1986); half of all above-plan turnover taxes collected in their area; and 10 percent of the profits of union-subordinate enterprises from the production and sale of consumer goods (Iusifov 1986).

Since the reforms have yet to be fully implemented, any assessment of the results must necessarily be provisional. Still, responses from the implementers themselves suggest that the experiments change certain types of incentives and behaviors but also create new problems. Shifting the target of the plan from output to contract-based sales means that, instead of negotiating for achievable production targets, enterprises and associations now have incentives to negotiate fewer but achievable contracts

(Tychina et al. 1985). Providing managers with more flexibility in allocating wages and bonuses allows wages and bonuses to rise even when real labor productivity does not, suggesting potential problems with inflation (Ragauskas 1985). Offering more discretion and flexibility to managers renders the prediction of economic outcomes and thus the planning process more difficult, at a time when planners are required to keep targets and normatives stable for the entire plan period.

In practice, the need to modify targets has won out, with frequent adjustments of sales, wage, and profit plans (Sherstneva 1986). And not all targets are adjusted downward: in some cases, enterprises in the experiment accumulated above-plan profits in incentive and research and development funds, and ministry officials want to soak up the unused funds for redistribution to other enterprises (Tychina et al. 1985). Some ministries in the experiment have in fact been accused of slipping old planning procedures in the back door, keeping a tight rein on material supplies, and substituting new plan targets for old ones, rather than cutting back on the amount of direction from above (*Izvestiia*, October 15, 1984, p. 2).

Other problems have emerged in efforts to evaluate the impact of and the allocation of rewards through the brigade system. Some brigades lack the equipment and measuring instruments they need to assess their specific consumption of raw materials and fuels; and some uncertainties exist in figuring overhead (such as administrative costs) into the brigade's costs and profits (ibid.).

The most important question, however, may be price reform, and the strategy to be used is as yet unclear. Improving managerial links to clients and managerial flexibility, increasing the emphasis placed on sales and on profits, and raising the material incentives for workers and managers may all serve to make enterprises more responsive to information from below. But if prices fail to reflect real costs of production, real scarcities, and real demand, enterprises will simply become more responsive to unrealistic information—and more effective at making the wrong choices.

For governments below the national level, the reforms pose additional problems. Calling on ministries to get prior local agreement (*soglasovanie*) on their plans still leaves local officials with the responsibility but not necessarily the means to participate. The requirement that ministries and local governments should agree has already been expressed in a series of decrees since 1979 (Ovchinnikov 1986). But the decrees have done little to foster such cooperation. Local governments still do lack full current information from relevant ministries, and still find many of their proposals ignored (Panskov and Velichko 1986; Ovchinnikov 1986).

Granting more discretion to enterprise managers may make coordination somewhat easier, by allowing local authorities to deal directly with managers. Yet discretion for managers also means, at least in theory, greater flexibility to respond to changing supplies, demand, costs, labor inputs, and the like—which will make planning more difficult for local governments (Shamsutdinov 1986; Sherstneva 1986).

Equally important, early experience with the reforms suggests that ministries have hardly surrendered real control over planning. Local leaders must therefore still contend with distant bureaucracies for whom the needs of the local economy are at best a secondary concern. Enterprise managers may want (or be under local pressure) to cooperate with local government, but the ministry's plan is still likely to predominate. The 1986 decree on greater local coordination seems to bear out this interpretation: the incentives to improve consumer goods and services focus on motivating local authorities to persuade union and republic-subordinate ministries in other branches to help with consumer goods where production capabilities permit. Local leaders are to accomplish this by mobilizing reserves and developing new uses for industrial byproducts and waste materials, hardly a major new allocation of resources to consumer goods.

There seem to be few incentives for the ministries themselves, whose primary plan targets lie in other areas. They do benefit from profits generated by the consumer goods they produce, but this is typically a small share of all their output. They also seem to be reluctant, where goods are profitable, to turn over the designated share of their profits to local budgets (Pabat 1985).

Even with cooperation between ministry, enterprise, and local government, the consumer sector presents other problems for local leaders. Big cities and highly industrialized oblasti may have diverse enough factories to supply the materials and equipment for new consumer goods, but it seems that the vast bulk of local governments do not have the makings of a self-sufficient consumer goods sector. Thus allotting them more power to coordinate intraregional production for local needs does not necessarily give them the resources to acquire needed equipment and raw materials from outside the locality (Ovchinnikov 1986).

Legalization of some forms of private enterprise in consumer goods and services may do much to alleviate such problems—and to absorb workers let go as part of the drive to cut unnecessary labor from public payrolls. However, where private producers will obtain supplies, and how the private sector will mesh with the public, are issues yet to be resolved.

Expansion of the private sector also promises a new and perhaps lucrative tax base for local governments, if private operations can be monitored and regulated effectively. This, in turn, suggests the need for larger local administrative staffs at a time when Moscow is pressing to reduce them.

There are, then, still too many unknowns to predict the net effect of the "large-scale economic experiment" on governments outside Moscow. What does seem clear is that the reforms, especially in the tax system, will reinforce the existing republic and local dependence on revenues from the primary and consumer sectors. The changes would also seem to heighten the dilemmas confronting republic and especially local leaders—creating even more pressure to coordinate economic activities within their jurisdiction, but with even fewer personnel and without advance information on all the plan changes from above. In effect, local authorities now seem likely to face more pressures to deliver both collective and private goods, but in a less certain environment.

Soviet Experience Compared

Comparative conclusions prove as troubling as predictions, especially when they touch on politics below the national level. The history of Soviet center-periphery relations admits few if any parallels. And the mechanisms of central control remain so elaborate that republic and local politicians are bound far more tightly to central interests than are any of their Western counterparts. Without independent powers of taxation or expenditure, and without an independent political base or constituency, they have very few options that are not defined by the center.

Yet this book suggests that even with the intricate controls over policy and personnel, Moscow has confronted dilemmas that are by no means unique to the USSR. Policy coordination among different levels of government and integration of branch and territorial interests prove difficult both in a highly centralized system and in more decentralized ones. The problem of finding a workable, comprehensive regional policy is not only a Soviet problem: capitalist systems have encountered some of the same obstacles in formulating and carrying through consistent policies on regional development (chapter 1). Pressures from subnational leaders and from competing central bureaucracies tend to widen the aims and adjust the impact of regional policies to incorporate a wide net of beneficiaries. The art of finding agreement among diverse bureaucratic contenders means a series of compromises that frequently level out central expenditures—as in the American case of aid to depressed areas, or Soviet five-year plans that promise something to a variety of regional interests.

The problem of optimal location choices also extends beyond the Soviet system. Empirical studies of industrial location in the West conclude that location decisions seldom match the outcome predicted by economic theory. Despite the impact of market forces, industries have been built in areas without the ideal mix of local resources, labor, and access to markets.

Similarly, Soviet problems with the revenue side of fiscal federalism also have their parallels outside the USSR. Republic and local governments are subject to externalities that create a mismatch between tax bases and expenditure needs, as in the United States, France, Britain, and other Western nations. The solutions, tax or revenue sharing, have been similar in principle, assigning the more lucrative sources of revenue—usually income taxes on individuals and corporations—to the national government. But in the USSR, the pattern has been turned upside down: given the traditional Soviet animus against direct personal taxes, such revenues have been less lucrative and have thus been assigned primarily to governments below the national level, where taxpayers can be more easily reminded of the social welfare functions their taxes support.

The findings here also suggest that although leaders in the Soviet periphery are tightly bound to the center, they have a few of the the political resources of their counterparts in the West. Even in the face of a powerful central bureaucracy, interdependence between center and periphery and integration across regions create opportunities to bring problems to the attention of central agencies and subtly rework central policies. Moreover, the sheer size of the central bureaucracy may also be an advantage, creating a fragmented administrative structure with multiple windows that officials below the national level can exploit to local advantage.

If Soviet dilemmas of center-periphery relations have analogs in noncommunist systems, then the problems can hardly be ascribed only to the USSR's unique history or penchant for extreme central controls. If coordination among multiple and overlapping levels of government is a problem under capitalism as well as communism; if formulating a coherent regional policy encounters political obstacles in France, Italy, or Japan as well as the USSR; if reorganization takes years and seldom achieves its expected goal; if location decisions rarely prove to be optimal; if decision-making is fragmented among bureaucratic agencies and interests, we can hardly be surprised that Soviet reforms replacing personnel or promising to upgrade republic and local authority have had only a limited impact on the problems they were meant to cure.

NOTES AND SOURCES ON
BUDGET AND INVESTMENT DATA

As several chapters make clear, Soviet data on budgets and investments are abundant but ambiguous, the more so as one dips below the national level. Much has been published over the years, but not necessarily in the same prices, using the same definitions, or covering the same items.

Budget data present the more serious problems for a study of appropriations below the national level, since they give no indication of what the central government spends in each region. Investment data offer a more complete picture, for they include central as well as republic and local expenditures, budget and nonbudget funds. But they have been subject to frequent changes in coverage and definitions, and price changes (Soviet sources report them in constant prices) that make it difficult to track investment expenditures over time. The following is an outline of the problems and the way I handled them here.

Budget Data

The most difficult questions about the Soviet budget typically revolve around defense spending. Given the Soviet penchant for understating how much is spent, can any budget data be trusted? If so, how does the problem of defense expenditures affect the data presented here? "Trust" in the data depends on how they measure up against what we know of the Soviet system, what we would predict from empirical studies of public finance, and what questions we want to answer. On the first two counts, the statistics appear to be generally reliable. As explained in the introduction, budgetary data fit well with the major political and economic trends since the 1920s, clearly recording the shifts in budgetary responsibilities imposed by Stalin, Khrushchev, and Brezhnev. Revenue data also fit with more general patterns of tax development, at least with respect to the mix of taxes and the distribution of revenues between levels of government.

But to say that the data are generally reliable is not to say that they are complete or well defined, as the problem of defense spending makes clear. This is not the place to review all the literature on the question; instead, I am specifically concerned with how the problem affects the findings in this book.

The answer seems to be that it does not have much of an impact, except for the data in figure 2.1. Since defense is so much a central rather than republic or local responsibility, the "hidden" components of budgetary defense expenditures appear to be concentrated in the all-union share of the budget—primarily in a large residual and in central allocations for "science" or research and development. These components are thus accounted for in central-versus-republic/local shares of the budget.

They do raise a question, however, about using officially reported defense expenditures for calculating central, republic, and local shares of *nondefense* spending. Here, their usefulness depends on the ratio of changes in total defense outlays to changes in reported outlays. If both are increasing or decreasing at approximately the same rate, then the hidden defense expenditures will have little effect on the data in figure 2.1. If total and reported spending change at different rates, they will throw off the data presented there.

To evaluate how this might affect the findings, I compared annual increases in reported defense spending with estimated total increases developed by Shishko and Nincic (cited in Zimmerman and Palmer 1983) for the years 1956–78 (See figure A.1.) For 14 years out of 23 (1956, 1960–72), the rate of increase is virtually identical, and thus the hidden expenditures have no significant effect on figure 2.1. For the other years, total defense expenditures tended to rise more rapidly than the reported military budget, and the republic/local share of nondefense spending would be slightly higher than is indicated in figure 2.1. The problem of military spending thus has relatively little impact on the findings presented here.

Other questions also crop up in dealing with Soviet budgetary statistics below the national level. The primary one is how to interpret statistics on

FIGURE A.1
Changes in Soviet Defense Spending, Official vs. Western Data

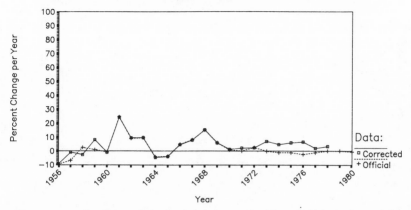

Year

Western (corrected) estimates calculated to include items omitted from official Soviet data on defense expenditures.
SOURCES: Zimmerman and Palmer (1983:365).
Gosbiudzhet (1962:19), (1966:1), (1972:25), (1976:23), 1982:23).

republic and local government expenditures. These count only what is spent directly by republic and local governments on the functions over which they exercise direct jurisdiction, and as the results in the book show, the functions are all too limited. Especially at the local level, official budgets are so small a portion of what the government actually spends that the data seriously underestimate real appropriations. The problem is most acute for expenditures on economic programs, where so much is centralized that republic and local budgets capture only a minor share of what each republic and locality actually receives, and where the degree of centralization differs from one program to another, so that the relative weight of the "hidden" central budget varies from each republic and locality to the next.

Thus budget data are inadequate for any appraisal of government appropriations on economic development across regions, or localities, and I rely instead on more comprehensive figures on total investment in each republic and oblast. The difference is substantial, as illustrated in figure A.2. The impact of budgetary organization is to overstate expenditure differences among republics.

Since the administrative and financial structure of social programs is

FIGURE A.2
A Comparison of Inequality in Republic Budgetary and Investment Data

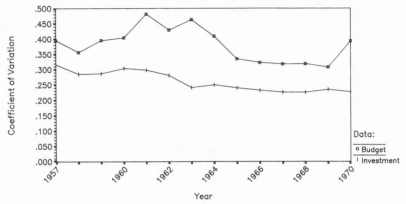

Year

Investment data represent total gross capital investment within the republic. Budget data represent the total spent by the republic government for economic development ("financing the economy").
SOURCES: For investment, see the sources listed in this appendix. For budget data, Bielasiak (1980).

relatively uniform across territorial units, and since most social spending is captured at the republic and local level, I rely on budgetary data to analyze appropriations for enlightenment and health care (chapter 4).

Investment Data

Investment data too present problems, but of a different sort. They overcome the dilemma of inadequate coverage, since they count all the funds spent in a given republic or locality, regardless of the source or level of government making the expenditure. But they are, of course, limited to capital outlays, thus giving no indication of how much is spent on subsidies for operating expenses or working capital. And rules for reporting on investment have not always been uniform: the data are typically reported in constant prices, but the price weights change often and thus create discrepancies from one year to the next. Definitions and coverage have been modified too, as the inclusion/exclusion of collective farm investment attests. To make the data even more complicated, statistics are published only for some years, sometimes aggregated by five-year plan period, sometimes annual—so that even identifying the discrepancies becomes problematic.

Thus any analysis based on investment data below the national level must cope with multiple gaps and inconsistencies. My approach, for the republics, has been to develop two time-series of investment, one annual and one based on five-year plan periods. For the annual statistics (chapter 4), I compared all the data on republic investment reported in each annual edition of *Narkhoz SSSR*, and reconciled disparate data by basing them all on prices reported for 1965. (At the outset, that was the midpoint of the time series.) For statistics by five-year periods, I collected data from republic statistical handbooks, all published in the late 1970s to minimize the problems of changing coverage and definitions. To my great relief, the two series showed the same basic trends by regions, so that whatever biases are introduced by my corrections of the annual data would seem to be minimal.

For local investment, the problems multiplied. Annual statistics by oblasti are published only sporadically for most areas, and my plan of developing a comprehensive yearly time-series for all of them had to be scaled down to a study of oblast investment within the Ukraine and Uzbekistan. These two provided annual data on all oblasti, and they offered examples of sufficiently different economic backgrounds and industrial structures to make any similarities more believable. In this case, I did not attempt to develop a consistent time-series for each oblast, since not only the data but even oblast' boundaries were inconsistent over time. Instead, I took the longest continuous series I could find in a single statistical handbook for each period. The breaks in the data are indicated in the tables in chapter 5 by solid horizontal lines.

Notes and Sources for Budget Data

Figures 2.1, 2.2, 3.1, 5.1

Data are net expenditures by republic and all subordiate local governments, with transfers from the all-union budget counted as expenditures at the republic/local level. All are measured in millions of rubles, with a post-1960 decimal.

Total expenditures (including reported defense outlays):

1924/25–1950	Plotnikov (1954:96, 131, 215, 255, 324, 377).
1951–55	*Gosbiudzhety* (1957:7).
1956–60	*Gosbiudzhet* (1962:5).
1961–65	*Gosbiudzhet* (1966:28).
1966–70	*Gosbiudzhet* (1972:32).
1971–75	*Gosbiudzhet* (1976:22).
1976–80	*Gosbiudzhet* (1982:22–23).

Total economic expenditures:

1924/25–1950	Plotnikov (1954:92, 132, 193, 255, 326, 407).
1951–55	*Gosbiudzhety* (1957:7).
1956–60	*Gosbiudzhet* (1962:27).
1961–65	*Gosbiudzhet* (1966:29).
1966–70	*Gosbiudzhet* (1972:33).
1971–75	*Gosbiudzhet* (1976:22).
1976–80	*Gosbiudzhet* (1982:22).

Total social-cultural expenditures:

1924/25–1932	Plotnikov (1954:92, 135).
1933–40	Plotnikov (1948:146, 218).
1941–50	Plotnikov (1954:340, 407).
1951–55	*Gosbiudzhety* (1957:7).
1956–60	*Gosbiudzhet* (1962:28).
1961–65	*Gosbiudzhet* (1966:30).
1966–70	*Gosbiudzhet* (1972:34).
1971–75	*Gosbiudzhet* (1976:22).
1976–80	*Gosbiudzhet* (1982:22).

Total republic expenditures:

1924/25–1937	Plotnikov (1954:96, 158, 215).
1938–40	Plotnikov (1948:228).
1940–45	Tamarchenko (1967:31).

1946–50	Plotnikov (1954:437, 440).
1951–55	*Gosbiudzhety* (1957:17).
1956–60	*Gosbiudzhet* (1962:26).
1961–65	*Gosbiudzhet* (1966:28).
1966–70	*Gosbiudzhet* (1972:32).
1971–75	*Gosbiudzhet* (1976:30).
1976–80	*Gosbiudzhet* (1982:20).

Total local expenditures:

1924/25–1932	Plotnikov (1954:96).
1933–37	Plotnikov (1947:173).
1938–39	Rovinskii (1939:15).
1940–45	Tamarchenko (1967:31).
1946–50	Plotnikov (1954:440).
1951–55	*Mestnye biudzhety* (1960:5).
1956–60	*Gosbiudzhet* (1962:94).
1961–65	*Gosbiudzhet* (1966:8).
1966–70	*Gosbiudzhet* (1972:103).
1971–75	*Gosbiudzhet* (1976:100).
1976–80	*Gosbiudzhet* (1982:20).

Total republic and local expenditures by type of program:

1950–55	*Gosbiudzhety* (1957:16).
1956–60	*Gosbiudzhet* (1962:71–73).
1961–65	*Gosbiudzhet* (1966:73).
1966–70	*Gosbiudzhet* (1972:79).
1971–75	*Gosbiudzhet* (1976:76).
1976–80	*Gosbiudzhet* (1982:49).

Total local expenditures by type of program:

1960–65	*Mestnye biudzhety* (1970).
1966–70	*Gosbiudzhet* (1972:103).

| 1971–75 | *Gosbiudzhet* (1976:100). |
| 1976–80 | *Gosbiudzhet* (1982:72). |

Republic expenditures on enlightenment and health care (excluding science), **for tables 4.4 and 4.5 and figure 4.1**:

1940, 1950, 1956–60	*Gosbiudzhet* (1962:29, 51, 55).
1961–65	*Gosbiudzhet* (1966:31, 53, 57).
1966–70	*Gosbiudzhet* (1972:36–37, 62–63).
1971–75	*Gosbiudzhet* (1976:34–35, 6–61).
1976–80	*Gosbiudzhet* (1982:34–35, 40–41).

Figure 2.3

Total revenues:

1924/25–1950	Plotnikov (1954:76, 106, 174, 236, 293, 377).
1951–55	*Gosbiudzhety* (1957:5).
1956–60	*Gosbiudzhet* (1962:7).
1961–65	*Gosbiudzhet* (1966:10).
1966–70	*Gosbiudzhet* (1972:11).
1971–75	*Gosbiudzhet* (1976:8).
1976–80	*Gosbiudzhet* (1982:10).

Total republic and local revenues:

1924/25–1933	*Sotialisticheskoe stroitel'stvo* (1935:661, 665, 675).
1940–45	Tamarchenko (1967:31).
1946–50	Plotnikov (1954:349).
1951–55	*Gosbiudzhety* (1957:15).
1956–60	*Gosbiudzhet* (1962:69).
1961–65	*Gosbiudzhet* (1966:72).
1966–70	*Gosbiudzhet* (1972:78).

1971–75   *Gosbiudzhet* (1976:75).
1976–80   *Gosbiudzhet* (1982:48).

Total transfers to republics (includes subventsii, dotatsii, and sredstva from the all-union budget; excludes shared taxes):

1925/26–1933   *Sotsialisticheskoe stroitel'stvo* (1935:661, 665).
1940   *Gosbiudzhet* (1962:69–70).
1941–45   Plotnikov (1948:348).
1950–54   *Gosbiudzhety* (1957:15).
1955–59   *Gosbiudzhet* (1962:69–70).
1960–65   *Gosbiudzhet* (1966:72).
1966–70   *Gosbiudzhet* (1972:78).
1971–75   *Gosbiudzhet* (1976:73–77).
1976–80   *Gosbiudzhet* (1982:48–50).

Notes and Sources for Investment Data

Annual Investment (figure 4.1, tables 4.1, 4.3):

Data were corrected to reflect a single set of prices (for 1965) and exclude investment in private housing.

1956–59   *Narkhoz 1959*:544–45, 554–58.
1960, 1964,
  1965   *Narkhoz 1965*:539–41.
1961   *Narkhoz 1961*:549–53.
1962–64   *Narknoz 1964*:520–22.
1966–68   *Narkhoz 1968*:527–28.
1969   *Narkhoz 1969*:509–10.
1970–75   *Narkhoz 1975*:514–15.
1976–77   *Narkhoz 1977*:360–61.
1978   *Narkhoz 1978*:349–50.
1979   *Narkhoz 1979*:373–74.

1980   *Narkhoz 1980*:343–44.
1981   *Narkhoz 1981*:375–76.

Data on republic shares of investment by five-year plan periods (table 4.2):

USSR	*Narkhoz SSSR 1922–1982*:365–75.
RSFSR	*Narkhoz RSFSR 1980*:205–209.
Ukraine	*Narkhoz UkSSR 1980*:215–21.
Belorussia	*Narkhoz BSSR 1981*:119–29.
Uzbekistan	*Narkhoz UzSSR 1980*:192–96.
Kazakhstan	*Narkhoz KaSSR 1980*:160–66.
	Narkhoz KaSSR 1976:133–35.
Georgia	*Narkhoz GruzSSR 1980*:124–29.
	Narkhoz GruzSSR 1978:120–28.
Azerbaidzhan	*Narkhoz AzSSR k 60-letiiu obrazovaniia SSSR.* (1982):169–75. 1980:215–21.
	Narkhoz AzSSR 1978:134.
Lithuania	*Narkhoz LiSSR 1981*:134.
	Narkhoz LiSSR 1978:147–54.
Moldavia	*Narkhoz MSSR 1981*:136–41.
	Narkhoz MSSR 1979:140–46.
Latvia	*Narkhoz LaSSR 1980*:198–206.
Kirgizia	*Narkhoz KiSSR 1980*:188–95.
Tadzhikistan	*Narkhoz TaSSR 1980*:168–73.
Armenia	*Narkhoz ArmSSR* (1977):116–23.
	Narkhoz ArmSSR (1981).
Turkmenia	*Narkhoz TuSSR 1980*:105–8.
Estonia	*Narkhoz ESSR 1980*:185–91.

Data and Variables for Regression Analysis (Tables 4.3 and 4.6)

Sources and definitions for the variables used in the regression analysis (chapter 4) are described below. The data were grouped, as chapter 4 describes, into eras corresponding to the Khrushchev and Brezhnev regimes. It should be emphasized that the cutpoints might well be different:

since Khrushchev promulgated several reforms in social services, wages, and pensions in the last months of his tenure, the implementation of some of his policy choices would only be felt in the first years of the Brezhnev era. Thus if the cutpoints were changed, the values of the regression coefficients for some of the variables (e.g., the constant term) would be different. However, the basic conclusions would remain the same.

It could also be that the effects of some political variables such as Politburo representation might in fact be cumulative, coming into play gradually as a republic leader gains experience and presumably greater influence. But tests of this hypothesis revealed no cumulative impact.

In the regression, all independent variables are lagged one year. The analysis relies on a combined cross-sectional, time-series general linear model. The variables are:

Level of economic development—measured as the value of retail trade in the republic, taken from annual editions of *Narkhoz SSSR*.

Population—size of total population, taken from Rakov (1969) up through 1968 and thereafter from annual editions of *Narkhoz SSSR*.

Skill of labor force—number of workers with a higher or secondary specialized education employed in the republic, taken from annual editions of *Narkhoz SSSR*. Data for 1978 and 1979 are interpolated.

Comparative natural resource endowment—an index of available natural resources calculated by Mints and Kokhanovskaia (1974).

Succession—a dummy variable with a value of one if the republic party boss (or, in the RSFSR, the premier) was replaced. Data are from Hodnett and Ogareff (1973); *Current Soviet Leaders; USSR Facts and Figures Annual*.

Native leadership—a dummy variable with a value of one if all four top republic leaders—first and second secretary, premier, and first deputy premier—are of the local nationality. Data are from Hodnett and Ogareff (1973).

Representation in Politburo—a dummy variable which equals one if a current republic leader is a full or candidate member of the CPSU Politburo.

Agricultural output—gross value of agricultural output in the republic, taken from annual editions of *Narkhoz SSSR*.

CODING AND SOURCES FOR
REPUBLIC AND LOCAL AGENDAS

Sampling

In analyzing the appeals presented in Moscow by republic and local leaders, I relied on several criteria for selecting a sample. One was to capture comments where central leaders themselves made up the audience, where appeals were in fact being transmitted directly to higher-ups. A second criterion was to insure geographical diversity, beyond the confines of the RSFSR or Ukraine alone (although local speakers from these two republics still predominate in the sample). Third, I wanted to sample appeals presented in the same format over time, in order to compare the same leaders at different points, compare successive republic and local delegates from the same regions, and compare the changes in agendas that emerged under different regimes.

The proceedings of CPSU congresses met all these conditions, and I therefore coded all speeches by republic and local delegates on plan directives from the Twentieth Congress (1956) through the Twenty-Seventh (1986). I used the full stenographic reports in Russian, except in the case of the 1986 congress, for which the only available data were the speeches published in *Pravda* and *Izvestiia*. I also reviewed the proceedings of earlier congresses, to develop a longer-term perspective on the concerns of leaders in the periphery; but formal coding of earlier data proved more difficult. I did not have a complete stenographic report of the Nineteenth Congress (1952) in Russian, and the abridged speeches published in English (*Current Soviet Policies* 1953) were inadequate for coding purposes. Stenographic reports of earlier congresses were available, but they posed the problem of identifying each speaker and his background. Biographical information before the mid-1950s is all too scarce.

A sample of budget convocations in the Supreme Soviet were also coded (for 1955, 1965, 1975, and 1983) to widen the pool of data and compare the differences in appeals between different national forums. The years were picked at slightly different intervals from those between congresses, in order to increase the number of years covered.

Only speakers formally representing a given territory were included; a factory director speaking on behalf on his industry's local needs, or a farm chairman discussing agricultural problems in a given oblast, were not counted as local officials. In a few instances, a delegate from a local party or soviet spoke and presented appeals on behalf of the entire union republic, and these were treated as republic rather than local presentations.

Coding Procedures

In the coding itself, I had hoped initially to count the number of appeals presented. But this approach proved to be unworkable, since appeals might be identical but be expressed in more or less specific wording. Some leaders offer a broad request, while others present a set of specific examples. A Solomentsev might ask for "more agricultural machinery" while a Kunaev might ask for "more tractors and harvesters"—but we could hardly conclude that Kunaev had presented twice as many demands. Similarly, it was impossible to develop a valid coding scheme that would capture the degree of intensity among different appeals or different speakers, without corresponding information on the urgency of the specific problem under appeal or the length of time it had been before central leaders.

The more compelling strategy was to count the *number of speakers* who raised each given issue, thus eliminating the problem of general versus specific wording of an individual request. I counted as appeals only those comments that asked directly for resources or assistance from above. Speakers who talked only about their own failings in a given field, or who mentioned only the successes, were not counted as presenting an appeal. Thus the data represent a frequency count of the number of speakers raising each cluster of issues.

Issues, in turn, were clustered because they were so often mentioned in tandem. The problem of water supplies was so frequently tied in with the state of local agriculture that it would be misleading to present them as separate categories. Appeals to develop fuels and minerals were so often mixed that they too could not easily be separated. It seemed that republic and local leaders were attempting to justify their requests by linking them together into a seemingly integrated package for "complex" local development.

Sources

For speeches:
XX S"ezd (1956)
XXI S"ezd (1959)
XXII S"ezd (1961)
XXIII S"exd (1966)
XXIV S"ezd (1971)
XXV S"ezd (1976)
XXVI S"ezd (1981)
Pravda (March–April 1986)
Izvestiia (March–April 1986)

Zasedaniia (1956)
Zasedaniia (1966)
Zasedaniia (1976)
Deviataia sessiia (1983)
For biographical information:
Deputaty (1959)
Deputaty (1963)
Deputaty (1967)
Deputaty (1970)
Deputaty (1979)
Ezhegodnik BSE (annual)
Lewytzky (1968)
Soviet Political Leaders (1957)
Radio Liberty Research (April 9 and 16, 1986)

NOTES

INTRODUCTION: THE LOCAL REVOLUTION

1. See, for example, work by Moses (1974), Miller (1977, 1983), Breslauer (1984), Hough (1971), Taubman (1973) Stewart (1968), and Biddulph (1983).

2. For example, Nechemias (1980), Gillula (1979), Koropeckyj (1972), Koropeckyj and Schroeder (1981), McAuley (1978), and Dellenbrant (1980).

3. Some regional statistical handbooks still omit this, especially in reporting within-republic investment.

4. Expenditures for social welfare (in Soviet terminology, "social-cultural programs") present less of a problem in this respect, since the breakdown between central and republic/local responsibilities is more or less uniform from one republic to another.

1. CENTER, PERIPHERY, AND POWER IN THE MODERN STATE

1. In 1982, for example, state and local governments accounted for all the property tax and for two-thirds of sales tax receipts in the United States, while the federal government collected 85 percent of individual income taxes and over 75 percent of corporate income taxes (Statistical Abstract of the United States, 1985, p. 263). Sharpe (1981:7–14) outlines a similar situation in most of Western Europe, where the "center takes the lion's share of the buoyant or income-elastic taxes." Scandinavia and Switzerland are exceptions, in that central governments permit local authorities a major share of income taxes; and the West German government allots approximately equal shares of income tax revenues between the federation and the lander (ACIR 1981).

2. Stanfield (1976) details the growth of coalitions and public-interest groups representing state and local governments in the United States: the Governors' Conference, the Conference of State Legislatures, the National League of Cities, the U.S. Conference of Mayors, the National Association of Counties, and the National League of Cities. This does not, of course, count the various lobbying offices established in Washington by individual states and cities or by regional interests.

3. The one major exception would seem to be the French socialist decentralization scheme adopted in 1981. But as Meny (1984:77) observes, the reforms were primarily a codification of the status quo: "they merely confirm processes which had been under way for the previous 10 to 15 years. They give legal blessing to a *de facto* situation—the accession to power of the major local elected representatives—and at the same time legitimise the increased intervention of local authorities in economic and social affairs."

4. Owens and Wade (1984) emphasize, however, that congressional appropriations for individual programs do reflect more specialized criteria. Welfare spending, for example, shows evidence of a redistributive bias; agriculture, the effects of geography and of the traditional influence structure in Congress; and public works, the universalism of logrolling.

5. Prud'homme (1974b) and Tarrow (1977) confirm that partisan ties do little to confer advantages or disadvantages for any region in Paris's allocation of public investment funds: regions represented by deputies from the majority party do neither better nor worse than any others.

6. The degree of redistrubution varies, however. For the United States, France, and Germany, the level of national expenditures corresponds roughly to the level of personal income, although government spending is more evenly distributed. In Canada, Australia, and the U.K., expenditures are inversely correlated with personal income: poorer regions get more national funds, owing largely to the territorial distribution of social security beneficiaries in Canada and Australia, and owing to redistributive capital grants and agricultural subsidies in the U.K. (Commission 1977).

7. Fainsod (1963:393) reports that there had been 18 ministries in 1936—8 all-union and 10 union-republic. By 1947, these had multiplied to a total of 59 ministries, 36 of them all-union and 23 union-republic. The total number dropped slightly in a consolidation campaign during Stalin's last years; but even so, there were still 51 ministries as late as 1952.

8. The Central Committee resolution condemning the antiparty group denounced them for being "against the widening of the rights of the union republics in the sphere of economic and cultural construction, and also against strengthening the role of local soviets in this sphere." And it suggested that they had opposed the idea of more rapid development in the "national republics." ("Ob antipartiinoi gruppe" 1960: 151)

9. This list does not include O. Kuusinen, the chairman of Karelia's Supreme Soviet, who was a Politburo member from 1953 to 1965.

10. According to Shafir (1968b) republic premiers had previously been included in the all-union Council of Ministers but without voting privileges.

11. The idea dated back to 1931, but Tsikulin's (1966) analysis suggests that such republic representatives carried very little weight in Moscow before the advent of Khrushchev.

12. However, the actual plans themselves did include a territorial section, largely a compilation by territory of the plans for individual ministries. What changed

was the degree of emphasis accorded to regional concerns in the party's overall directives.

13. See, e.g., the comments by Sverdlovsk first secretary Iu. V. Petrov (*Pravda*, March 2, 1986, p. 6), and Gorkii's Iu. I. Khristoradnov (*Pravda*, March 4, 1986, p. 2).

14. Of course, protecting republic and regional interests has its limits, as the purges in Georgia and Azerbaidzhan in the early 1970s and the more recent cleanup campaigns in Central Asia under Gorbachev all demonstrate.

15. The practice has a venerable history, going back at least to the 1920s when some appeals were couched in terms of vanquishing the Left or the Right—which would lead to the "correct" path of allocating more resources for local needs. See, e.g., comments at the Fifteenth Party Congress by Uzbekistan's Ikramov (*XV S"ezd 1928:148–53*). Others raised the defense issue—see comments by Andronnikov (ibid.:895–99).

16. But regional politicians and economists defend the system of republic administration as optimal (if only the republics and localities were allowed more power). Osminin (1979:40–41) writes that only the republics have the administrative structure and the required scale to succeed at regional planning; and others (Maniushis 1978; Kochumov 1982; Khaburzaniia 1978) seem to be equally vigorous in defense of republic rights.

2. THE EVOLUTION OF SOVIET FISCAL FEDERALISM

1. Technically, local budgets were considered separate from the "state budget" of the union and the republics until 1938, although in practice local finances were regulated from above. In 1938, the de jure situation was brought into line with actual practice, and all levels were consolidated into a system of unified budgetary accounts. Since then data on the state budget of each union republic have included all subordinate local finances. All the references and data here on "republic budgets" thus include all subordinate local finances. Transfers are treated as revenues of the donor, and as expenditures of the recipient level of government.

2. An account is provided in a Central Committee resolution, "O grubykh narusheniiakh gosudarstvennoi distsipliny v ispol'zovanii kapital'nykh vlozhenii i faktakh proiavleniia mestnichestva so storony otdel'nykh rukovoditelei sovnarkhozov," reprinted in *Spravochnik sekretaria PPO* (1960:199–203).

3. Note that the housing and municipal expenditures in figure 2.2 represent the republic and local share of the state budget for these items; they do not include resources allocated by ministries to house their own employees.

4. Sabirov (1966:207) demonstrates the effect in Uzbekistan with rare data cc mparing total budget expenditures in the republic versus expenditures only through the republic budget. Total expenditures on Uzbek industrial development were 83.5 million rubles in 1951–55, but only 21.8 percent of the total (18.2 million rubles) was channeled through the republic's own budget. In 1956–58, total budget spending on Uzbek industrial development reached 163.2 million rubles, but now 135.3 million rubles (82.9 percent of the total) were channeled

through the republic's budget. Had we looked only at the increase in the amount of the republic budget, we would conclude—erroneously—that industrial expenditures had grown sevenfold in just a few years. In reality, total expenditures only doubled, but with more of the total counted in the republic's own budget.

5. In the RSFSR, the republic's budget expenditures on industry dropped from 7.6 to 2.1 billion rubles just between 1965 and 1966; and in the Ukraine, the republic budget for industry dropped from 2.7 to 2.3 billion rubles (*Gosbiudzhet* 1972:110, 118). But total investment in industry (by central as well as republic agencies) increased in both regions (see *Narkhoz* 1967:625)

6. Ironically, tax rates and payment schedules grew very complex very quickly. By 1938, Soviet officials were complaining that the turnover tax had 2,500 assessment rates, and that individual producers often found themselves paying varying amounts even for similar items. The Commissariat of the Food Industry, e.g., had to contend with 1,387 rates for its different products (*Second Session* 1938:20).

7. In contrast, the other major revenue source, profit payments, created something of a problem for financial officials, since profitability varied not only with plan fulfillment but with costs of production, and these were more difficult to anticipate in drawing up plan and budget for the following year.

8. This includes profit payments from republic-subordinate enterprises, farms, and trade establishments; income taxes on cooperatives and collectives; and agricultural taxes (*Gosbiudzhet* 1982:46–48).

9. Some accounts of budgetary policies during the prewar years also include shared taxes under the label "transfers," making the total appear to be much higher.

10. D'iachenko (1978) shows that the bulk of such grants, at least for the 1920s, went to Central Asia, and that they amounted to as much as half of some republic budgets.

11. In 1967, for example, Ukrainian budget figures indicate receipt of 577.8 million rubles in "means" from the central budget; but in the same year the Ukraine also transferred 1,045.3 million rubles *to* the central budget in connection with the recentralization of industry (*Gosbiudzhet* 1972:117–118). See also the accounts of other republic budgets in *Gosbiudzhet* (1972).

12. This is not true for local budgets, however. Despite continual warnings in the budgetary literature that subsidies undermine fiscal responsibility, revenue bases for many local governments continue to be too low to support expenditure needs, and subsidies are common below the republic level. For a discussion of the problems, see Khesin (1976) and Rusin (1974).

3. REGIONAL INFLUENCE AND SOVIET BUDGETARY DECISION-MAKING

1. One of the most intriguing sources is Khrushchev's memoirs, recounting some of the budget battles over science, defense, and consumer goods. See Khrushchev (1971, 1976).

2. Thus the Politburo itself reportedly was involved in planning for the Kama

River complex (F. A. Tabeev, *XXV S"ezd* 1976: 1:380–86). And individual Politburo members concentrate on special problems—Khrushchev monitored housing construction plans, and Kosygin signed off on all major allocations of pipe, a perennial deficit item. These examples were mentioned to me in personal interviews with economic officials who emigrated to the West.

3. Gosplan or the Council of Ministers ratifies plans directly for some key regions and cities, while other plans below the union-republic level—e.g., for oblasti and cities—are approved by the union-republics (Zenchenko 1979; Nekrasov 1975). However, Soviet authors are not in total agreement about the list of regional and city plans that get singled out for ratification at the national level. Kutafin (1976) reports that for the Ninth and Tenth Five-Year Plans (1971–75 and 1976–80), the Council of Ministers had to approve plan targets for Krasnoiarsk krai, Chita oblast, and the Far East economic region, while Gosplan USSR had to sign off on targets for Moscow, Leningrad, and Sverdlovsk. Todorskii (1982) reports that the Council of Ministers approved plans for the Far East and East Siberian economic regions, Krasnoiarsk, Tiumen, and Moscow; and that plans for Leningrad and Sverdlovsk were left to Gosplan for ratification. Apparently two sets of criteria are used in selecting such areas: (1) Moscow and Leningrad are subordinate directly to the central government (and not to the RSFSR), so their plans must be approved by central agencies; (2) the other regions are areas with heavy investment in natural resource development, a key sector over which central authorities sought to exercise more stringent control.

4. Compare, for example, the allocation of revenues to local governments in the RSFSR and Belorussia as reported in *Odinnadtsataia sessiia* (1980:188–95; with *Trinadtsataia sessiia* (1980:461–66).

5. Some indication of the differences is provided in the official guidelines for plan formulation (*Metodicheskie ukazaniia* 1980).

6. Khrushchev (1976:138) acknowledged that central party leaders were well aware of this process, as in the case of assigning the Virgin Lands program directly to all-union control: "We didn't want to channel our investments through the Republic [that is, Kazakh] government or planning commission because we were afraid that resources earmarked for the Virgin Lands might end up in other branches of the Kazakh economy. Such a temptation always exists, so we decided to bypass the Republic administration."

7. Dyker (1983) reports, however, that the recentralization after Khrushchev brought with it more stringent control over such expenditures, and the room for regional and local officials to maneuver thus grew narrower.

8. V. P. Orlov, deputy premier of the RSFSR, complained in 1983 that the Russian republic had compiled a comprehensive plan for developing small and medium-sized towns east of the Urals, but neither Gosplan nor the relevant central ministries were willing to cooperate in carrying it out (*Deviataia sessiia* 1983:66).

9. Both the Council of Minsters and Gosplan do, however, have "interbranch" commissions for examining the relevants parts of ministerial plans in key areas of the country such as Siberia and the Far East (Azovkin and Sheremet 1985). And individual ministries have some departments or glavki set up by region—though

each ministry follows its own regionalization scheme, making it difficult to co-ordinate territorial planning. For details about major ministry subdivisions, one useful source is *Moskva 1973*.

10. See, for example, remarks by Kirgiz premier K. D. Dikambaev to the June 1959 plenum (*Plenum TsK KPSS* 1959:701).

11. Instances of initiative from below include remarks by Kirgizia's first secretary, T. U. Usubaliev, proposing a major new effort to develop northeast Kirgizia's gold, wolfram, molybdenum, and other minerals, and to create a resort zone near Lake Issyk-Kul (*XXVI S"ezd* 1981: 1:268–72); by Turkmenia's D. Rasulov noting that republic planners had worked out proposals to develop mineral sites and viticulture to employ the rapidly growing pool of labor in Turkmenia (*XXV S"ezd* 1976: 1:309–13); and by Moldavia's I. I. Bodiul proposing that Moldavia should develop light, electronics, and instrument-building industries in order to take advantage of their low resource costs but highly labor-intensive operations (*XXIII S"ezd* 1966: 1:417–25).

12. Belorussia's Mazurov (*XXII S"ezd* 1961: 1:290–303) and the Ukraine's Scherbitskii (*XXIII S"ezd* 1966: 2:69–75) are among the examples.

13. The only exceptions were Karelia's O. V. Kuusinen and Lithuania's P. P. Grishkiavicius. Every other republic party boss (and in the RSFSR, premier) who spoke raised at least one appeal during his appearances.

14. At the Twentieth Congress, Brezhnev (*XX S"ezd* 1956: 1:213–20) advocated greater development of Kazakhstan's natural resources and argued that the Ministry of Ferrous and Nonferrous Metallurgy had underestimated Kazakhstan's potential; advocated better use of mineral by-products; asked for a caustic soda plant; noted that the Academy of Sciences, Ministry of Agriculture, and Institute of Agricultural Sciences should do more to recognize unique local circumstances in agriculture; and requested more funds for irrigation to solve Kazakhstan's water shortage.

15. By the time of the Twenty-Seventh Congress, an increasing number of appeals for energy had come to focus on developing atomic power plants—as one solution to the territorial imbalance between industry and population on one hand and energy resources on the other. Note the comments by Tataria's G. I. Usmanov (*Pravda* March 3, 1986, pp. 2–3); Krasnodar's I. K. Polozkov (*Pravda* March 1, 1986, p. 2); and Gorkii's Iu. I. Khristoradnov (*Pravda* March 4, 1986, p. 2).

16. In fact, the preoccupation with water supplies appeared as early as the Seventeenth Congress (*XVII S"ezd* 1934:436–39), when Kazakhstan's Isaev reminded his listeners that his region needed more investment in agriculture, and especially in irrigation and reclamation.

17. *XXIII S"ezd* 1966: 1:148–57; *XXV S"ezd* 1976: 1:137–44; *XXVI S"ezd* 1981: 1:122–29.

18. The available information on the Nineteenth Congress showed general trends, but was too limited to allow 1952 to be included in tables 3.3 and 3.4. The only copy of the stenographic report that I could find was an abridged version in English (*Current Soviet Policies* 1953). Nor was it possible to find sufficient biographical data to identify the regional and local officials who spoke.

19. Kazakhstan's D. A. Kunaev alluded to the "subjective, unfounded approach" that had recently characterized agricultural policy; Belorussia's P. Masherov noted the urgent necessity of correcting problems in the leadership of agriculture (*XXIII S"ezd* 1966: 1:148–57, 173–80).

20. Armenia's M. O. Muradian expressed concern to the Supreme Soviet (*Izvestiia* December 2, 1978, p. 5) over the draft 1979 plan and budget, and Georgia's D. L. Kartvelashvili (*Deviataia sessiia* 1983:103–9) registered complaints about the draft 1984 plan and budget.

21. Note the comments by RSFSR deputy premiers V. P. Orlov and V. I. Kazakov (*Deviataia sessiia* 1983:63–69, 136–41) and by Tadzhik delegate R. Nabiev (*Izvestiia* October 30, 1978:, pp. 5–6) to the Supreme Soviet.

22. See comments by the Ukraine's A. Kolomiets and Lithuania's R. I. Songaila and S. K. Grossu to the Supreme Soviet in 1983 (*Deviataia sessiia* 1983:131–36, 171–79).

23. These same issues go back even further on regional agendas: what appeals there were in Stalin's time focused largely on farm problems and the development of energy resources and minerals (*Current Soviet Policies* 1953), for the same reasons that later appeals focused on them. Although the share of funds channeled to republic and local governments was much more modest, the tax reforms of the 1930s had made governments outside Moscow dependent on the primary sectors and on agricultural and consumer goods for most of their revenues; and the administrative structure gave them a slightly larger role in these sectors than in other branches of the economy.

24. For a description of the process, see Maniushis (1978).

25. Apparently appeals also go to the Central Committee, but I could find no evidence of any direct request yielding more resources from the committee. Moscow city party chief B. N. Eltsin (*Pravda* February 27, 1986, pp. 2–3) has, however, lamented that the Central Committee spends too much of its time coping with economic bottlenecks, responding to problems raised by ministries and by leaders in the periphery.

26. These examples were culled by comparing the initial draft plans with the final versions adopted at the end of the party congresses. They include only the cases where a republic official stated a request and the request was subsequently incorporated into the plan directives. I did not count any other amendments even if they were geared to specific republics, since it was not clear whether any republic leader had asked for the change or even supported it.

27. See the speeches by Estonia's I. G. Kebin, Tadzhikistan's D. Rasulov, Belorussia's K. Mazurov, Turkmenia's B. Ovezov, and Moldavia's I. I. Bodiul (*XXII S"ezd* 1961: 1:290–303, 414–21, 438–45, 465–72)

28. Gosplan, the Council of Ministers, and the Ministry of Finance also review and apparently must agree to any budget changes approved by the Supreme Soviet. Judging from the procedures at other points in the plan-budget process, they most likely hold back a small reserve of funds to cover the Supreme Soviet's amendments.

29. But of course they also discount the appeals, since each request has most likely been fattened in anticipation of receiving only partial funding.

30. This was a major theme of the Twenty-Seventh Congress (and of party plenums earlier in the Gorbachev era), which called for more effective follow-through in the implementation of Politburo decisions. It was echoed by Tadzhikistan's new first secretary, K. Makhkamov (*Pravda* March 1, 1986, p. 4), who reminded his audience that the Politburo had passed a resolution in 1984 on the further development of Dushanbe—but some ministries had failed to comply with the Politburo's directives.

31. Thus, for example, Azerbaidzhan's S. G. Ragimov complained that the Ministry of Tractors and Agricultural Machinery evaded a Central Committee/Council of Ministers order to build cotton cultivators in Azerbaidzhan (*XX S"ezd* 1956:333–40). Kurgan oblast's G. F. Sizov noted that after the Council of Ministers resolved to build a textile complex in his oblast, Gosplan refused to go ahead with the project (*Zasedaniia* 1965:182–87). And Moscow's mayor V. F. Promyslov pointed out that Gosplan and the Ministry of Rail and Transport Construction had ignored a Council of Ministers decision to expand the Moscow metro (*Zasedaniia* 1975:136–41).

32. In the Lithuanian case cited above, the republic Council of Ministers had presented several requests for housing to Moscow while Lithuania's light industry was under expansion. However, the appeals brought a response only when the new plants were supposed to be operating but could not attract workers (Maniushis 1978).

33. The five-million-ruble grant equaled 3 percent of the Lithuanian republic budget for industrial development in 1973 (*Gosbiudzhet* 1976:155).

4. POLITICS, REGIONAL COMPETITION, AND BUDGET POLICIES

1. Rykov (*XV S"ezd* 1928:769–70) complained that the draft was was far too ambitious in its goals, since the Sovnarkom and Council of Labor and Defense (STO) sat for whole days trying to find additional funds just to raise investment on a given project by a single percentage point. And he noted too that the draft plan did not have a clearly defined regional component, since it gave all-union figures but none by region.

2. Some local leaders also complained about the opposite problem. Arkhangel's Bergavinov (*XV S"ezd* 1928:815–16) reported that forestry development in his region was being slighted in central appropriations, because, he suggested, the All-Union Lumber Trust was situated in Arkhangel and not in Moscow.

3. This and other figures for the 1930s are in old rubles.

4. A request which the Central Finance Commissariat cut back by over 50 percent (A. G. Zverev, *Second Session* 1938:363–64).

5. This is not to say that no additional funds were ever granted. In the deliberations over the 1938 budget, the Supreme Soviet did dole out marginal amounts to the Georgian, Armenian, Turkmen, and Tadzhik SSRs (*Second Session* 1938:16–17).

6. Note Molotov's comments to the Seventeenth Congress (*XVII S"ezd* 1934:648–50).

7. Uzbekistan's N. A. Mukhitdinov referred to proposals for energy development and irrigation; Brezhnev, as Kazakh first secretary, described proposals to develop iron ore and phosphates; Azerbaidzhan's I. D. Mustafaev called for an oil-shale processing plant (*XX S"ezd* 1956: 1:180–86, 213–20, 538–44).

8. See, for example, Tulebaev (1973); Iskanderov (1969); Zhikhareva (1979); Organov, Struev, Chernyshev, and Maniakhin (*XX S"ezd* 1956: 1:366–73, 381–87, 2:206–12.)

9. See work by Pavlenko (1983), Azovkin and Sheremet (1985), and Mukoed (1981), and the complaints to the Twenty-Sixth Congress by Komi ASSR first secretary, I. P. Morozov (*XXVI S"ezd* 1981: 3:10–14); and to the Twenty-Seventh Congress by Krasnoiarsk's P. S. Fedirko, Kazakhstan's N. A. Nazarbaev, and Yakutia's Iu. N. Prokop'ev (*Pravda* March 5, 1986, pp. 2–5).

10. For a sample of locational principles, see work by Gosplan's Chistiakov and Morozov (1971); and by Nekrasov (1975).

11. Note the complaints about transportation expenses by Sverdlovsk oblast first secretary K. K. Nikolaev (*XXIII S"ezd* 1966: 1:332–38) and by Belorussian economist V. Udovenko (1983).

12. For example, V. I. Dolgikh's defense of eastern development, while serving as first secretary in Krasnoiarsk krai (*XXIV S"ezd* 1971: 1:229–36); Turkmenian first secretary S. A. Niiazov's similar arguments at the Twenty-Seventh Congress (*Pravda* March 2, 1986, p. 5); and Chistiakov and Morozov's (1971) discussion of on-site raw materials costs.

13. And each one seems to carry a different weight at different times. Koropeckyj (1967) suggests that priorities shifted in 1927 from attempts at a proportional allocation of industry to efforts to stress defense and efficiency, thus moving industrial development eastward; and priorities shifted again in 1939 to encourage self-sufficiency and cut transport costs. The Eighteenth Congress that year (*XVIII S"ezd* 1939:660) underscored complex development of different regions, and put special emphasis on securing local fuels, minerals, and consumer goods so as to reduce dependency on long hauls.

14. At party congresses, it appears to be spokesmen from border regions who use defense needs to legitimize their requests. In 1986, for example, Primorskii krai's D. N. Gagarov referred to his area's vulnerability and need for economic reinforcement in the face of Western hostility; and as noted in chapter 1, Turkmeniia's S. A. Niiazov complained that inadequate water supplies would threaten the success of the Food Program—which had serious implications for a distant border region (*Pravda* March 2, 1986, pp. 4–5).

15. Regional and even central leaders sometimes refer to the "internal departmentalism" of Gosplan and central ministries. Leningrad's I. V. Spiridonov summed up the problem at the Twenty-First Congress (*XXI S"ezd* 1959:243–50)—"This is planning? This is chaos!" And note the same frustruations expressed in Premier N. Ryzhkov's address to the Twenty-Seventh Congress (*Pravda* March 4, 1986:2).

16. These three republics also had the highest rate of economic growth during 1960–75 (Koropeckyj 1981:96–97).

17. Since the dependent variable is the percentage increase in investment for

each year, a significant constant term indicates that the rate of increase was very similar from year to year and from region to region.

18. This would explain the drop in the percentage of variance explained (R^2) by the models in table 4.3 from Khrushchev to Brezhnev: as the Brezhnev era unfolded, average increases in investment for each region grew smaller and also less stable.

19. As noted above, efforts to contain large city growth have a long and not totally successful history. Plan directives as far back as 1939 (XVIII S"ezd 1939) urged the same limits, and directives in the intervening years have used almost identical language (e.g., *Pravda* April 11, 1971, pp. 1–6).

20. However, Siberia's share of oil, gas, and coal production did increase dramatically. According to Shniper (1980:75), Siberia accounted for negligible amounts of the country's oil and gas production, and 23.1 percent of its coal output in 1960; but by 1975, East and West Siberia produced 30.1 percent of the oil, 13.3 percent of the gas, and 29.0 percent of the coal.

21. Note, however, that noncapital appropriations for enlightenment and health are determined largely on the basis of norms for specific line-items (e.g., a certain amount per day per patient for food, medicine, and linens, a set amount per pupil or school for food and supplies in the schools, a fixed amount for staff). Thus if we were to compare expenditures per pupil in primary schools or per patient in general practice clinics, we would find even less variation than is evident in figure 4.1. And the variations that do arise stem largely from a different mix of services (different types of hospitals and clinics, and different types of schools, have different norms) and from differential rates of construction and repair of facilities.

5. LOCAL AGENDAS AND LOCAL BUDGETS

1. Note that Moscow and Leningrad are not formally subordinate to the RSFSR; but many of their economic and social programs must still be coordinated with republic organs.

2. Pavlenko (1983) reports that the reform, designed with the best of intentions, was never fully implemented. Similar conclusions are offered by Trehub (1985) and Teague (1986).

3. Two economists from Gosplan RSFSR suggest that part of the reason lies with the local suggestions themselves: since local planners often lack data or guidelines on developing complex plans, they "cannot analyze the process of complex local development very deeply" and have little opportunity to come up with well-documented, well-argued proposals (Singur and Shtulberg 1978). The authors also note that the RSFSR has begun to encourage local officials to submit proposals and appeals further in advance, in order to provide more careful consideration of local needs.

4. By one estimate (Revaikin and Troshina 1985:53), only 25 percent of the housing in Amur oblast belonged to the local soviets in 1980; in Yakutia, the figure was 9 percent.

5. Apparently some republics were allowed to adopt an experiment in 1981 whereby republic Councils of Ministers were accorded greater power to coordinate funds to local governments for construction in the nonproductive sphere (Azovkin and Sheremet 1985). But I was unable to find any assessment of the results.

6. Kutafin (1980:223) reports that in Saratov, with a population of 850,000, the city planning commission (Gorplan) has a staff of only eleven—fewer workers than in 1952, when the city had only 470,000 residents.

7. According to Azovkin and Sheremet (1985), this has created a proliferation of only partially integrated plans in many localities, with separate documents for construction materials, education, health care, etc.

8. As recorded in *Moskva 1973*.

9. In 1980, the turnover tax and taxes/fees on agriculture, trade, and light industries accounted for 48 percent of local budget revenues (*Gosbiudzhet* 1982:70–71).

10. The one exception is Rostov oblast, which ranked fifth in population in 1981, but did not have speakers on the podium in 1961 or 1971.

11. These mixed criteria do not seem to include rewarding the general secretary's old "home" region. Under Brezhnev, for example, Dnepropetrovsk was represented on the podium at only two of four congresses (in 1966 and 1976); and under Gorbachev, Stavropol' krai had no speaker on the agenda for the Twenty-Seventh Congress.

12. El'tsin did, however, lobby energetically during his tenure as first secretary of Sverdlovsk oblast. At the Twenty-Sixth Congress, he suggested that the 387 different construction agencies in Sverdlovsk, which were then subject to 36 different ministries and organizations, be amalgamated and put under local jurisdiction. He also advocated the same solution for wood and timber enterprises, and went on the emphasize the need for complex development and infrastructure to balance out the growth of Sverdlovsk's heavy industry. (*XXVI S"ezd* 1981: 1:230–35)

13. The cases presented include all the overlaps for all the congresses since 1956. There were no instances of overlapping requests in 1966 or 1971, nor were there any for republics outside the RSFSR and Ukraine.

14. Thus, for example, local appeals are a major part of the deliberations of republic central committees and supreme soviets. See *Zasedaniia Verkhovnogo Soveta Kirgizskoi SSR* (1978), *Zasedaniia Verkhovnogo Soveta Armianskoi SSR* (1960); *Odinnatsadtaia sessiia Verkhovnogo Soveta Belorusskoi SSR* (1979).

15. Presumably this rule does not hold for Moscow or Leningrad, or for the other oblasti whose plans are approved directly by the center (see chapter 3).

16. As noted, except for the 1983 data on the Ukraine, these Soviet investment figures do not include investment by collective farms, which represents a sizable component of allocations in the most backward areas. If these data were included, the degree of intraregional inequality would be lower, and the coefficients of variation, smaller than those reported.

17. The data are sketchy, since city statistical handbooks appear so sporadically outside Moscow and Leningrad, and since investment data are scarcer still. But a

comparison of total investment per capita for Baku, Tbilisi, Erevan, Leningrad, Moscow, and Kiev suggests some convergence in investment levels at least up through the mid–1960s. The following data are based on an index of 100, representing Baku:

	1950	1955	1960	1965
Baku	100	100	100	100
Erevan			74.4	93.2
Kiev	41.0	76.3	129.1	107.3
Leningrad	32.3	52.4	85.6	96.8
Moscow				120.2
Tbilisi	18.6	44.4	67.8	75.0

These data are not corrected for price changes or for differences in coverage from one city or one year to another, and should be taken only as rough indicators of the trend in big city investment. Data on Kiev are for 1951 rather than 1950 and for 1964 rather than 1965; on Moscow, for 1966 rather than 1965; and on Leningrad, for 1961 rather than 1960. Sources are:
Baku—*Baku v tsifrakh* (1967):7, 39.
Erevan—*Erevan k 50-letiiu* (1967):27, 67.
Kiev—*Kiiv v tsifrakh* (1966):7, 53.
Leningrad, 1950–55—*Narkhoz Leningrada* (1957):7, 61.
Moscow—*Moskva v tsifrakh* (1967):13, 41.
Tbilisi—*Tbilisi k 40-letiiu* (1961):15, 44.

6. RETHINKING POLITICS BELOW THE NATIONAL LEVEL

1. Central agencies can also respond by reallocating funds in the course of the year, providing a temporary cure but also prompting another appeal from the "donor" region.

2. Such violations might, of course, be ordered by the Politburo or secretariat, leaving the ministries and Gosplan to become the scapegoats. They might also be unavoidable by-products of orders from above that preempt resources for higher priority projects. But the few ex-employees of ministries and of Gosplan whom I have been able to interview confirm that their organizations constantly reallocated funds themselves.

3. Kushnirsky (1982:33) estimates that in 1970, the 35,000 construction projects under way were three times more than the capacity of the Soviet economy.

4. Nove (1983) also suggests other sources of overinvestment: preoccupation with large and spectacular projects without a realistic estimate of maintenance or repair costs; a bias in central planning for bigger but fewer projects to cut the administrative problems of dealing with many smaller objects; a lack of unambiguous criteria for making investment decisions; and bureaucratic competition for funds.

5. But this approach is not without its risks: given authorization from above, regional or local authorities may find their "reserves" by reprogramming funds away from other central priorities.

6. For careful and persuasive assessments of the impacts, see McAuley (1979), Gillulla (1979, 1981) and Koropeckyj (1981).

7. This does not, of course, deny that natives and imports may split dramatically on other, noneconomic issues, such as affirmative action for the local population or language use.

BIBLIOGRAPHY

Abouchar, Alan. 1979. "Investment at Regional Level: Industrial and Consumer." In NATO Economics Directorate and Information Directorate, eds., *Regional Development in the USSR: Trends and Prospects*. Newtonville, MA: Oriental Research Partners.

Advisory Commission on Intergovernmental Relations (ACIR). 1981. *Studies in Comparative Federalism: Australia, Canada, the United States, and West Germany*. Washington.

Aiushiev, A. D. and V. P. Ivanitskii. 1978. "Istochniki finansirovania kapitalovlozheniia." *Finansy SSSR* no. 6, pp. 36–39.

Alampiev, P. M. 1960. "Problems of General Regionalization at the Present Stage." *Soviet Geography: Review and Translation* 1:3–16.

Allakhverdian, D. A. 1976. *Finansovo-kreditnyi mekhanizm razvitogo sotsializma*. Moscow: Finansy.

Allakhverdian, D. A. et al. 1966. *Soviet Financial System*. Moscow: Progress.

Al'peravichus, S. E. 1971. *Gosudarstvenno-pravovye osnovy predstavitel'stva soiuznykh respublik v organakh soiuza SSSR*. Autoreferat cand. diss. Moscow: Vsesoiuznyi Nauchno-Issledovatel'skii Institut Sovetskogo Zakonodatel'stva.

Armstrong, John. 1959. *The Soviet Bureaucratic Elite*. New York: Praeger.

Arnold, R. Douglas. 1979. *Congress and the Bureaucracy*. New Haven: Yale University Press.

Ashford, Douglas. 1977. "Are Britain and France 'Unitary'?" *Comparative Politics* 9(4):483–99.

—— 1979. "Territorial Politics and Equality: Decentralization and the Modern State." *Political Studies* 27(1):71–83.

—— 1981. *British Dogmatism and French Pragmatism: Central-Local Policy-Making in the Welfare State*. London: Allen and Unwin.

Aspaturian, Vernon. 1950. "Theory and Practice of Soviet Federalism." *Journal of Politics* 12(1):20–51.

Astakhov, A. A. 1972. *Kapital'noe vlozhenie v vysshuiu shkolu.* Moscow.

Avetisian, I. A. 1979. *Voprosy territorial'nogo finansovogo planirovaniia.* Erevan: Izd-vo Erevanskogo Universiteta.

Azovkin, I. A. and K. F. Sheremet. 1985. *Sovety narodnykh deputatov i ekonomika.* Moscow: Nauka.

Bagdasarian, A. M. 1975. *Pod'em i vyravnivanie urovnei ekonomicheskogo razvitiia soiuznykh respublik.* Moscow: Vysshaia shkola.

Bahl, Roy. 1984. *Financing State and Local Government in the 1980s.* New York: Oxford University Press.

Bahry, Donna. 1980. "Measuring Communist Priorities: Budgets, Investment, and the Problem of Equivalence." *Comparative Political Studies* 13(3):267–92.

Bahry, Donna and Carol Nechemias. 1981. "Half Full or Half Empty: The Debate Over Soviet Regional Equality." *Slavic Review* 40(3):366–83.

Baianov, E. B. 1977. *Upravlenie promyshlennost'iu respublikanskogo podchineniia.* Alma-ata: Nauka.

Baiseitov, R. S. 1980. "Finorgany Kazakhstana v bor'be za mobilizatsiiu reservov sotsialisticheskoi ekonomiki." *Finansy SSSR* no. 8, pp. 13–19.

Baku v tsifrakh. 1967. Baku: TsSU g. Baku.

Bandera, V. N. and Z L. Melnyk, eds. 1973. *The Soviet Economy in Regional Perspective.* New York: Praeger.

Becquart-Leclercq, J. 1977. "Relational Power and Center-Periphery Linkages in French Local Politics." *Sociology and Sociological Research* 62:21–42.

Beer, Samuel. 1976. "The Adoption of General Revenue Sharing: A Case Study in Public Sector Politics." *Public Policy* 24(2):127–95.

Bell, Michael and Paul Lande. 1982. *Regional Dimensions of Industrial Policy.* Lexington, MA: Lexington Books.

Bennett, R. J. 1980. *The Geography of Public Finance: Welfare Under Fiscal Federalism and Local Government Finance.* New York: Methuen.

Bergson, Abram. 1964. *The Economics of Soviet Planning.* New Haven: Yale.

Bescherevnykh, V. V. 1960. *Razvitie sovetskogo biudzhetnogo prava.* Moscow: Izd-vo Moskovskogo Universiteta.

—— 1976. *Kompetentsiia Soiuza SSR v oblasti biudzheta*. Moscow: Iuridicheskaia literatura.

Bialer, Seweryn. 1980. *Stalin's Successors*. New York: Cambridge University Press.

Biddulph, Howard. 1983. "Local Interest Articulation at CPSU Congresses." *World Politics* 36(1):28–52.

Bielasiak, Jack. 1980. "Policy Choices and Regional Equality Among Soviet Republics." *American Political Science Review* 74(2):

Birman, Igor. 1978. "From the Achieved Level." *Soviet Studies* 30(2):153–73.

—— 1982. *Secret Incomes of the Soviet State Budget*. The Hague: Martinus Nijhoff.

Bisher, I. D. 1973. "Ministerstva soiuznykh respublik: Nazrevshie problemy." *Sovetskoe gosudarstvo i pravo* no. 5, pp. 28–35.

Bobrovnikov, A. A., ed. 1977. *Gosudarstvennyi biudzhet rossiiskoi federatsii za 60 let sovetskoi vlasti*. Moscow: Finansy.

Bogalenko, V. A., S. I. Ishchuk, and A. V. Stepanenko. 1980. *Kompleksnoe planirovanie sotsial'no-ekonomicheskogo razvitiia goroda*. Kiev: Izd-vo Vishcha shkola.

Borshchevshii, L. M. 1969. "Peredacha prav vyshestoiashchikh organov upravleniia nizhestoiashchim." *Sovetskoe gosudarstvo i pravo*, no. 8, pp. 58–63.

Brand, Jack. 1976. "Reforming Local Government: Sweden and England Compared." In Richard Rose, ed., *The Dynamics of Public Policy*. Beverly Hills: Sage.

Break, George F. 1980. *Financing Government in a Federal System*. Washington: Brookings.

Breslauer, George. 1982. *Khrushchev and Brezhnev as Leaders: Building Authority in Soviet Politics*. London: Allen and Unwin.

—— 1984. "Is There A Generation Gap in the Soviet Political Establishment? Demand Articulation by RSFSR Provinicial Party First Secretaries." *Soviet Studies* 36(1):1–25.

Brezhnev, L. I. 1972. *The Fiftieth Anniversary of the Union of Soviet Socialist Republics*. Moscow: Novosti.

—— 1976. In *Materialy XXV S"ezda KPSS*. Moscow.

Brzezinski, Zbigniew and Samuel P. Huntington. 1965. *Political Power: USA/USSR*. New York: Viking.

Buchanan, James M. 1950. "Federalism and Fiscal Equity." *American Economic Review* 40(4):583–97.

—— 1952. "Federal Grants and Resource Allocation." *Journal of Political Economy* 40:208–17.

Bulganin, N. A. 1956. *Report to the 20th Congress of the CPSU on the Directives for the Sixth Five-Year Plan, 1956–60.* Moscow.

Bunce, Valerie. 1979. "Leadership Succession and Policy Innovation in the Soviet Republics." *Comparative Politics* 11(4):379–402.

Bykovskii, D. Ia., and E. I. Koliushin. 1982. *Mestnye sovety i planirovanie kompleksnogo razvitiia territorii.* Moscow: Iuridicheskaia literatura.

Campbell, Robert. 1966. *Soviet Economic Power.* 2d ed. New York: Houghton Mifflin.

—— 1978. "Economic Reform and Adaptation of the CPSU." In Karl Ryavec, ed., *Soviet Society and the Communist Party.* Amherst: University of Massachusetts Press.

Catsambas, Thanos. 1978. *Regional Impacts of Federal Fiscal Policies: Theory and Estimation of Economic Incidence.* Lexington, MA: Lexington Books.

Cattell, David. 1964. "Local Government and the Sovnarkhoz Reform in the USSR." *Soviet Studies* 15(4):430–42.

—— 1968. *Leningrad: A Case Study of Soviet Urban Government.* New York: Praeger.

—— 1983. "Local Government and the Provision of Consumer Goods and Services." In Everett M. Jacobs, ed., *Soviet Local Politics and Government,* pp. 172–85. London: Allen and Unwin.

Cherkashin, L. V. 1969. *Planirovanie kul'turnogo stroitel'stva.* Moscow: Ekonomika.

Chernenko, K. U. 1984. "Sixty Years of Fraternal Friendship of Nationalities." In *Izbrannye rechi i stat'i,* pp. 558–73. Moscow: Izd-vo politicheskoi literaturi.

Chistiakov, E. G. 1982. *Metody sochetaniia otraslevogo i territorial'nogo planirovaniia.* Moscow: Nauka.

Chistiakov, M. I. and P. T. Morozov 1971. *Planirovanie v SSSR.* Moscow: Ekonomika.

Cohen, Stephen, Alexander Rabinowich, and Robert Sharlet, eds. 1980. *The Soviet Union Since Stalin.* Bloomington: Indiana University Press.

Commission of the European Communities, Directorate-General for Economic and Financial Affairs. 1977. *Report of the Study Group on the Role of Public Finance in European Integration.* Brussels.

Current Soviet Leaders. A Cumulative Guide to Officials and Notables in the USSR. Serial. Oakville, Ontario: Mosaic Press.

Current Soviet Policies: The Documentary Record of the Nineteenth Communist Party Congress and the Reorganization After Stalin's Death. 1953. New York: Praeger.

Darkov, G. V. and G. I. Maksimov. 1969. *Finansovaia statistika.* Moscow: Finansy.

Davies, R. W. 1958a. *The Development of the Soviet Budgetary System.* Cambridge: Cambridge University Press.

—— 1958b. "The Decentralization of Industry: Some Notes on the Background." *Soviet Studies* 9(4):353–67.

—— 1974. "A Note on Defense Aspects of the Ural-Kuznetsk Combine." *Soviet Studies* 26(2):272–73.

Dellenbrant, Jan Ake. 1980. *Soviet Regional Policy.* Stockholm: Almqvist and Wiksell.

Deputaty Verkhovnogo Soveta SSSR. 1959, 1963, 1967, 1970, 1979. Moscow: Izdanie Verkhovnogo Soveta SSSR.

Derthick, Martha. 1974. *Between State and Nation.* Washington: Brookings.

Derzhavin, V. 1986. "Kakovy vozmozhnosti gorodskogo soveta." *Sovety narodnykh deputatov* no. 4, pp. 44–50.

Deviataia sessiia Verkhovnogo Soveta SSSR. 10-yi sozyv. Stenograficheskii otchet. 1983. Moscow: Izdanie Verkhovnogo Soveta SSSR.

D'iachenko, V. P. 1957. "Sovetskaia sistema finansov i kredita v bor'be za sotsialisticheskoe pereustroistvo ekonomiki i postroenie kommunizma v SSSR." In L. M. Gatovskii, ed., *Sovetskaia sotsialisticheskaia ekonomika, 1917–1957.* Moscow: Politicheskaia literatura.

—— 1978. *Istoriia finansov SSSR 1917–1950.* Moscow: Nauka.

Diamant, Alfred. 1981. "Bureaucracy and Public Policy in Neocorporatist Settings." *Comparative Politics* 14:101–24.

Dienes, Leslie. 1971. "Issues in Soviet Energy Policy and Conflicts over Fuel Costs in Regional Development." *Soviet Studies* 23:26–58.

—— 1972. "Investment Priorities in Soviet Regions." *Annals of the Association of American Geographers* 62:437–54.

—— 1982. "The Development of Siberian Regions: Economic Profiles, Income Flows, and Strategies for Growth." *Soviet Geography: Review and Translation* 23:205–44.

210   BIBLIOGRAPHY

—— 1983. "Regional Economic Development." In Abram Bergson and Herbert Levine, eds., *The Soviet Economy: Toward the Year 2000*, pp. 218–68. Boston: Allen and Unwin.

Dmitriev, Iv. and A. Zenkovich. 1980. "Territorial'nye aspekty kompleksnogo plana ekonomicheskogo i sotsial'nogo razvitiia." *Voprosy ekonomiki* no. 1, pp. 71–77.

Dolotov, K. 1982. "Mestnaia promyshlennost' i potrebnosti naseleniia." *Planovoe khoziaistvo* no. 12, pp. 35–40.

Dosymbekov, S. N. 1971. "Uchastie soiuznykh respublik v upravlenii promyshlennost'iu soiuznogo podchineniia." *Sovetskoe gosudarstvo i pravo* no. 2, pp. 62–69.

—— 1974. *Problemy gosudarstvennogo upravleniia promyshlennost'iu v soiuznoi respublike.* Moscow: Nauka.

Dyker, David. 1970. "Industrial Location in the Tadzhik Republic." *Soviet Studies* 21:485–506.

—— 1983. *The Process of Investment in the Soviet Union.* Cambridge: Cambridge University Press.

Emelianov, A. S., ed. 1976. *Sovershenstvovanie territorial'nogo planirovaniia v soiuznoi respublike.* Moscow: Ekonomika.

Erevan k 50-letiiu Velikogo Oktiabria. 1967. Erevan: TsSU g. Erevana.

Ermakov, V. 1980. "Vliianie mestnykh planovykh organov na formirovanii planov ekonomicheskogo i sotsial'nogo razvitiia." *Planovoe khoziaistvo* no. 12, pp. 89–93.

Evdokimov, V. 1962. *Finansirovanie ministerstv, vedomstv, i sovnarkhozov.* Moscow: Gosfinizdat.

—— 1974. *Kontrol' za ispolneniem gosudarstvennogo biudzheta SSSR.* Moscow: Finansy.

Evstigneev, V. P. 1976. "The Location of Metal-Intensive and Labor-Intensive Industries in the Eastern Regions." *Soviet Geography: Review and Translation* 17(5):314–24.

—— 1985. *Effektivnost' razmeshcheniia obshchestvennogo proizvodstva. Metodologiia i metodika.* Moscow: Nauka.

Ezhegodnik Bol'shoi Sovetskoi Entsiklopedii. Annual. Moscow: Sovetskaia entsiklopediia.

Fainsod, Merle. 1958. *Smolensk Under Soviet Rule.* Cambridge, MA: Harvard University Press.

—— 1963. *How Russia Is Ruled.* Cambridge, MA: Harvard University Press.

Fedorenko, N. P. 1979. *Nekotorye voprosy teorii i praktiki planirovaniia i upravleniia.* Moscow: Nauka.

—— 1984. "O putiakh razvitiia ekonomiko-matematicheskogo napravleniia sovetskoi ekonomicheskoi nauki." *Ekonomika i matematicheskie metody* 20:18–27.

Filimonov, B. I. 1975. "Sovershenstvovanie sostavleniia mestnykh biudzhetov." *Finansy SSSR* no. 11, pp. 39–44.

Frank, Peter. 1974. "Constructing a Classified Ranking of CPSU Obkoms." *British Journal of Political Science* 4:217–30.

Frears, J. R. 1983. "The Decentralization Reform in France." *Parliamentary Affairs* 36(2):56–66.

Gallik, Daniel, Czestmir Jesina, and Stephen Rapawy. 1968. *The Soviet Financial System.* International Population Statistics Reports, Series P-90, no. 23. Washington: U.S. Bureau of the Census, Foreign Demographic Analysis Division.

Gillulla, James. 1979. "The Economic Interdependence of Soviet Republics." In U.S. Congress, Joint Economic Committee, *Soviet Economy in a Time of Change* 1:618–55. Washington.

—— 1981. "The Growth and Structure of Fixed Capital." In I. S. Koropeckyj and Gertrude Schroeder, eds., *Economics of Soviet Regions*, pp. 157–96. New York: Praeger.

Goss, Carol F. 1973. "Military Committee Membership and Defense-Related Benefits in the House of Representatives." *Western Political Quarterly* 25(2):215–33.

Gosudarstvennyi biudzhety soiuznykh respublik. Statisticheskii sbornik. 1957. Moscow: Gosfinizdat.

Gosudarstvennyi biudzhet SSSR i biudzhety soiuznykh respublik. Statisticheskii sbornik. 1962. Moscow: Gosfinizdat.

Gosudarstvennyi biudzhet SSSR i biudzhety soiuznykh respublik, 1961–1965 gg. Statisticheskii sbornik. 1966. Moscow: Finansy.

Gosudarstvennyi biudzhet SSSR i biudzhety soiuznykh respublik. 1966–1970 gg. Statisticheskii sbornik. 1972. Moscow: Finansy.

Gosudarstvennyi biudzhet SSSR i biudzhety soiuznykh respublik. 1971–1975 gg. Statisticheskii sbornik. 1976. Moscow: Finansy.

Gosudarstvennyi biudzhet SSSR i biudzhety soiuznykh respublik. 1976–1980 gg. Statisticheskii sbornik. 1982. Moscow: Finansy i statistika.

Gosudarstvennyi piatiletnyi plan razvitiia narodnogo khoziaistva SSSR na 1971–1975 gody. 1972. Moscow: Izd-vo politicheskoi literatury.

Gourevitch, Peter. 1977. "The Reform of Local Government: A Political Analysis." *Comparative Politics* 10(1):69–88.

Granberg, A. G. 1984. "The Economic Interaction of Soviet Republics." *Problems of Economics* 26:3–25. Translated from: "Ekonomicheskoe vzaimodeistvie sovetskikh respublik," *Ekonomika i organizatsiaa promyshlennogo proizvodstva* (1982) no. 12, pp. 3–37.

—— 1986. "Structural Changes and Intensification in Siberian Industry." *Problems of Economics* 29(3):39–60.

Grant, Wyn. 1982. *The Political Economy of Industrial Policy.* London: Butterworth's.

Grebnev, L. 1986. "The Application of Contractual Relationships in the Production-Planning System." *Problems of Economics* 29(4):18–31. Translated from "Primenenie dogovornykh otnoshenii v sisteme planirovaniia proizvodstva." *Voprosy ekonomiki* (1985) no. 11, pp. 3–10.

Grin'ko, G. T. 1936. *The Five-Year Plan of the Soviet Union.* New York: International Publishers.

Grodzins, Morton. 1972. "The Federal System." In Peter Woll, ed., *American Government: Readings and Cases.* Boston: Little Brown.

Grossman, Gregory. 1963. "Notes for a Theory of the Command Economy." *Soviet Studies* 15:101–15.

Gulian, P. V. 1982. *Latvia v sisteme narodnogo khoziaistva SSSR.* 2d edition. Riga: Zinatne.

Gustafson, Thane. 1981. *Reform in Soviet Politics: The Lessons of Recent Policies on Land and Water.* New York: Cambridge University Press.

Hahn, Werner G. 1972. *The Politics of Soviet Agriculture.* Baltimore: Johns Hopkins University Press.

Haider, Donald. 1974. *When Governments Come to Washington: Governors, Mayors, and Inter-Governmental Lobbying.* New York: Free Press.

Hale, George E. and Marian Leif Palley. 1979. "Federal Grants to the States: Who Governs?" *Administration and Society* 11:3–26.

—— 1981. *The Politics of Federal Grants.* Washington: Congressional Quarterly Press.

Hall, John Stuart. 1985. "Local Implementation of National Domestic Policy in the 1980s: The Bottom Line." Paper presented to the APSA, New Orleans, 1985.

Hamilton, F. E. Ian. 1970. "Aspects of Spatial Behavior in Planned Economies." *Papers of the Regional Science Association* 25:83–105.

Hanf, Kenneth and Fritz W. Scharpf, eds. 1978. *Interorganizational Policy*

Making: Limits to Coordination and Central Control. Sage Modern Politics Series, no. 1. Beverly Hills: Sage.

Heclo, Hugh and Aaron Wildavsky. 1974. *The Private Government of Public Money*. Berkeley: University of California Press.

Hill, Ronald J. 1977. *Soviet Political Elites: The Case of Tiraspol*. London: Martin Robertson.

—— 1983. "The Development of Soviet Local Government Since Stalin's Death." In Everett Jacobs, ed., *Soviet Local Politics and Government*, pp. 18–33. London: Allen and Unwin.

Hodnett, Grey. 1975. "Succession Contingencies in the Soviet Union," *Problems of Communism* 24(2):1–21.

Hodnett, Grey and Val Ogareff. 1973. *Leaders of the Soviet Republics*. Canberra: Australian National University.

Hoffman, Erik P. 1980. "Changing Soviet Perspectives on Leadership and Administration." In Stephen Cohen, Alexander Rabinowich, and Robert Sharlet, eds., *The Soviet Union Since Stalin*, pp. 71–92. Bloomington: Indiana University Press.

Holubnychy, Vsevolod. 1965. "Introduction." In Z. L. Melnyk, *Soviet Capital Formation: Ukraine, 1928/29–1932*. Munich: Ukrainian Free University Press.

—— 1975. "Teleology of the Macroregions in the Soviet Union's Long Range Plans, 1920–90." In Andrew Burghart, ed., *Development Regions in the Soviet Union, Eastern Europe, and Canada*, pp. 82–150. New York: Praeger.

Holzman, Franklyn D. 1955. *Soviet Taxation*. Cambridge, MA: Harvard University Press.

—— 1975. *Financial Checks on Soviet Defense Expenditures*. Lexington, MA: Lexington Books.

Hoover, Edgar M. 1948. *The Location of Economic Activity*. New York: McGraw-Hill.

Hough, Jerry F. 1969. *The Soviet Prefects: The Role of Local Party Organs in Industrial Decision-Making*. Cambridge, MA: Harvard University Press.

—— 1971. "The Party Apparatchiki." In H. Gordon Skilling and Franklyn Griffiths, eds., *Interest Groups in Soviet Politics*, pp. 47–92. Princeton: Princeton University Press.

Hough, Jerry and Merle Fainsod. 1979. *How the Soviet Union Is Governed*. Cambridge, MA: Harvard University Press.

Hutchings, Raymond. 1983. *The Soviet Budget*. Albany: State University of New York Press.

Huzinec, George. 1977. "A Reexamination of Soviet Industrial Location Theory." *The Professional Geographer* 29:259–65.

Il'in, I. K. 1976. "Peredacha predpriiatii, organizatsii, i uchrezhdenii." *Sovetskoe gosudarstvo i pravo* no. 4, pp. 50–57.

Il'nitskii, V. 1969. "Rabota oblfinotdela v novykh usloviiakh." *Finansy SSSR* no. 1, pp. 20–23.

Ingram, Helen. 1977. "Policy Implementation through Bargaining: The Case of Federal Grants-in-Aid." *Public Policy* 25:499–526.

Iskanderov, I. 1969. *Problemy razvitiia tekstil'noi promyshlennosti v Uzbekistane*. Tashkent: Fan.

Iusifov, F. G. 1986. "Ob ukreplenii dokhodnoi bazy mestnykh biudzhetov." *Finansy SSSR* no. 7, pp. 38–40.

Jackson, Marvin R. 1971. "Information and Incentives in Planning Soviet Investment Projects." *Soviet Studies* 23(1):3–25.

Jacobs, Everett M., ed. 1983. *Soviet Local Politics and Government*. London: Allen and Unwin.

Johnson, Nevil. 1983. *State Government in the Federal Republic of Germany: The Executive at Work*. 2d ed. Oxford: Pergamon.

Jones, Ellen. 1981. "Evaluating Levels of Centralization in the Soviet Administrative System." Paper presented to the Annual Meeting of the AAASS,

—— 1984. "Committee Decision Making in the Soviet Union." *World Politics* 36(2):165–88.

Kalinin, N. G. 1973. *Organizatsiia upravleniia v sisteme ministerstva*. Moscow: Izd-vo Moskovskogo Universiteta.

Kaplan, Norman. 1951. *Capital Investment in the Soviet Union, 1924–1951*. RAND Research Memorandum RM-735. Santa Monica: RAND.

Katsuk, M. and N. Onipko. 1961. "Struggle Against Localism." *Current Digest of the Soviet Press* 13(2):30–31. Translated from *Sotsialisticheskaia zakonnost'* (1960) no. 11, pp. 47–50.

Kazakov, S. 1982. *Metodologicheskie voprosy planirovaniia v soiuznoi respublike*. Frunze: Ylym.

Kazankova, K. A., V. P. Ignamushkin, and V. I. Ukin. 1971. *Finansy ministerstv i ob"edinenii v novykh usloviiakh khoziaistvovaniia*. Moscow: Finansy.

Kazanskii, N. N. and B. S. Khorev. 1976. "Problems of Economic Regionalization at the Present Stage." *Soviet Geography: Review and Translation* 17:637–46. Translated from *Izvestiia Akademii Nauk, seria geograficheskaia* (1975) no. 4, pp. 10–19.

Kee, Woo Sik. 1977. "Fiscal Decentralization and Economic Development." *Public Finance Quarterly* 5(1):79–97.

Kellerman, B. G., and L. Ia. Osipovich. 1983. "Problemy upravleniia otraslevymi finansami v soiuzno-respublikanskom ministerstve." *Finansy SSSR* no. 3, pp. 18–22.

Kesselman, Mark. 1974. "Research Perspectives in Comparative Local Politics: Pitfalls, Prospects, and Notes on the French Case." In Terry N. Clark, ed., *Comparative Community Politics.* New Jersey: Halsted.

Ketebaev, K. K. 1986. "Nekotorie voprosy sostavleniia finansovogo balansa respubliki." *Finansy SSSR* no. 1, pp. 46–50.

Khaburzaniia, L. Ia. 1978. *Sotsial'no-ekonomicheskie aspekty proportsional'nosti razvitiia sotsialisticheskogo obshchestva.* Tbilisi: Sabchota sakartvelo.

Khachaturov, T. S. 1979. "Effektivnost' kapital'nogo vlozheniia v neproizvodstvennoi sfere." *Voprosy ekonomiki* no. 1, pp. 47–58.

Khesin, Ia. B. 1974. "Puti resheniia problem mestnykh biudzhetov." *Finansy SSSR* no. 9, pp. 72–76.

—— 1976. *Puti povysheniia ustoichivosti dokhodnoi bazy mestnykh biudzhetov.* Moscow: Finansy.

Khimicheva, N. I. 1966. *Pravovye osnovy biudzhetnogo protsessa v SSSR.* Saratovsk: Izd-vo Saratovskogo Universiteta.

Khrushchev, Nikita S. 1959. *Seven-Year Plan Target Figures.* Soviet Booklet no. 47. London: Soviet Booklets.

—— 1971. *Khrushchev Remembers.* New York: Bantam Books.

—— 1976. *Khrushchev Remembers: The Last Testament.* New York: Bantam Books.

Kiiv v tsifrakh. 1966. Kiev: Statistika.

Kim, I. L. 1975. *Sovershenstvovanie poriadka sostavleniia biudzheta.* Moscow: Finansy.

Kirilenko, I. and V. Kozlova. 1973. "Perspektivnyi plan gorodskogo soveta." *Sovety deputatov trudiashchikhsia* no. 10, pp. 59–67.

Kistanov, V. V. 1978. "Predplanovye issledovaniia territorial'noi organizatsii narodnogo khoziaistva v SSSR." *Planovoe khoziaistvo* no. 11, pp. 104–8.

—— 1981. *Territorial'naia organizatsiia proizvodstva.* Moscow: Ekonomika.

Kochumov, Ia. Kh. 1982. *Konstitutsiia SSSR i problemy upravleniia ekonomicheskim i sotsial'nim razvitiem soiuznoi respubliki.* Ashkhabad: Ylym.

Kokhonov, F. 1977. "Sovershenstvovanie planirovaniia khoziaistva respubliki." *Planovoe khoziaistvo* no. 6, pp. 20–31.

Koliushin, K. I. 1979. "Mestnye sovety i kompleksnoe planirovanie." *Sovetskoe gosudarstvo i pravo* no. 7, pp. 87–95.

Korenevskaia, E. I. 1973. "Gorodskie sovety i kompleksnoe planirovanie razvitiia gorodov." *Sovetskoe gosudarstvo i pravo* no. 9, pp. 66–69.

Koropeckyj, Iwan S. 1967. "The Development of Soviet Location Theory Before the Second World War." *Soviet Studies* 19:1–28, 232–44.

—— 1971. *Location Problems in Soviet Industry: The Case of the Ukraine.* Chapel Hill: University of North Carolina Press.

—— 1972. "Equalization of Regional Development in Socialist Countries: An Empirical Study." *Economic Development and Cultural Change* 21(1):68–86.

—— 1981. "Growth and Productivity." In Iwan S. Koropecky and Gertrude Schroeder, eds., *Economics of Soviet Regions*, pp. 92–117. New York: Praeger.

Koropeckyj, Iwan S., and Gertrude Schroeder, eds. 1981. *Economics of Soviet Regions.* New York: Praeger.

Kostennikov, V. 1972. "Territorial'noe razdelenie truda i vyravnivanie urovnei ekonomicheskogo razvitiia soiuznykh respublik." *Planovoe khoziaistvo* no. 12, pp. 19–29.

Kosygin, A. N. 1965. *Pravda*, September 28, 1965, p. 1.

Kotov, F. I. 1974. *Organizatsiia planirovaniia narodnogo khoziaistva SSSR.* Moscow: Ekonomika.

Kotov, V. V. 1980. "Iz istorii stanovleniia otechestvennoi teorii faktorov razmeshcheniia promyshlennosti." *Izvestiia Akademii Nauk SSSR, seriia geograficheskaia* no. 4, pp. 95–108.

KPSS v rezoliutsiiakh i resheniiakh s"ezdov, konferentsii i plenumov TsK, 1978–1980. 1981. Moscow: Izd-vo politicheskoi literatury.

Kress, John H. 1980. "Representation of Positions on the CPSU Politburo." *Slavic Review* 39(2):218–38.

Kudriashov, R. A. 1962. *Raspredelenie dokhodov mezhdu biudzhetami.* Moscow: Gosfinizdat.

Kushnirsky, Fyodor. 1982. *Soviet Economic Planning, 1965–1980.* Boulder: Westview.

Kutafin, O. E. 1976. *Mestnye sovety i narodno-khoziaistvennoe planirovanie.* Moscow: Izd-vo Moskovskogo universiteta.

—— 1980. *Planovaia deiatel'nost' sovetskogo gosudarstva. Gosudarstvenno-pravovoi aspekt.* Moscow: Iuridicheskaia literatura.

Leningrad za 50 let. 1967. Leningrad: Lenizdat.

Lewis-Beck, Michael S. and Tom W. Rice. 1985. "Government Growth in the United States." *Journal of Politics* 47:2–30.

Lewytzky, Boris. 1968. *The Soviet Political Elite.* Stanford: Hoover Institution.

Liberman, Ia. G. 1970. *Gosudarstvennyi biudzhet v novykh usloviiakh kho-ziaistvovaniia.* Moscow: Nauka.

Liebowitz, Ronald. 1984. "Soviet Investment Policy: An Ethno-Spatial Analysis." Paper presented to the annual meeting of the AAASS, New York.

Linge, G. J. R. et al. 1978. "An Appraisal of the Soviet Concept of the Territorial Production Complex," *Soviet Geography: Review and Translation* 19:

Lowenhardt, John. 1982. *The Soviet Politburo.* New York: St. Martin's.

Lychagin, V. A. 1975. *Ekonomicheskie problemy razvitiia natsiei i natsion-al'nykh otnoshenii v SSSR na stadii razvitogo sotsializma.* Saransk: Mordovskoe knizhnoe izd-vo.

McAuley, Alastair. 1978. *Economic Welfare in the Soviet Union.* Madison: University of Wisconsin Press.

McAuley, Mary. 1974. "The Hunting of the Hierarchy: RSFSR Obkom First Secretaries and the Central Committee." *Soviet Studies* 26:473–501.

Maniushis, A. Iu. 1978. *Sovershenstvovanie upravleniia narodnym khoziaist-vom soiuznoi respubliki.* Vil'nius: Mintis.

Mariakhin, G. L. 1964. *Ocherki istorii nalogov naseleniia v SSSR.* Moscow: Finansy.

Maslov, P. P., ed. 1974. *Statistika finansov.* Moscow: Statistika.

Materialy XXIV S''ezda KPSS. 1971. Moscow: Politizdat.

Materialy XXVI S''ezda KPSS. 1981. Moscow: Izd-vo politicehskoi literatury.

Mazanova, M. E. 1974. *Territorial'nye proportsii narodnogo khoziaistva SSSR.* Moscow: Nauka.

Medvedkova, E. A. 1984. "Issues in Perfecting a Lower-Level Economic

Regionalization in the USSR." *Soviet Geography: Review and Translation* 25:75–87. Translated from *Geografiia i prirodnye resursy* (1983) no. 1, pp. 140–50.

Melnyk, Z. L. 1965. *Soviet Capital Formation: Ukraine, 1928/29–1932.* Munich: Ukrainian Free University Press.

Meltsner, Arnold. 1971. *The Politics of City Revenue.* Berkeley: University of California Press.

Meny, Yves. 1984. "Decentralization in Socialist France: The Politics of Pragmatism." *West European Politics* 7:65–79.

Meskhiia, Ia., ed. 1979. *Aktual'nye problemy sovershenstvovaniia planirovaniia i upravleniia narodnogo khoziaistva.* Tbilisi: NII Ekonomiki i planirovaniia pri Gosplane Gruzinskoi SSSR.

Mestnye biudzhety SSSR. Statisticheskii sbornik. 1960. Moscow: Gosfinizdat.

Mestnye biudzhety SSSR. Statisticheskii sbornik. 1970. Moscow: Finansy.

Metodicheskie ukazaniia k razrabotke gosudarstvennykh planov ekonomicheskogo i sotsial'nogo razvitiia SSSR. 1980. Moscow: Ekonomika.

Mezhevich, M. 1978. "Kompleksnoe planirovanie krupnykh gorodov." *Planovoe khoziaistvo* no. 3, pp. 110–15.

Milch, Jerome. 1978. "Urban Government in France: Municipal Policy-Making in the Centralized State." *Administration and Society* 9(4):

Millar, James R. 1975. "History and Analysis of Soviet Domestic Bond Policy." *Soviet Studies* 27(4):598–614.

Millar, James R. and Donna Bahry. 1979. "Financing Development and Tax Structure Change in the USSR." *Canadian Slavonic Papers* 21(2):166–74.

Miller, John. 1977. "Cadres Policy in Nationality Areas." *Soviet Studies* 29:3–30.

—— 1983. "Nomenklatura: Check on Localism?" In T. H. Rigby and Bogdan Harasymiw, eds., *Leadership Selection and Patron-Client Relations in the USSR and Yugoslavia,* pp. 63–97. London: Allen and Unwin.

Mints, A. A. 1972. *Ekonomicheskaia otsenka estestvennykh resursov.* Moscow: Mysl'.

—— 1976. "A Predictive Hypothesis of Economic Development in the European Part of the USSR." *Soviet Geography: Review and Translation* 17(1):1–28. Translated from *Resursy, sredstva, rasselenie.* Moscow: Nauka, 1974.

Mints, A. A. and G. D. Kokhanovskaia. 1974. "An Attempt at a Quantitative Evaluation of the Natural Resource Potential of Regions in the USSR." *Soviet Geography: Review and Translation* 15(9):554–65. Translated from *Izvestiia Akademii Nauk SSSR, seriia geograficheskaia* (1973) no. 5, pp. 55–65.

Miroshchenko, S. M. 1974. "O nekotorykh voprosakh naloga s oborota." *Finansy SSSR* no. 10, pp. 23–31.

Mochalov, B., ed. 1980. *Territorial'no-otraslevoi printsip planirovaniia. Teoriia i praktika.* Moscow: Mysl'.

Moldokulov, A. M., ed. 1978. *Otraslevoe i territorial'noe raspredelenie kapital'nykh vlozhenii v promyshlennosti Kirgizii.* Frunze: Ylym.

Morton, Henry W. 1983. "Local Soviets and the Attempt to Rationalize the Delivery of Urban Services: The Case of Housing." In Everett Jacobs, ed., *Soviet Local Politics and Government*, pp. 186–203. London: Allen and Unwin.

Mosashvili, T. I. 1981. *Izvestiia*, November 20, p. 4.

Moses, Joel. 1974. *Regional Party Leadership and Policy-Making in The USSR.* New York: Praeger.

Moskva 1973: Kratkaia adresno-spravochnaia kniga. 1973. Moscow: Moskovskii rabochii.

Moskva v tsifrakh za gody Sovetskoi vlasti (1917–1967). 1967. Moscow: Statistika.

Mukoed, A. L. 1981. "Rol' mestnykh sovetov v razvitii territorial'no-proizvodstvennykh kompleksov." *Sovetskoe gosudarstvo i pravo* no. 2, pp. 12–19.

Mushketik, L. M. 1974. *Kompleksnyi territorial'nyi plan v usloviiakh otraslevogo upravleniia.* Kiev: Naukova dumka.

Narodnoe khoziaistvo Armianskoi SSR. (*Narkhoz Arm. SSR*) Annual. Erevan: Aiastan.

Narodnoe khoziaistvo Belorusskoi SSR. (*Narkhoz BSSR*) Annual. Minsk: Belarus.

Narodnoe khoziaistvo Estonskoi SSR. (*Narkhoz ESSR*) Annual. Tallinn: Eesti raamat.

Narodnoe khoziaistvo goroda Leningrada. 1957. Moscow: Gosstatizdat.

Narodnoe khoziaistvo Gruzinskoi SSR. (*Narkhoz GruzSSR*) Annual. Tbilisi: Sabchota sakartvelo.

Narodnoe khoziaistvo Kazakhskoi SSR. (*Narkhoz KaSSR*) Annual. Alma-ata: Kazakhstan.

Narodnoe khoziaistvo Kirgizskoi SSR. (*Narkhoz KiSSR*) Annual. Frunze: Kyrgyzstan.

Narodnoe khoziaistvo Latviiskoi SSR. (Narkhoz LaSSR) Annual. Riga.

Narodnoe khoziaistvo Litovskoi SSR. (Narkhoz LiSSR) Annual. Vilna: Mintis.

Narodnoe khoziaistvo Moldavskoi SSR. (Narkhoz MSSR) Annual. Kishinev: Kartia moldovenske.

Narodnoe khoziaistvo RSFSR. (Narkhoz RSFSR) Annual. Moscow: Finansy i statistika.

Narodnoe khoziaistvo Tadzhikskoi SSR. (Narkhoz TaSSR) Annual. Dushanbe: Irfon.

Narodnoe khoziaistvo Turkmenskoi SSR. (Narkhoz TuSSR) Annual. Ashkhabad: Turkmenistan.

Narodne gospodarstvo Ukrainskoi RSR. Annual. Kiev.

Narodnoe khoziaistvo Ukrainskoi SSR. (Narkhoz UkSSR) Annual. Kiev: Tekhnika.

Narodnoe khoziaistvo Uzbekskoi SSR. (Narkhoz UzSSR) Annual. Tashkent: Uzbekistan.

Narodnoe khoziaistvo Uzbekskoi SSR za 60 let. 1984. Tashkent: Uzbekistan.

Narodnoe khoziaistvo SSSR. Statisticheskii sbornik. (Narkhoz) Annual. Moscow.

Nathan, Richard P., et al. 1975. Monitoring Revenue Sharing. Washington: Brookings.

Nathan, Richard P. and Fred C. Doolittle. 1984. "The Untold Story of Reagan's 'New Federalism'." The Public Interest.

Nathan, Richard P., Fred C. Doolittle, and associates. 1983. The Consequences of Cuts: The Effects of the Reagan Domestic Program on State and Local Governments. Princeton: Princeton Urban and Regional Research Center.

Nechemias, Carol. 1980. "Regional Differentiation of Living Standards in the RSFSR: The Issue of Inequality." Soviet Studies 32(3):366–78.

Nekrasov, N. N. 1975. Regional'naia ekonomika. Moscow: Ekonomika.

—— 1978. "Problemy razmeshcheniia proizvoditel'nykh sil SSSR," Voprosy ekonomiki no. 11, pp. 3–12.

Nelidov, A. A. 1962. Istoriia gosudarstvennykh uchrezhdenii SSSR, 1917–1936 gg. Moscow: Moskovskii gosudarstvennyi istoriko-arkhivnyi institut.

Nelson, Daniel N. 1979. "Dilemmas of Local Politics in Communist States." Journal of Politics 41:23–54.

Nikitina, L. 1963. *Gosudarstvennyi biudzhet Moldavskoi SSR.* Kishinev: Kartia Moldovenske.

Nishanov, N. N. 1973. *Effektivnost' razvitiia legkoi promyshlennosti v Uzbekistane.* Tashkent: Uzbekistan.

North, Robert N. 1972. "Soviet Northern Development: The Case of NW Siberia." *Soviet Studies* 24(2):171–99.

Nove, Alec. 1980. *Political Economy and Soviet Socialism.* London: Allen and Unwin.

—— 1981. "An Overview." In I. S. Koropeckyj and Gertrude Schroeder, eds., *Economics of Soviet Regions*, pp. 1–10. New York: Praeger.

—— 1983. *The Economics of Feasible Socialism.* London: Allen and Unwin.

Nove, Alec and J. A. Newth. 1967. *The Soviet Middle East.* New York: Praeger.

Oates, Wallace E., ed. 1977. *The Political Economy of Fiscal Federalism.* Lexington, MA: Lexington Books.

"Ob antipartiinoi gruppe Malenkova G. M., Kaganovicha L. M., Molotova V. M." 1960. In *Spravochnik sekretaria PPO*, pp. 150–56. Moscow: Politicheskaia literatura.

Odinnadtsataia sessiia Verkhovnogo Soveta BSSR. 1979. Minsk: Belarus.

Odinnadtsataia sessiia Verkhovnogo Soveta RSFSR. 1980. Moscow: Izdanie Verkhovnogo Soveta RSFSR.

Okrostvaridze, I. E. 1973. *Biudzhetnaia sistema i biudzhetnye prava Gruzinskoi SSR.* Tbilisi: Metsniereba.

"O merakh po dal'neishemu povysheniiu roli i usilieniiu otvetsvennosti sovetov narodnykh deputatov za uskorenie sotsial'no-ekonomicheskogo razvitiia v svete reshenii XXVII S"ezda KPSS" 1986. *Sovety narodnykh deputatov* no. 9, pp. 5–13.

Osminin, V. A. 1979. *Planirovanie v respublike: teoriia, metodologiia, praktika.* Tashkent: Uzbekistan.

Ovchinnikov, I. 1986. "Oblastnyi sovet i proizvodstvo tovarov narodnogo potrebleniia." *Sovety narodnykh deputatov* no. 2, pp. 98–103.

Owens, John R. and Larry L. Wade. 1984. "Federal Spending in Congressional Districts." *Western Political Quarterly* 37(3):404–23.

Pabat, M. G. 1985. "Rol' biudzhetnoi sistemy v razvitiia ekonomiki regiona." *Finansy SSSR* no. 9, pp. 41–45.

Panskov, V. G. and L. S. Velichko. 1986. "Zadachi ukrepleniia dokhodnoi bazy mestnykh sovetov." *Finansy SSSR* no. 3, pp. 18–25.

Pavlenko, V. F. 1975. *Territorial'noe planirovanie v SSSR.* Moscow: Ekonomika.

—— 1983. "The Potential of the Territory." *Pravda,* May 5, p. 2. Translated in *Current Digest of the Soviet Press* (June 1, 1983) 35:5, 14.

Perlo, Victor. 1961. *How the Soviet Economy Works: An Interview with A. I. Mikoyan, First Deputy Premier of the USSR.* New York: International Publishers.

Pervaia sessiia Verkhovnogo Soveta SSSR. 9-ogo sozyva. Stenograficheskii otchet. 1979. Moscow: Izdanie Verkhovnogo Soveta.

Peshekhonov, Iu V. et al. 1978. *Razvitie i finansirovanie obshchestvennykh fondov potrebleniia.* Moscow: Finansy.

Piskotin, M. I. 1971. *Sovetskoe biudzhetnoe pravo.* Moscow: Iuridicheskaia literatura.

—— 1981. "Demokraticheskii tsentralizm i problemy sochetaniia tsentralizatsii i detsentralizatsii." *Sovetskoe gosudarstvo i pravo* no. 5, pp. 39–49.

"Planirovanie i territorial'noe razvitie ekonomiki." 1977. *Planovoe khoziaistvo* no. 6, pp. 3–7.

Plenum TsK KPSS, 24–29 Iuniia 1959 g. Stenograficheskii otchet. 1959. Moscow: Gosudarstvennoe izd-vo politicheskoi literatury.

Plotnikov, K. N. 1947. "Gosudarstvennyi biudzhet Sovetskogo Soiuza." In N. N. Rovinskii, ed., *Finansy SSSR za XXX let.* Moscow: Gosfinizdat.

—— 1948. *Biudzhet sotsialisticheskogo gosudarstva.* Moscow: Gosfinizdat.

—— 1954. *Ocherki istorii biudzheta sovetskogo gosudarstva.* Moscow: Gosfinizdat.

Poliak, G. B. 1978. *Biudzhet goroda.* Moscow: Finansy.

Pommerehne, Werner W. 1977. "Quantitative Aspects of Federalism: A Study of Six Countries." In Wallace Oates, ed., *The Political Economy of Fiscal Federalism,* pp. 275–355. Lexington, MA: Lexington Books.

Popov, G. A. 1976. *Ekonomika i planirovanie zdravookhraneniia.* Moscow: Izd-vo Moskovskogo gosudarstvennogo universiteta.

Potichnyj, Peter. 1983. "Permanent Representatives (Postpredstva) of Union Republics in Moscow." In Peter Potichnyj and Jane Shapiro Zacek, eds., *Politics and Participation Under Communist Rule,* pp. 50–83. New York: Praeger.

Pressman, Jeffrey and Aaron Wildavsky. 1973. *Implementation.* Berkeley: University of California Press.

Probst, A. E. 1965. "Ratsional'noe razmeshchenie energoemkikh otraslei." *Planovoe khoziaistvo* no. 1, pp. 42–50.

Prokoshin, B. A. 1977. *Rukovodstvo mestnykh sovetov promyshlennost'iu.* Moscow:

Prud'homme, Remy. 1974a. "Critique de la Politique d'Amenagement du Territoire." *Revue D'Economie Politique* no. 6, pp. 921–35.

—— 1974b. "Regional Economic Policy in France, 1962–72." In Niles Hansen, ed., *Public Policy and Regional Economic Development.* Boston: Ballinger.

—— 1977. "France: Central Government Control over Public Investment Expenditure." In Warren Oates, ed., *The Political Economy of Fiscal Federalism.* Lexington, MA: Lexington Books.

Radio Liberty Research Bulletin (RFE/RL Research). Serial. Munich: Radio Free Europe/Radio Liberty.

Ragauskas, P. V. 1985. "Nekotorye itogi i problemy raboty v usloviiakh ekonomicheskogo eksperimenta." *Finansy SSSR* no. 7, pp. 32–33.

Rakov, A. A. *Naselenie BSSR.* 1969. Minsk: Nauka i tekhnika.

Rakowska-Harmstone, ed. 1979. *Perspectives for Change in Communist Societies.* Boulder: Westview.

Ray, Bruce A. 1981. "Military Committee Membership in the House of Representatives and the Allocation of Defense Department Outlays." *Western Political Quarterly* 34(2):222–34.

Revaikin, I. S. and T. V. Proshina. 1985. *Regional'nye osobennosti formirovaniia i ispol'zovaniia obshchestvennykh fondov potrebleniia.* Moscow: Nauka.

Richardson, H. W. 1973. *Regional Growth Theory.* New York: Macmillan.

Ritt, Leonard. 1976. "Committee Position, Seniority, and the Distribution of Government Expenditures." *Public Policy* no. 24, pp. 463–89.

Rodgers, A. 1974. "The Locational Dynamics of Soviet Industry." *Annals of the Association of American Geographers* 64(2):226–40.

Rovinskii, N. N. 1939. *Gosudarstvennyi biudzhet SSSR.* Moscow: Gosfinizdat.

Ruban, G. I. 1979. *Sovershenstvovanie upravleniia proizvodstvom v ekonomike raiona.* Moscow: Ekonomika.

Ruble, Blair A. 1982. "Policy Innovation and the Soviet Political Process: The Case of Socio-Economic Planning in Leningrad." *Canadian Slavonic Papers* 24:161–74.

Rumer, Boris. 1982a. "The Investment Process in Siberian Industry. Soviet Industrial Investments: Problems of the 1981–85 Plan." Interim report to the National Council for Soviet and East European Research.

—— 1982b. "Current Problems in the Industrialization of Siberia." Final report to the National Council for Soviet and East European Research.

—— 1984. *Investment and Reindustrialization in the Soviet Economy.* Boulder: Westview.

Runova, T. G. 1976. "The Location of the Natural Resource Potential of the USSR in Relation to the Geography of Productive Forces." *Soviet Geography: Review and Translation* 17(2):73–85.

Rusin, Z. E. 1974. "O regulirovanii biudzhetov gorodov, raionov gorodskogo podchineniia i poselkov." *Finansy SSSR* no. 5, pp. 72–74.

Sabirov, Kh. 1966. *Iz istorii gosudarstvennykh finansov Uzbekistana.* Tashkent:

Sagers, Matthew 1984a. "Regional Distribution of Industrial Employment in the USSR." *Soviet Geography: Review and Translation* 25:166–76.

—— 1984b. "Structural Change and the Spatial Distribution of Industry in Belorussia." *Soviet Geography: Review and Translation* 25:328–53.

Sagers, Matthew J. and Milford Green. 1979. "Industrial Dispersion in the Soviet Union: An Application of Entropy Measures." *Soviet Geography: Review and Translation* 20:567–86.

Samuels, Richard J. 1983. *The Politics of Regional Policy in Japan: Localities Incorporated?* Princeton: Princeton University Press.

Schain, Martin A. 1979. "Communist Control of Municipal Councils and Urban Political Change in France." *Studies in Comparative Communism* 12:351–70.

—— 1985. *French Communism and Local Power: Urban Politics and Political Change.* London: Frances Pinter.

Schapiro, Leonard. 1960. *The Communist Party of the Soviet Union.* New York: Vintage Books.

Schueller, George K. 1965. "The Politburo." In Harold Lasswell and Daniel Lerner, eds., *World Revolutionary Elites.* Cambridge, MA: MIT Press.

Second Session of the Supreme Soviet of the USSR. 1938. New York: International Publishers.

Semina, R. T. and L. I. Tatevosova 1980. "Economic Evaluation of the Factors of Industrial Location over the Long Term." *Soviet Geography:*

Review and Translation 21:581–91. Translated from *Izvestiia Akademiia Nauk SSSR, seria geograficheskaia* (1979) no. 5, pp. 50–59.

XV S"ezd Vsesoiuznoi Kommunisticheskoi partii(b). *Stenograficheskii otchet*. 1928. Moscow: Gosudarstvennoe izdatel'stvo.

XVII S"ezd Vsesoiuznoi Kommunisticheskoi partii(b). *Stenograficheskii otchet*. 1934. Moscow: Partizdat.

XVIII S"ezd VKP(b). *Stenograficheskii otchet*. 1939. Moscow: Gosudarstvennoe izdatel'stvo politicheskoi literatury.

XX S"ezd KPSS. *Stenograficheskii otchet*. 1956. Moscow: Politizdat.

XXI S"ezd KPSS. *Stenograficheskii otchet*. 1959. Moscow: Politizdat.

XXII S"ezd KPSS. *Stenograficheskii otchet*. 1961. Moscow: Politizdat.

XXIII S"ezd KPSS. *Stenograficheskii otchet*. 1966. Moscow: Politizdat.

XXIV S"ezd KPSS. *Stenograficheskii otchet*. 1971. Moscow: Politizdat.

XXV S"ezd KPSS. *Stenograficheskii otchet*. 1976. Moscow: Politizdat.

XXVI S"ezd KPSS. *Stenograficheskii otchet*. 1981. Moscow: Izdatel'stvo Politicheskoi literatury.

Shabad, Theodore 1969. *Basic Industrial Resources of the USSR*. New York: Columbia University Press.

—— 1980. "Soviet Regional Policy and CMEA Integration." In Paul Marer and J. M. Montias, eds., *East European Integration and East-West Trade*, pp. 223–51. Bloomington: Indiana University Press.

—— 1983. "Soviet, After Studies, Shelves Plan to Turn Siberian Rivers." *New York Times*, December 16, pp. 1, 7.

Shafir, M. A. 1968a. *Kompetentsiia SSSR i soiuznykh republik*. Moscow.

—— 1968b. "Federativnye nachala v strukture organov SSSR." *Sovetskoe gosudarstvo i pravo* no. 11:36–46.

Shamsutdinov, R. G. 1986. "Perspektivy sovershenstvovaniia dokhodnoi bazy mestnykh biudzhetov." *Finansy SSSR* no. 3, pp. 26–28.

Sharpe, L. G., ed. 1981. *The Local Fiscal Crisis in Western Europe: Myths and Realities*. Beverly Hills: Sage.

Shatilo, B. 1986. "Biudzhet mestnyi, interes obshchii." *Sovety narodnykh deputatov* no. 9, pp. 32–37.

Shekhovtsov, G. K. 1976. *Svodnoe biudzhetnoe planirovanie*. Moscow: Finansy.

Sherstneva, L. A. 1985. "Rol' finansov v povyshenii ekonomicheskoi zainteresovannosti mestnykh sovetov." *Finansy SSSR* no. 4, pp. 49–52.

Shirkevich, N. A. 1972. *Rol' biudzheta v razvitii ekonomiki i kul'tury soiuznykh respublik*. Moscow: Finansy.

Shitarev, G. 1953. "Demokraticheskii tsentralizm i rukovodiashchaia deiatel'nost' partiinykh organov." *Kommunist* no. 18, pp. 51–66.

Shniper, R. I. 1980. *Tendentsii ekonomicheskogo razvitiia sibiri, 1961–75 gg.* Novosibirsk: Nauka.

Silaev, E. and A. Baramidze. 1980. "Vliianie proizvodstvennykh faktorov na ekonomicheskii rost soiuznykh respublik." *Voprosy ekonomiki* no. 4, pp. 104–12.

Singur, N. and B. Shtulberg. 1978. "Metodicheskie voprosy territorial'nogo kompleksnogo planirovaniia." *Planovoe khoziaistvo* no. 11, pp. 53–60.

Skrypnik, V. 1986. "Eto ukrepliaet mestnyi biudzhet." *Sovety narodnykh deputatov* no. 11, pp. 25–26.

Sotsialisticheskoe stroitel'stvo SSSR. 1935. Moscow: Tsentral'noe upravlenie narodno-khoziaistvennogo ucheta.

Soviet Political Leaders. 1957. No author or place of publication given. (Included in a file of U.S. government publications at the Harvard Russian Research Center.)

Spravochnik partiinogo rabotnika. 1957. Moscow: Izd-vo politicheskoi literatury.

Spravochnik sekretaria PPO. 1960. Moscow: Izd-vo politicheskoi literatury.

Stanfield, Rochelle. 1976. "The PIGS: Out of the Sty, Into Lobbying with Style." *National Journal*, August 14, pp. 1134–39.

Stephens, G. Ross. 1974. "State Centralization and the Erosion of Local Autonomy." *Journal of Politics* 36:44–76.

——— 1985. "State Centralization Revisited." Paper presented to the annual meeting of the APSA, New Orleans.

Sternheimer, Stephen. 1980. "Running Soviet Cities: Bureaucratic Degeneration, Bureaucratic Politics, or Urban Management?" In Gordon Smith, ed., *Public Policy and Public Administration in the Soviet Union*, pp. 79–108. New York: Praeger.

Stewart, Philip D. 1968. *Political Power in the Soviet Union.* Indianapolis: Bobbs-Merrill.

Sullivant, Robert. 1962. *Soviet Politics and the Ukraine, 1917–57.* New York: Columbia University Press.

Sundquist, James L. and Hugh Mields, Jr. 1980. "Regional Growth Policy in the US." In Kevin Allen, ed., *Balanced National Growth*, pp. 305–30. Lexington, MA: Lexington Books.

Swearer, Howard R. 1959. "Khrushchev's Revolution in Industrial Management." *World Politics* 12:45–59.

—— 1964. *The Politics of Succession in the USSR.* Boston: Little Brown.

Taaffe, Robert N. 1980. "Soviet Regional Development." In Stephen Cohen, Alexander Rabinowich, and Robert Sharlet, eds., *The Soviet Union Since Stalin,* pp. 155–78. Bloomington: Indiana University Press.

—— 1984. "The Conceptual, Analytical and Planning Framework of Siberian Development." In Roland Fuchs and George Demko, eds., *Geographical Studies on the Soviet Union: Essays in Honor of Chauncey Harris,* pp. 157–87. Chicago: University of Chicago.

Tamarchenko, M. L. 1967. *Sovetskie finansy v period Velikoi Otechestvennoi Voiny.* Moscow: Finansy.

Tarasenko, M. N. 1980. "Vzaimodeistvie mestnykh sovetov i ministerstv." *Sovetskoe gosudarstvo i pravo* no. 8, pp. 74–82.

Targets of the Seven-Year Plan for Soviet Economy 1959–1965. 1958. Soviet Booklet no. 43. London: Soviet Booklets.

Tarschys, Daniel. 1979. *The Soviet Political Agenda: Problems and Priorities, 1950–1970.* White Plains, NY: M. E. Sharpe.

Tarrow, Sidney. 1974. "Local Constraints on Regional Reform: A Comparison of Italy and France." *Comparative Politics* 7(1):1–36.

—— 1977. *Between Center and Periphery.* New Haven: Yale University Press.

Tarrow, Sidney, Peter Katzenstein, and Luigi Graziano, eds. 1978. *Territorial Politics in Industrial Nations.* New York: Praeger.

Taubman, William. 1973. *Governing Soviet Cities: Bureaucratic Politics and Urban Development in the USSR.* New York: Praeger.

Tbilisi k 40-letiiu Sovetskoi vlasti v Gruzii. 1961. Tbilisi: Gosstatizdat.

Teague, Elizabeth. 1986. "Gorbachev's Speech to the Twenty-Seventh Party Congress: The Role of Local Soviets." Research report 100/86 (February 26). Munich: Radio Free Europe/Radio Liberty Research.

Thompson, Joel A. 1985. "Bringing Home the Bacon: The Politics of Pork Barrel in the North Carolina Legislature." Paper delivered to the annual meeting of the APSA, New Orleans.

Todorskii, Iu. V. 1979. "Relations of Territorial and Regional Soviets with Associations Not Subordinate to Them." *Soviet Geography: Review and Translation* 18:61–78. Translated from "Vzaimootnosheniia kraevykh, oblastnykh sovetov s nepodvedomstvennymi ob"edineniiami." *Sovetskoe gosudarstvo i pravo* (1978), no. 9.

——— 1982. *Rukovodstvo mestnykh sovetov razvitiem sotsialisticheskoi promyshlennosti.* Moscow: Nauka.

Tokareva, T. A. 1979. "Mestnye biudzhety na sovremennom etape." *Finansy SSSR* no. 4, pp. 29–34.

Trehub, Aaron. 1985. "Housing: More Power to the City Soviets?" Research report 387/85 (November 19). Munich: Radio Free Europe/Radio Liberty Research.

Trinadtsataia sessiia Verkhovnogo Soveta BSSR. 1980. Minsk: Belarus.

Tsikulin, V. A. 1966. *Istoriia gosudarstvennykh uchrezhdenii SSSR, 1936–1965 gg.* Moscow: Moskovskii Gosudarstvennyi Istoriko-Arkhivnyi Institut.

Tsipkin, S. D. 1973. *Dokhody gosudarstvennogo biudzheta SSSR. Pravovye voprosy.* Moscow: Iuridicheskaia literatura.

Tulebaev, T. T. 1960. *Gosudarstvennyi biudzhet sovetskogo Kazakhstana.* Moscow: Gosfinizdat.

——— 1963. *Voprosy teorii i praktiki planirovaniia biudzhetov soiuznykh respublik.* Moscow: Ekonomicheskaia literatura.

——— 1969. *Biudzhetnoe planirovanie v soiuznoi respublike.* Moscow: Finansy.

——— 1973. *Problemy territorial'nogo kompleksnogo finansirovaniia.* Alma-ata: Kazakhstan.

Tychina, V. G. et al. 1985. "Minpishcheprom UkSSR v usloviiakh ekonomicheskogo eksperimenta." *Finansy SSSR* no. 9, pp. 12–16.

Udovenko, V. G. 1968. In Akademiia Nauk SSSR, Institut Ekonomiki, *Problemy ekonomicheskoi effektivnosti razmeshcheniia sotsialisticheskogo proizvodstva v SSSR.* Moscow: Nauka.

——— 1983. "Razmeshchenie proizvoditel'nykh sil i effektivnost' obshchestvennogo proizvodstva." *Voprosy ekonomiki* no. 7, pp. 73–83.

USSR Facts and Figures Annual. Annual. Gulf Breeze, FL: Academic International Press.

USSR: Measures of Economic Growth and Development, 1950–80. 1982. Studies prepared for the use of the U.S. Congress, Joint Economic Committee. Washington.

Vasil'ev, V. I. 1973. *Demokraticheskii tsentralizm v sisteme sovetov.* Moscow: Iuridicheskaia literatura.

Vasilik, O. D. 1980. "Planirovanie raskhodov na soderzhanie VUZov v usloviiakh OASU." *Finansy SSSR* no. 7, pp. 44–48.

——— 1982. *Gosudarstvennyi biudzhet SSSR.* Kiev: Vishcha shkola.

Volobuev, M. 1928. "Do problemy Ukrainskoi ekonomiki." *Bilshovyk Ukrainy* 3:46–72.

Voluiskii, N. M. 1970. *Svodnyi finansovyi plan.* Moscow: Finansy.

Vvedensky, G. A. 1958. "The New Economic Setup: The Organization of Soviet Industry, 1917–58." *Caucasian Review* no. 6, pp. 37–53.

Wagener, Hans-Jurgen. 1973. "Rules of Location and the Concept of Rationality: The Case of the USSR." In V. M. Bandera and Z. L. Melnyk, eds., *The Soviet Economy in Regional Perspective,* pp. 63–103. New York: Praeger.

White, Stephen. 1982. "The Supreme Soviet and Budgetary Politics in the USSR." *British Journal of Political Science* 12:75–94.

Wood, David M. 1985. "The Member of Parliament and Economic Policy: Is There a Territorial Imperative?" Paper presented to the annual meeting of the APSA, New Orleans.

Zakumbaev, A. K. 1975. *Metody otsenki urovnia ekonomicheskoi razvitii soiuznoi respublik i raionov.* Alma-ata: Nauka.

—— 1977. *Ekonomicheskoe razvitie soiuznykh respublik i raionov.* Alma-ata: Nauka.

Zasedaniia Verkhovnogo Soveta ArSSR. 9-aia sessiia. 1960. Erevan: Izdanie Verkhovnogo Soveta ArSSR.

Zasedaniia Verkhovnogo Soveta KiSSR. 9-ogo sozyva, 7-aia sessiia. 1978. Frunze: Izdanie Verkhovnogo Soveta KiSSR.

Zasedaniia Verkhovnogo Soveta SSSR. 1-aia sessiia. 1950. Moscow: Izdanie Verkhovnogo Soveta SSSR.

Zasedaniia Verkhovnogo Soveta SSSR. 4-ogo sozyva, 4-aia sessiia. Stenografishceskii otchet. 1956. Moscow: Izdanie Verkhovnogo Soveta SSSR.

Zasedaniia Verkhovnogo Soveta SSSR. 5-ogo sozyva, 1-aia sessiia. Stenografishceskii otchet. 1958. Moscow: Izdanie Verkhovnogo Soveta SSSR.

Zasedaniia Verkhovnogo Soveta SSSR. 5-ogo sozyva, 3-aia sessiia. Stenografishceskii otchet. 1959. Moscow: Izdanie Verkhovnogo Soveta SSSR.

Zasedaniia Verkhovnogo Soveta SSSR. 5-ogo sozyva, 5-aia sessiia. Stenografishceskii otchet. 1961. Moscow: Izdanie Verkhovnogo Soveta SSSR.

Zasedaniia Verkhovnogo Soveta SSSR. 6-ogo sozyva, 7-aia sessiia. Stenografishceskii otchet. 1966. Moscow: Izdanie Verkhovnogo Soveta SSSR.

Zasedaniia Verkhovnogo Soveta SSSR. 8-ogo sozyva. Stenografishceskii otchet. 1970. Moscow: Izdanie Verkhovnogo Soveta SSSR.

Zasedaniia Verkhovnogo Soveta SSSR. 9-ogo sozyva, 4-aia sessiia. Stenografishceskii otchet. 1976. Moscow: Izdanie Verkhovnogo Soveta SSSR.

Zenchenko, N. S. 1979. *Sochetanie territorial'nogo i otraslevogo planirovaniia*. Moscow: Ekonomika.

—— 1982. *Planirovanie v soiuznoi respublike*. Moscow: Ekonomika.

—— 1983. "Aktual'nye zadachi mestnykh planovykh organov." *Planovoe khoziaistvo* no. 6, pp. 20–30.

Zhamin, V. A. 1965. *Aktual'nye voprosy ekonomiki narodnogo obrazovaniia*. Moscow: Prosveshchenie.

—— 1969. *Ekonomika obrazovaniia*. Moscow: Prosveshchenie.

Zhikhareva, V. I. 1979. *Territorial'noe razdelenie truda i effektivnost' promyshlennogo proizvodstva*. Alma-ata: Nauka.

Ziiadullaev, S. K. 1972a. *Planirovanie i razvitie ekonomiki Uzbekskoi SSR*. Tashkent: Uzbekistan.

—— 1972b. "Territorial'nyi aspekt planirovaniia." *Ekonomicheskaia gazeta* no. 26, pp. 9–10.

Zimmerman, William and G. Palmer. 1983. "Words and Deeds in Soviet Foreign Policy." *American Political Science Review* 77(2): 358–67.

Zlobin, I. D. et al. 1975. *Soviet Finance*. Moscow: Progress.

Zverev, A. G. 1946. *Gosudarstvennyi biudzhet SSSR 1938–45*. Moscow: Gosfinizdat.

—— 1950. *O gosudarstvennom biudzhete na 1950 g. i ob ispolneniem gosudarstvennogo biudzheta za 1948 i 1949 gg*. Moscow: Gospolitizdat.

INDEX

Abramov, G. G. (Moscow), 142
Administrative fragmentation: and center-regional coordination, 17, 72–75, 105, 106, 109, 171–72; and compromise over appropriations, 95–96, 147, 155, 158–59, 162–65; and delays in planning process, 92–96, 147, 155; and local governments, 129–34, 154–55
Agriculture: as an issue on republic and local agendas, 81–88, 142–43; Ministry/Commissariat of, 30; as a revenue base for republic and local governments, 58–61
Akhundov, V. Iu. (Azerbaidzhan), 82
Aliev, G. A. (Azerbaidzhan), 78
All-union ministries, see Ministries, all-union
Altai krai, 148, 164
Andropov, Yuri, 31
Annamukhamedova, G. (Turkmenia), 76
Antiparty group, and regional politics, 27, 192n8
Appeals by republic and local officials: by career background of leaders, 82–83, 143–44; coding of, 187–89; concerns shared by republic and local officials, 147–48; continuity of, 85–88, 144–47, 161; issues involved in, 75–88, 140–48, 160–62, 197n23; limitations on, 32–33, 78–81, 92, 93–96, 109; by members and nonmembers of Politburo, 83–84; by old versus new leaders under Gorbachev, 84; proposals for new projects, 100n11; resolution of 35, 65–66, 79–80, 88–99, 120–22, 148–50
Armenia, investment in, 115, 165
Armstrong, John, 166

Associations, see Ob"edinenie reforms
Atomic energy, see Energy
Azerbaidzhan: appeals to central authorities, 78, 82; investment in, 115

Bashkir ASSR, 147
Beer, Samuel, 18
Belorussia: appeals to central authorities, 30, 34, 101, 164; investment in, 104, 114–15

Bialer, Seweryn, 2, 39, 122
Birman, Igor, 64
Boitsov, I. P. (Stavropol), 140
Bondarenko, I. A. (Rostov), 144, 146, 166
Breslauer, George, 6
Brezhnev, Leonid: as Kazakh first secretary, 35, 82, 85, 152, 166, 196n14; on the need for regional initiative, 32; on regional development, 3, 30–31, 164–65; on regional interdependence, 36
Budgetary centralization: in capitalist countries, 13–20; in the USSR, 1–2, 4, 10, 32, 35, 37, 42–61, 64–75
Budgetary powers: of localities, 129–35, 193n1; of republics, 42–52, 66–72
Budget data, reliability of, 8–10, 41–42, 135, 175–78, 191n3, 193n4
Bulganin, Nikolai, 26

Campbell, Robert, 33
Canada, provincial and local share of expenditures, 14–15